NARCOTICS
ANONYMOUS

Other Publications Available from NA World Services

Books

Just for Today
Living Clean: The Journey Continues
It Works: How and Why
Guiding Principles: The Spirit of Our Traditions
The NA Step Working Guides
Sponsorship

General

Who, What, How, & Why (IP 1)
Another Look (IP 5)
Just for Today (IP 8)
Living the Program (IP 9)
The Triangle of Self-Obsession (IP 12)
One Addict's Experience... (IP 14)
Self-Acceptance (IP 19)
Money Matters: Self-Support in NA (IP 24)

New Members

NA White Booklet
An Introductory Guide to NA
Recovery and Relapse (IP 6)
Am I an Addict? (IP 7)
Sponsorship (IP 11)
For the Newcomers (IP 16)
For Those in Treatment (IP 17)
Welcome to NA (IP 22)
An Introduction to NA Meetings (IP 29)

Youth

By Young Addicts, For Young Addicts (IP 13)
For the Parents or Guardians of Young People in NA (IP 27)

Public Relations

Membership Survey
Information about NA
*NA & Persons Receiving
Medication-Assisted Treatment*
NA: A Resource in Your Community
PI and the NA Member (IP 15)
H&I Service and the NA Member (IP 20)

Service

Twelve Concepts for NA Service
The Group Booklet
The Group (IP 2)
Funding NA Services (IP 28)

Special

Behind the Walls
In Times of Illness
The Loner — Staying Clean in Isolation (IP 21)
Staying Clean on the Outside (IP 23)
Accessibility for Those with Additional Needs (IP 26)

For a complete list of NA literature in all languages, visit our website at **www.na.org**.

NARCOTICS ANONYMOUS

SIXTH EDITION

Narcotics Anonymous World Services, Inc.
Chatsworth, California

Twelve Steps and Twelve Traditions
reprinted for adaptation by permission of AA World Services, Inc.

World Service Office
PO Box 9999
Van Nuys, CA 91409 USA
T 818.773.9999
F 818.700.0700
Website: www.na.org

World Service Office–CANADA
Mississauga, Ontario

World Service Office–EUROPE
Brussels, Belgium
T +32/2/646 6012

World Service Office–IRAN
Tehran, Iran
www.na-iran.org

Published 1983. Second Edition 1983. Third Edition 1984.
Third Edition (Revised) 1986. Fourth Edition 1987. Fifth Edition 1988.
Sixth Edition 2008.

Printed in China.

21   20   19   39   38   37

ISBN 9781557767349 (Hardcover)   WSO Catalog Item No. 1101
ISBN 9781557767356 (Softcover)   WSO Catalog Item No. 1102
ISBN 9781557767868 (Pocket-sized Softcover) WSO Catalog Item No. 1106
ISBN 9781557767851 (Gift Edition)   WSO Catalog Item No. 1107
ISBN 9781557768896 (ePub)   WSO Catalog Item No. 1108
ISBN 9781557768322 (Large-Print)   WSO Catalog Item No. 1101LP
ISBN 9781633800618 (line-Numbered)   WSO Catalog Item No. 1101LN

This is NA Fellowship-approved literature.

Table of Contents

Our Program: Narcotics Anonymous

Our Members Share

Beginnings

> The short passages that begin this section are excerpted from sto-
> ries in previous editions of the Basic Text.

> When he was using he went from one "mother" to another—from
> his mother's house to the military to marriage—until his wife
> tired of the insanity and found the only NA meeting in the world.
> In his story from our First Edition, this addict admits that it took
> him time but finally he learned to take action and be responsible
> for himself.

> He lived in a place that many call paradise, but in his story from
> our First Edition, this beachcomber shares that for an addict, "skid
> row is in the mind." Through NA, he has found a sense of peace
> and a new way of life.

> After a lifetime of using, this "southern gentleman" learned that
> the most gracious thing he could do was open the doors to an NA
> meeting. In this story from our First Edition, he recalls that the
> first time a man told him he loved him was in Narcotics Anony-
> mous.

> In this story originally published in our Little White Book and
> added to the Basic Text at the Second Edition, a mother learns
> that she can come out of the paralyzing fear of addiction and turn
> her whole life around. She claims her seat as a woman in NA and
> hopes that one day more women will find recovery.

> This addict found freedom behind bars through the Fellowship of
> Narcotics Anonymous. This is a story from our First Edition.

Coming Home

Regardless of ...

Life on Life's Terms

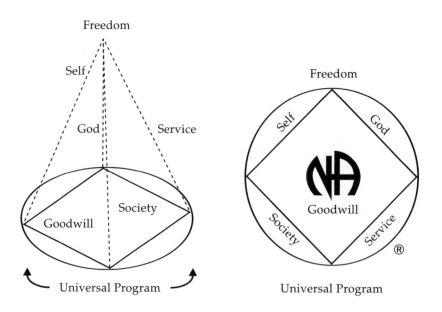

Our Symbol

Simplicity is the key to our symbol; it imitates the simplicity of our Fellowship. All sorts of occult and esoteric connotations can be found in its simple outlines, but foremost in the minds of the Fellowship are easily understood meanings and relationships.

The outer circle denotes a universal and total program that has room within it for all manifestations of the recovering person.

The square, whose lines are defined, is easily seen and understood, but there are other unseen parts of the symbol. The square base denotes Good will, the ground of both the Fellowship and the members of our society. Good will is best exemplified in service; proper service is "Doing the right thing for the right reason." When Good will supports and motivates both the individual and the Fellowship, we are fully whole and wholly free. Probably the last to be lost to freedom will be the stigma of being an addict.

It is the four pyramid sides that rise from the base in a three-dimensional figure that represent Self, Society, Service, and God. All rise to the point of Freedom. All parts are closely related to the needs and aims of the addict who is seeking recovery, and to the purpose of the Fellowship which is to make recovery available to all. The greater the base, (as we grow in unity in numbers and in fellowship) the broader the sides of the pyramid, and the higher the point of freedom.

Preface to the Sixth Edition

Many of us have never known recovery without the Basic Text. Our meetings open with readings found in its pages; it sits on the literature tables in our groups; and the book itself has been a constant in our recovery through the months or years or decades. Since the first edition of *Narcotics Anonymous*, our Basic Text, was published, NA has grown and changed in countless ways. In many respects, the Basic Text has been instrumental in that evolution. There are over 70,000 weekly NA meetings today; in 1982, the year the World Service Conference approved the Basic Text, there were about 2,700. Most places in the world did not offer an NA meeting every night of the week. In fact, most places didn't offer a meeting *any* night of the week. Now NA is in 144 countries and we speak 82 languages. The Basic Text itself is translated into 30 languages.[1]

Certainly NA's growth cannot be attributed to the power of this book alone. But the fact is the Basic Text is one of the most effective means we have of carrying the message. Where it is published and distributed, NA grows, not just in numbers but in breadth of recovery and experience. As our members stay clean ten, twenty, thirty years and more, our fellowship has more and more experience dealing with challenges beyond "not picking up the first drug." In the Sixth Edition, you will read stories of addicts who stayed clean through the loss of loved ones, serious illnesses, raising children, marriage, divorce, getting an education, pursuing careers, and much more. The common thread through all of these varied experiences is that we draw strength from the

---

[1] The numbers in this paragraph are updated regularly. These figures are as of May 2018.

NA program regardless of how long we have been clean or what life situation we are facing. Over the decades our members have lived a lot of life on life's terms and have learned a lot about what it means to recover from addiction in that context.

Now, with the publication of our Sixth Edition Basic Text, we can say NA has, in many respects, come of age. That process has not been without growing pains, however. From 1983 to 1988, we published five editions and a revision of the Basic Text. For years afterward, the fellowship as a whole was unwilling to undertake another revision. Many of us thought we would never see the day that a new edition of the Basic Text could be welcomed by the fellowship. And so, the publication of a Sixth Edition is something to celebrate and a real marker of our ability, as a fellowship, to grow and change.

Chapters One through Ten remain as they were in the Fifth Edition. These ten chapters speak to many of us in a way that no other literature does, in a voice that is difficult, if not impossible, to duplicate. What is significantly different in the Sixth Edition text, however, in addition to this new preface, is the personal experience that follows Chapters One through Ten.

It would be impossible to list all of the ways in which the face of NA has changed over the years, and this new edition doesn't pretend to be a mirror, reflecting back a perfect image of our membership. But it does aim to represent the richness of our differences as well as it can. The Basic Text already tells us that any addict is welcome in NA regardless of what we look like, how old we are, and what kind of spiritual beliefs we hold. Addiction is a disease that does not discriminate, and neither does the program of NA. Admittedly there is a stereotype of the "typical" candidate for NA—urban, criminal, a needle-user—and that narrow vision does describe some of us, but we are also professionals, and parents, and students, and so on, living in cities, small towns, and rural communities in countries all over the world. We can only hope to gesture at our diversity in the space of one book. Even our name itself, *Narcotics* Anonymous, may not fully describe our membership. Addiction has nothing to do with where we come from or the specific substances we used.

Our members come from every walk of life. We are not contained within political or geographic boundaries, nor are we limited by any individual differences in faith or philosophy. No matter what conflicts are unfolding in the world at large, we aspire to an ideal of unity: Our common welfare should come first. Our text explains that this unity of purpose helps us "to achieve the true spirit of anonymity" where all of us are equal as members of the group. With that as our foundation, we as individual recovering addicts are each able to find our own distinct voice and to sing a song that is uniquely ours. This new edition presents some of those voices.

We hope the Sixth Edition Basic Text will offer a vision of recovery for addicts around the world—those who have already found the rooms of NA and those who will walk through our doors tomorrow. Over the years our fellowship has changed and our literature has expanded and been revised, but the message remains the same: An addict, any addict, can stop using drugs, lose the desire to use, and find a new way to live. You are welcome here. Please stay and be part of our growth, change, and recovery.

Preface to the First Edition

"The full fruit of a labor of love lives in the harvest, and that always comes in its right season..."

The material for this book was drawn from the personal experiences of addicts within the Fellowship of Narcotics Anonymous. This Basic Text is based on an outline derived from our "white book," *Narcotics Anonymous.* The first eight chapters are based on the topic headings in the white book and carry the same title. A ninth chapter has been included, Just for Today, as well as a tenth chapter, More Will Be Revealed. Following is a brief history of the book.

Narcotics Anonymous was formed in July 1953, with the first meeting held in Southern California. The Fellowship grew erratically but quickly spread to various parts of the United States. From the beginning, the need was evident for a book on recovery to help strengthen the Fellowship. The white book, *Narcotics Anonymous,* was published in 1962.

The Fellowship still had little structure, however, and the 1960s were a period of struggle. Membership grew rapidly for a time and then began to decline. The need for more specific direction was readily apparent. NA demonstrated its maturity in 1972, when a World Service Office (WSO) was opened in Los Angeles. The WSO has brought the needed unity and sense of purpose to the Fellowship.

The opening of the WSO brought stability to the growth of the Fellowship. Today, there are recovering addicts in thousands of meetings all across the United States and in many foreign countries. Today the World Service Office truly serves a worldwide Fellowship.

Narcotics Anonymous has long recognized the need for a complete Basic Text on addiction—a book about addicts, by addicts and for addicts.

This effort was strengthened, after the formation of WSO, with the publication of *The NA Tree,* a pamphlet on service work. This pamphlet was the original service manual of the Fellowship. It has been followed by subsequent and more comprehensive volumes, and now the *NA Service Manual.*

The manual outlined a service structure that included a World Service Conference (WSC). The WSC, in turn, included a Literature Committee. With the encouragement of WSO, several members of the Board of Trustees, and the Conference, work began.

As the cry for literature, particularly a comprehensive text, became more widespread, the WSC Literature Committee developed. In October 1979, the first World Literature Conference was held in Wichita, Kansas, followed by conferences in Lincoln, Nebraska; Memphis, Tennessee; Santa Monica, California; Warren, Ohio; and Miami, Florida.

The WSC Literature Subcommittee, working in conference and as individuals, has collected hundreds of pages of material from members and groups throughout the Fellowship. This material has been laboriously catalogued, edited, assembled, dismembered and reassembled. Dozens of area and regional representatives working with the Literature Committee have dedicated thousands of man-hours to produce the work presented here. But more importantly, those members have conscientiously sought to ensure a "group conscience" text.

In keeping with the spirit of anonymity, we, the WSC Literature Subcommittee, feel it appropriate to express our special gratitude and appreciation to the Fellowship as a whole, especially the many who contributed material for inclusion in the book. We feel that this book is a synthesis of the collective group conscience of the Fellowship and that every single idea submitted is included in the work in some form or another.

This volume is intended as a textbook for every addict seeking recovery. As addicts, we know the pain of addiction, but we also know the joy of recovery we have found in the Fellowship of Narcotics Anonymous. We believe the time has come to share our recovery, in written form, with all who desire what we have found. Appropriately, this book is devoted to informing every addict:

JUST FOR TODAY, YOU NEVER HAVE TO USE AGAIN!

Therefore,

With gratitude in our recovery, we dedicate our NA book to the loving service of our Higher Power. That through the development of a conscious contact with God, no addict seeking recovery need die without a chance to find a better way of life.

We remain trusted servants in gratitude and loving service,

LITERATURE SUBCOMMITTEE
WORLD SERVICE CONFERENCE
NARCOTICS ANONYMOUS

We cannot change the nature of the addict or addiction. We can help to change the old lie "Once an addict, always an addict," by striving to make recovery more available. God, help us to remember this difference.

Introduction

This book is the shared experience of the Fellowship of Narcotics Anonymous. We welcome you to read this text, hoping that you will choose to share with us the new life that we have found. We have by no means found a cure for addiction. We offer only a proven plan for daily recovery.

In NA, we follow a program adapted from Alcoholics Anonymous. More than one million people have recovered in A.A., most of them just as hopelessly addicted to alcohol as we were to drugs. We are grateful to the A.A. Fellowship for showing us the way to a new life.

The Twelve Steps of Narcotics Anonymous, as adapted from A.A., are the basis of our recovery program. We have only broadened their perspective. We follow the same path with a single exception; our identification as addicts is all-inclusive with respect to any mood-changing, mind-altering substance. Alcoholism is too limited a term for us; our problem is not a specific substance, it is a disease called addiction. We believe that as a fellowship, we have been guided by a Greater Consciousness, and are grateful for the direction that has enabled us to build upon a proven program of recovery.

We come to Narcotics Anonymous by various means and believe that our common denominator is that we failed to come to terms with our addiction. Because of the variety of addicts found within our Fellowship, we approach the solution contained within this book in general terms. We pray that we have been searching and thorough, so that every addict who reads this volume will find the hope that we have found.

Based on our experience, we believe that every addict, including the potential addict, suffers from an incurable disease of body, mind, and spirit. We were in the grip of a hopeless dilemma, the solution of which is spiritual in nature. Therefore, this book will deal with spiritual matters.

We are not a religious organization. Our program is a set of spiritual principles through which we are recovering from a seemingly hopeless state of mind and body. Throughout the compiling of this work, we have prayed:

"GOD, grant us knowledge that we may write according to Your Divine precepts. Instill in us a sense of Your purpose. Make us servants of Your will and grant us a bond of selflessness, that this may truly be Your work, not ours—in order that no addict, anywhere, need die from the horrors of addiction."

Everything that occurs in the course of NA service must be motivated by the desire to more successfully carry the message of recovery to the addict who still suffers. It was for this reason that we began this work. We must always remember that as individual members, groups and service committees, we are not and should never be in competition with each other. We work separately and together to help the newcomer and for our common good. We have learned, painfully, that internal strife cripples our Fellowship; it prevents us from providing the services necessary for growth.

It is our hope that this book will help the suffering addict find the solution that we have found. Our purpose is to remain clean, just for today, and to carry the message of recovery.

Our Program

NARCOTICS ANONYMOUS

Many books have been written about the nature of addiction. This book primarily concerns itself with the nature of recovery. If you are an addict and have found this book, please give yourself a break and read it!

Chapter One

Who Is an Addict?

Most of us do not have to think twice about this question.
WE KNOW! *Our whole life and thinking was centered in drugs*
in one form or another—the getting and using and finding
ways and means to get more. We lived to use and used to
live. Very simply, an addict is a man or woman whose life is
controlled by drugs. We are people in the grip of a continuing
and progressive illness whose ends are always the same: jails,
institutions and death.

Those of us who have found the Program of Narcotics Anonymous do not have to think twice about the question: Who is an
addict? We know! The following is our experience.

As addicts, we are people whose use of any mind-altering,
mood-changing substance causes a problem in any area of life.
Addiction is a disease that involves more than the use of drugs.
Some of us believe that our disease was present long before the
first time we used.

Most of us did not consider ourselves addicted before coming
to the Narcotics Anonymous Program. The information available to us came from misinformed people. As long as we could
stop using for a while, we thought we were all right. We looked
at the stopping, not the using. As our addiction progressed, we
thought of stopping less and less. Only in desperation did we
ask ourselves, "Could it be the drugs?"

We did not choose to become addicts. We suffer from a disease
that expresses itself in ways that are anti-social and that makes
detection, diagnosis and treatment difficult.

Our disease isolated us from people except when we were getting, using and finding ways and means to get more. Hostile, resentful, self-centered and self-seeking, we cut ourselves off from the outside world. Anything not completely familiar became alien and dangerous. Our world shrank and isolation became our life. We used in order to survive. It was the only way of life that we knew.

Some of us used, misused and abused drugs and still did not consider ourselves addicts. Through all of this, we kept telling ourselves, "I can handle it." Our misconceptions about the nature of addiction included visions of violence, street crime, dirty needles and jail.

When our addiction was treated as a crime or moral deficiency, we became rebellious and were driven deeper into isolation. Some of the highs felt great, but eventually the things that we had to do to continue using reflected desperation. We were caught in the grip of our disease. We were forced to survive any way that we could. We manipulated people and tried to control everything around us. We lied, stole, cheated and sold ourselves. We had to have drugs regardless of the cost. Failure and fear began to invade our lives.

One aspect of our addiction was our inability to deal with life on life's terms. We tried drugs and combinations of drugs to cope with a seemingly hostile world. We dreamed of finding a magic formula that would solve our ultimate problem—ourselves. The fact was that we could not use any mind-altering or mood-changing substance, including marijuana and alcohol, successfully. Drugs ceased to make us feel good.

At times, we were defensive about our addiction and justified our right to use, especially when we had legal prescriptions. We were proud of the sometimes illegal and often bizarre behavior that typified our using. We "forgot" about the times when we sat alone and were consumed by fear and self-pity. We fell into a pattern of selective thinking. We only remembered the good drug experiences. We justified and rationalized the things that we did to keep from being sick or going crazy. We ignored the times when life seemed to be a nightmare. We avoided the reality of our addiction.

Higher mental and emotional functions, such as conscience and the ability to love, were sharply affected by our use of drugs. Living skills were reduced to the animal level. Our spirit was broken. The capacity to feel human was lost. This seems extreme, but many of us have been in this state of mind.

We were constantly searching for the answer—that person, place or thing that would make everything all right. We lacked the ability to cope with daily living. As our addiction progressed, many of us found ourselves in and out of institutions.

These experiences indicated that there was something wrong with our lives. We wanted an easy way out. Some of us thought of suicide. Our attempts were usually feeble and only helped to contribute to our feelings of worthlessness. We were trapped in the illusion of "what if," "if only" and "just one more time." When we did seek help, we were only looking for the absence of pain.

We had regained good physical health many times, only to lose it by using again. Our track record shows that it is impossible for us to use successfully. No matter how well we may appear to be in control, using drugs always brings us to our knees.

Like other incurable diseases, addiction can be arrested. We agree that there is nothing shameful about being an addict, provided we accept our dilemma honestly and take positive action. We are willing to admit without reservation that we are allergic to drugs. Common sense tells us that it would be insane to go back to the source of our allergy. Our experience indicates that medicine cannot cure our illness.

Although physical and mental tolerance play a role, many drugs require no extended period of use to trigger allergic reactions. Our reaction to drugs is what makes us addicts, not how much we use.

Many of us did not think that we had a problem with drugs until the drugs ran out. Even when others told us that we had a problem, we were convinced that we were right and the world was wrong. We used this belief to justify our self-destructive behavior. We developed a point of view that enabled us to pursue our addiction without concern for our own well-being or the well-being of others. We began to feel that the drugs were killing us long before we could ever admit it to anyone else. We noticed that if we tried to stop using, we couldn't. We suspected that we had lost control over the drugs and had no power to stop.

Certain things followed as we continued to use. We became accustomed to a state of mind that is common to addicts. We forgot what it was like before we started using; we forgot about social graces. We acquired strange habits and mannerisms. We forgot how to work; we forgot how to play; we forgot how to express ourselves and how to show concern for others. We forgot how to feel.

While using, we lived in another world. We experienced only periodic jolts of reality or self-awareness. It seemed that we were at least two people instead of one, Dr. Jekyll and Mr. Hyde. We ran around and tried to get our lives together before our next run. Sometimes we could do this very well, but later, it was less important and more impossible. In the end, Dr. Jekyll died and Mr. Hyde took over.

Each of us has a few things that we never did. We cannot let these things become excuses to use again. Some of us feel lonely because of differences between us and other members. This feeling makes it difficult to give up old connections and old habits.

We all have different tolerances for pain. Some addicts needed to go to greater extremes than others. Some of us found that we had enough when we realized that we were getting high too often and it was affecting our daily lives.

At first, we were using in a manner that seemed to be social or at least controllable. We had little indication of the disaster that the future held for us. At some point, our using became uncontrollable and anti-social. This began when things were going well, and we were in situations that allowed us to use frequently. This was usually the end of the good times. We may have tried to moderate, substitute or even stop using, but we went from a state of drugged success and well-being to complete spiritual, mental and emotional bankruptcy. This rate of decline varies from addict to addict. Whether it occurs in years or days, it is all downhill. Those of us who don't die from the disease will go on to prison, mental institutions or complete demoralization as the disease progresses.

Drugs had given us the feeling that we could handle whatever situation might develop. We became aware, however, that drug usage was largely responsible for some of our worst predicaments. Some of us may spend the rest of our lives in jail for a drug-related crime.

We had to reach our bottom, before we were willing to stop. We were finally motivated to seek help in the latter stage of our addiction. Then it was easier for us to see the destruction, disaster and delusion of our using. It was harder to deny our addiction when problems were staring us in the face.

Some of us first saw the effects of addiction on the people closest to us. We were very dependent on them to carry us through life. We felt angry, disappointed and hurt when they found other interests, friends and loved ones. We regretted the past, dreaded the future, and we weren't too thrilled about the present. After years of searching, we were more unhappy and less satisfied than when it all began.

Our addiction enslaved us. We were prisoners of our own mind and were condemned by our own guilt. We gave up the hope that we would ever stop using drugs. Our attempts to stay clean always failed, causing us pain and misery.

As addicts, we have an incurable disease called addiction. The disease is chronic, progressive and fatal. However, it is a treatable disease. We feel that each individual has to answer the question, "Am I an addict?" How we got the disease is of no immediate importance to us. We are concerned with recovery.

We begin to treat our addiction by not using. Many of us sought answers but failed to find any workable solution until we found each other. Once we identify ourselves as addicts, help becomes possible. We can see a little of ourselves in every addict and see a little of them in us. This insight lets us help one another. Our future seemed hopeless until we found clean addicts who were willing to share with us. Denial of our addiction kept us sick, but our honest admission of addiction enabled us to stop using. The people of Narcotics Anonymous told us that they were recovering addicts who had learned to live without drugs. If they could do it, so could we.

The only alternatives to recovery are jails, institutions, dereliction and death. Unfortunately, our disease makes us deny our addiction. If you are an addict, you can find a new way of life through the NA Program. We have become very grateful in the course of our recovery. Through abstinence and through working the Twelve Steps of Narcotics Anonymous, our lives have become useful.

We realize that we are never cured, and that we carry the disease within us for the rest of our lives. We have a disease, but we do recover. Each day we are given another chance. We are convinced that there is only one way for us to live, and that is the NA way.

Chapter Two

What Is the
Narcotics Anonymous Program?

NA is a nonprofit Fellowship or society of men and women for whom drugs had become a major problem. We are recovering addicts who meet regularly to help each other stay clean. This is a program of complete abstinence from all drugs. There is only one requirement for membership, the desire to stop using. We suggest that you keep an open mind and give yourself a break. Our program is a set of principles written so simply that we can follow them in our daily lives. The most important thing about them is that they work.

There are no strings attached to NA. We are not affiliated with any other organizations, we have no initiation fees or dues, no pledges to sign, no promises to make to anyone. We are not connected with any political, religious or law enforcement groups, and are under no surveillance at any time. Anyone may join us, regardless of age, race, sexual identity, creed, religion or lack of religion.

We are not interested in what or how much you used or who your connections were, what you have done in the past, how much or how little you have, but only in what you want to do about your problem and how we can help. The newcomer is the most important person at any meeting, because we can only keep what we have by giving it away. We have learned from our group experience that those who keep coming to our meetings regularly stay clean.

Narcotics Anonymous is a Fellowship of men and women who are learning to live without drugs. We are a nonprofit society and have no dues or fees of any kind. Each of us has paid the price of membership. We have paid for the right to recover with our pain.

Surviving against all odds, we are addicts who meet regularly. We respond to honest sharing and listen to the stories of our members for the message of recovery. We realize that there is hope for us at last.

We make use of the tools that have worked for other recovering addicts who have learned in NA to live without drugs. The Twelve Steps are positive tools that make our recovery possible. Our primary purpose is to stay clean and to carry the message to the addict who still suffers. We are united by our common problem of addiction. By meeting, talking, and helping other addicts, we are able to stay clean. The newcomer is the most important person at any meeting, because we can only keep what we have by giving it away.

Narcotics Anonymous has many years of experience with literally hundreds of thousands of addicts. This firsthand experience in all phases of illness and recovery is of unparalleled, therapeutic value. We are here to share freely with any addict who wants to recover.

Our message of recovery is based on our experience. Before coming to the Fellowship, we exhausted ourselves by trying to use successfully, and wondering what was wrong with us. After coming to NA, we found ourselves among a very special group of people who have suffered like us and found recovery. In their experiences, freely shared, we found hope for ourselves. If the program worked for them, it would work for us.

The only requirement for membership is a desire to stop using. We have seen the program work for any addict who honestly and sincerely wants to stop. We don't have to be clean when we get here, but after the first meeting, we suggest that newcomers keep coming back and come back clean. We don't have to wait for an overdose or a jail sentence, to get help from Narcotics Anonymous. Addiction is not a hopeless condition from which there is no recovery.

We meet addicts like ourselves who are clean. We watch, listen and realize that they have found a way to live and enjoy life without drugs. We don't have to settle for the limitations of the past. We can examine and re-examine our old ideas. We can constantly improve our old ideas or replace them with new ones. We are men and women who have discovered and admitted that we are powerless over our addiction. When we use, we lose.

When we discovered that we could not live with or without drugs, we sought help through NA, rather than prolong our suffering. The program works a miracle in our lives. We become different people. Working the steps and maintaining abstinence give us a daily reprieve from our self-imposed life sentences. We become free to live.

We want our place of recovery to be a safe place, free from outside influences. For the protection of the Fellowship, we insist that no drugs or paraphernalia be brought to any meeting.

We feel totally free to express ourselves within the Fellowship, because law enforcement agencies are not involved. Our meetings have an atmosphere of empathy. In accordance with the principles of recovery, we try not to judge, stereotype or moralize with each other. We are not recruited and membership does not cost anything. NA does not provide counseling or social services.

Our meetings are a process of identification, hope and sharing. The heart of NA beats when two addicts share their recovery. What we do becomes real for us when we share it. This happens on a larger scale in our regular meetings. A meeting happens when two or more addicts gather to help each other stay clean.

At the beginning of the meeting, we read NA literature that is available to anyone. Some meetings have speakers, topic discussions or both. Closed meetings are for addicts or those who think they might have a drug problem. Open meetings welcome anyone wishing to experience our fellowship. The atmosphere of recovery is protected by our Twelve Traditions. We are fully self-supporting through voluntary contributions from our members. Regardless of where the meeting takes place, we remain unaffiliated. Meetings provide a place to be with fellow addicts. All we need are two addicts, caring and sharing, to make a meeting.

We let new ideas flow into us. We ask questions. We share what we have learned about living without drugs. Though the principles of the Twelve Steps may seem strange to us at first, the most important thing about them is that they work. Our program is a way of life. We learn the value of spiritual principles such as surrender, humility and service from reading the NA literature, going to meetings and working the steps. We find that our lives steadily improve, if we maintain abstinence from mind-altering, mood-changing chemicals and work the Twelve Steps to sustain our recovery. Living this program gives us a relationship with a Power greater than ourselves, corrects defects and leads us to help others. Where there has been wrong, the program teaches us the spirit of forgiveness.

Many books have been written about the nature of addiction. This book concerns itself with the nature of recovery. If you are an addict and have found this book, please give yourself a break and read it.

Chapter Three

Why Are We Here?

Before coming to the Fellowship of NA, we could not manage our own lives. We could not live and enjoy life as other people do. We had to have something different and we thought we had found it in drugs. We placed their use ahead of the welfare of our families, our wives, husbands, and our children. We had to have drugs at all costs. We did many people great harm, but most of all we harmed ourselves. Through our inability to accept personal responsibilities we were actually creating our own problems. We seemed to be incapable of facing life on its own terms.

Most of us realized that in our addiction we were slowly committing suicide, but addiction is such a cunning enemy of life that we had lost the power to do anything about it. Many of us ended up in jail, or sought help through medicine, religion and psychiatry. None of these methods was sufficient for us. Our disease always resurfaced or continued to progress until in desperation, we sought help from each other in Narcotics Anonymous.

After coming to NA we realized we were sick people. We suffered from a disease from which there is no known cure. It can, however, be arrested at some point, and recovery is then possible.

We are addicts seeking recovery. We used drugs to cover our feelings, and did whatever was necessary to get drugs. Many of us woke up sick, unable to make it to work or went to work loaded. Many of us stole to support our habit. We hurt the ones we loved. We did all these things and told ourselves, "I can handle it." We were looking for a way out. We couldn't face life on life's terms. In the beginning, using was fun. For us using became a habit and finally was necessary for survival. The progression of the disease was not apparent to us. We continued on the path of destruction, unaware of where it was leading us. We were addicts and did not know it. Through drugs, we tried to avoid reality, pain and misery. When the drugs wore off, we realized that we still had the same problems, and they were becoming worse. We sought relief by using again and again—more drugs, more often.

We sought help and found none. Often doctors didn't understand our dilemma. They tried to help by giving us medication. Our husbands, wives and loved ones gave us what they had and drained themselves in the hope that we would stop using or would get better. We tried substituting one drug for another but this only prolonged our pain. We tried limiting our usage to social amounts without success. There is no such thing as a social addict. Some of us sought an answer through churches, religions or cultism. Some sought a cure by geographic change. We blamed our surroundings and living situations for our problems. This attempt to cure our problems by moving gave us a chance to take advantage of new people. Some of us sought approval through sex or change of friends. This approval-seeking behavior carried us further into our addiction. Some of us tried marriage, divorce or desertion. Regardless of what we tried, we could not escape from our disease.

We reached a point in our lives where we felt like a lost cause. We had little worth to family, friends or on the job. Many of us were unemployed and unemployable. Any form of success was frightening and unfamiliar. We didn't know what to do. As the feeling of self-loathing grew, we needed to use more and more to mask our feelings. We were sick and tired of pain and trouble. We were frightened and ran from the fear. No matter how far we ran, we always carried fear with us. We were hopeless, useless and lost. Failure had become our way of life and self-esteem was non-existent. Perhaps the most painful feeling of all was the desperation. Isolation and denial of our addiction kept us moving along this downhill path. Any hope of getting better disappeared. Helplessness, emptiness and fear became our way of life. We were complete failures. Personality change was what we really needed. Change from self-destructive patterns of life became necessary. When we lied, cheated or stole, we degraded ourselves in our own eyes. We had had enough of self-destruction. We experienced our powerlessness. When nothing relieved our paranoia and fear, we hit bottom and became ready to ask for help.

We were searching for an answer when we reached out and found Narcotics Anonymous. We came to our first NA meeting in defeat and didn't know what to expect. After sitting in a meeting, or several meetings, we began to feel that people cared and were willing to help. Although our minds told us that we would never make it, the people in the Fellowship gave us hope by insisting that we could recover. We found that no matter what our past thoughts or actions were, others had felt and done the same. Surrounded by fellow addicts, we realized that we were not alone anymore. Recovery is what happens in our meetings. Our lives are at stake. We found that by putting recovery first, the program works. We faced three disturbing realizations:

1. We are powerless over addiction and our lives are unmanageable;
2. Although we are not responsible for our disease, we are responsible for our recovery;
3. We can no longer blame people, places and things for our addiction. We must face our problems and our feelings.

The ultimate weapon for recovery is the recovering addict. We concentrate on recovery and feelings not what we have done in the past. Old friends, places and ideas are often a threat to our recovery. We need to change our playmates, playgrounds and playthings.

When we realize that we are not able to manage without drugs, some of us immediately begin experiencing depression, anxiety, hostility and resentment. Petty frustrations, minor setbacks and loneliness often make us feel that we are not getting any better. We find that we suffer from a disease, not a moral dilemma. We were critically ill, not hopelessly bad. Our disease can only be arrested through abstinence.

Today, we experience a full range of feelings. Before coming into the Fellowship, we either felt elated or depressed. Our negative sense of self has been replaced by a positive concern for others. Answers are provided, and problems are solved. It is a great gift to feel human again.

What a change from the way that we used to be! We know the NA Program works. The program convinced us that we needed to change ourselves, instead of trying to change the people and situations around us. We discovered new opportunities. We found a sense of self-worth. We learned self-respect. This is a program for learning. By working the steps, we come to accept a Higher Power's will. Acceptance leads to recovery. We lose our fear of the unknown. We are set free.

Chapter Four

How It Works

If you want what we have to offer, and are willing to make the effort to get it, then you are ready to take certain steps. These are the principles that made our recovery possible.

1. *We admitted that we were powerless over our addiction, that our lives had become unmanageable.*

2. *We came to believe that a Power greater than ourselves could restore us to sanity.*

3. *We made a decision to turn our will and our lives over to the care of God as we understood Him.*

4. *We made a searching and fearless moral inventory of ourselves.*

5. *We admitted to God, to ourselves, and to another human being the exact nature of our wrongs.*

6. *We were entirely ready to have God remove all these defects of character.*

7. *We humbly asked Him to remove our shortcomings.*

8. *We made a list of all persons we had harmed, and became willing to make amends to them all.*

9. *We made direct amends to such people wherever possible, except when to do so would injure them or others.*

10. *We continued to take personal inventory and when we were wrong promptly admitted it.*

11. *We sought through prayer and meditation to improve our conscious contact with God as we understood Him, praying only for knowledge of His will for us and the power to carry that out.*

12. *Having had a spiritual awakening as a result of these steps, we tried to carry this message to addicts, and to practice these principles in all our affairs.*

*This sounds like a big order, and we can't do it all at once. We didn't become addicted in one day, so remember—*easy does it.

There is one thing more than anything else that will defeat us in our recovery; this is an attitude of indifference or intolerance toward spiritual principles. Three of these that are indispensable are honesty, open-mindedness and willingness. With these we are well on our way.

We feel that our approach to the disease of addiction is completely realistic for the therapeutic value of one addict helping another is without parallel. We feel that our way is practical, for one addict can best understand and help another addict. We believe that the sooner we face our problems within our society, in everyday living, just that much faster do we become acceptable, responsible, and productive members of that society.

The only way to keep from returning to active addiction is not to take that first drug. If you are like us you know that one is too many and a thousand never enough. We put great emphasis on this, for we know that when we use drugs in any form, or substitute one for another, we release our addiction all over again.

Thinking of alcohol as different from other drugs has caused a great many addicts to relapse. Before we came to NA many of us viewed alcohol separately, but we cannot afford to be confused about this. Alcohol is a drug. We are people with the disease of addiction who must abstain from all drugs in order to recover.

These are some of the questions we have asked ourselves: Are we sure we want to stop using? Do we understand that we have no real control over drugs? Do we recognize that in the long run, we didn't use drugs—they used us? Did jails and institutions take over the management of our lives at different times? Do we fully accept the fact that our every attempt to stop using or to control our using failed? Do we know that our addiction changed us into someone we didn't want to be: dishonest, deceitful, self-willed people at odds with ourselves and our fellow man? Do we really believe that we have failed as drug users?

When we were using, reality became so painful that oblivion was preferable. We tried to keep other people from knowing about our pain. We isolated ourselves, and lived in prisons that we built with loneliness. Through this desperation, we sought help in Narcotics Anonymous. When we come to NA we are physically, mentally, and spiritually bankrupt. We have hurt so long that we are willing to go to any length to stay clean.

Our only hope is to live by the example of those who have faced our dilemma and have found a way out. Regardless of who we are, where we came from, or what we have done, we are accepted in NA. Our addiction gives us a common ground for understanding one another.

As a result of attending a few meetings, we begin to feel like we finally belong somewhere. It is in these meetings that we are introduced to the Twelve Steps of Narcotics Anonymous. We learn to work the steps in the order that they are written and to use them on a daily basis. The steps are our solution. They are our survival kit. They are our defense against addiction which is a deadly disease. Our steps are the principles that make our recovery possible.

Step One

"We admitted that we were powerless over our addiction, that our lives had become unmanageable."

It doesn't matter what or how much we used. In Narcotics Anonymous, staying clean has to come first. We realize that we cannot use drugs and live. When we admit our powerlessness and our inability to manage our own lives, we open the door to recovery. No one could convince us that we were addicts. It is an admission that we have to make for ourselves. When some of us have doubts, we ask ourselves this question: "Can I control my use of any form of mind or mood-altering chemicals?"

Most addicts will see that control is impossible the moment it is suggested. Whatever the outcome, we find that we cannot control our using for any length of time.

This would clearly suggest that an addict has no control over drugs. Powerlessness means using drugs against our will. If we can't stop using, how can we tell ourselves we are in control? The inability to stop using, even with the greatest willpower and the most sincere desire, is what we mean when we say, "We have absolutely no choice." However, we do have a choice after we stop trying to justify our using.

We didn't stumble into this Fellowship brimming with love, honesty, open-mindedness or willingness. We reached a point where we could no longer continue using because of physical, mental, and spiritual pain. When we were beaten, we became willing.

Our inability to control our usage of drugs is a symptom of the disease of addiction. We are powerless not only over drugs, but over our addiction as well. We need to admit this fact in order to recover. Addiction is a physical, mental and spiritual disease that affects every area of our lives.

The physical aspect of our disease is the compulsive use of drugs: the inability to stop using once we have started. The mental aspect of our disease is the obsession, or overpowering desire to use, even when we are destroying our lives. The spiritual part of our disease is our total self-centeredness. We felt that we could stop whenever we wanted to, despite all evidence to the contrary. Denial, substitution, rationalization, justification, distrust of others, guilt, embarrassment, dereliction, degradation, isolation, and loss of control are all results of our disease. Our disease is progressive, incurable and fatal. Most of us are relieved to find out we have a disease instead of a moral deficiency.

We are not responsible for our disease, but we are responsible for our recovery. Most of us tried to stop using on our own, but we were unable to live with or without drugs. Eventually we realized that we were powerless over our addiction.

Many of us tried to stop using on sheer willpower. This action was a temporary solution. We saw that willpower alone would not work for any length of time. We tried countless other remedies—psychiatrists, hospitals, recovery houses, lovers, new towns, new jobs. Everything that we tried, failed. We began to see that we had rationalized the most outrageous sort of nonsense to justify the mess that we made of our lives with drugs.

Until we let go of our reservations, no matter what they are, the foundation of our recovery is in danger. Reservations rob us of the benefits that this program has to offer. In ridding ourselves of all reservations, we surrender. Then, and only then, can we be helped to recover from the disease of addiction.

Now, the question is: "If we are powerless, how can Narcotics Anonymous help?" We begin by asking for help. The foundation of our program is the admission that we, of ourselves, do not have power over addiction. When we can accept this fact, we have completed the first part of Step One.

A second admission must be made before our foundation is complete. If we stop here, we will know only half the truth. We are great ones for manipulating the truth. We say on one hand, "Yes, I am powerless over my addiction," and on the other hand, "When I get my life together, I can handle drugs." Such thoughts and actions led us back to active addiction. It never occurred to us to ask, "If we can't control our addiction, how can we control our lives?" We felt miserable without drugs, and our lives were unmanageable.

Unemployability, dereliction and destruction are easily seen as characteristics of an unmanageable life. Our families generally are disappointed, baffled and confused by our actions and often desert or disown us. Becoming employed, socially acceptable and reunited with our families does not make our lives manageable. Social acceptability does not equal recovery.

We have found that we had no choice except to completely change our old ways of thinking or go back to using. When we give our best, it works for us as it has worked for others. When we could no longer stand our old ways, we began to change. From that point forward, we began to see that every clean day is a successful day, no matter what happens. Surrender means not having to fight anymore. We accept our addiction and life the way it is. We become willing to do whatever is necessary to stay clean, even the things we don't like doing.

Until we took Step One, we were full of fear and doubt. At this point, many of us felt lost and confused. We felt different. Upon working this step, we affirmed our surrender to the principles of NA. Only after surrender are we able to overcome the alienation of addiction. Help for addicts begins only when we are able to admit complete defeat. This can be frightening, but it is the foundation on which we built our lives.

Step One means that we do not have to use, and this is a great freedom. It took a while for some of us to realize that our lives had become unmanageable. For others, the unmanageability of their lives was the only thing that was clear. We knew in our hearts that drugs had the power to change us into someone that we didn't want to be.

Being clean and working this step, we are released from our chains. However, none of the steps work by magic. We do not just say the words of this step; we learn to live them. We see for ourselves that the program has something to offer us.

We have found hope. We can learn to function in the world in which we live. We can find meaning and purpose in life and be rescued from insanity, depravity and death.

When we admit our powerlessness and inability to manage our own lives, we open the door for a Power greater than ourselves to help us. It is not where we were that counts, but where we are going.

Step Two

"We came to believe that a Power greater than ourselves could restore us to sanity."

The Second Step is necessary if we expect to achieve ongoing recovery. The First Step leaves us with a need to believe in something that can help us with our powerlessness, uselessness, and helplessness.

The First Step has left a vacuum in our lives. We need to find something to fill that void. This is the purpose of the Second Step.

Some of us didn't take this step seriously at first; we passed over it with a minimum of concern, only to find the next steps would not work until we worked Step Two. Even when we admitted that we needed help with our drug problem, many of us would not admit to the need for faith and sanity.

We have a disease: progressive, incurable and fatal. One way or another we went out and bought our destruction on the time payment plan! All of us, from the junkie snatching purses to the sweet little old lady hitting two or three doctors for legal prescriptions, have one thing in common: we seek our destruction a bag at a time, a few pills at a time, or a bottle at a time until we die. This is at least part of the insanity of addiction. The price may seem higher for the addict who prostitutes for a fix than it is for the addict who merely lies to a doctor. Ultimately both pay for their disease with their lives. Insanity is repeating the same mistakes and expecting different results.

Many of us realize when we get to the program that we have gone back time and again to using, even though we knew that we were destroying our lives. Insanity is using drugs day after day knowing that only physical and mental destruction comes when we use. The most obvious insanity of the disease of addiction is the obsession to use drugs.

Ask yourself this question, Do I believe it would be insane to walk up to someone and say, "May I please have a heart attack or a fatal accident?" If you can agree that this would be an insane thing, you should have no problem with the Second Step.

In this program, the first thing we do is stop using drugs. At this point, we begin to feel the pain of living without drugs or anything to replace them. The pain forces us to seek a Power greater than ourselves that can relieve our obsession to use.

The process of coming to believe is similar for most addicts. Most of us lacked a working relationship with a Higher Power. We begin to develop this relationship by simply admitting to the possibility of a Power greater than ourselves. Most of us have no trouble admitting that addiction had become a destructive force in our lives. Our best efforts resulted in ever greater destruction and despair. At some point, we realized that we needed the help of some Power greater than our addiction. Our understanding of a Higher Power is up to us. No one is going to decide for us. We can call it the group, the program, or we can call it God. The only suggested guidelines are that this Power be loving, caring and greater than ourselves. We don't have to be religious to accept this idea. The point is that we open our minds to believe. We may have difficulty with this, but by keeping an open mind, sooner or later, we find the help we need.

We talked and listened to others. We saw other people recovering, and they told us what was working for them. We began to see evidence of some Power that could not be fully explained. Confronted with this evidence, we began to accept the existence of a Power greater than ourselves. We can use this Power long before we understand it.

As we see coincidences and miracles happening in our lives, acceptance becomes trust. We grow to feel comfortable with our Higher Power as a source of strength. As we learn to trust this Power, we begin to overcome our fear of life.

The process of coming to believe restores us to sanity. The strength to move into action comes from this belief. We need to accept this step to start on the road to recovery. When our belief has grown, we are ready for Step Three.

Step Three

"We made a decision to turn our will and our lives over to the care of God as we understood Him."

As addicts, we turned our will and our lives over many times to a destructive power. Our will and our lives were controlled by drugs. We were trapped by our need for instant gratification that drugs gave us. During that time, our total being—body, mind and spirit—was dominated by drugs. For a time, it was pleasurable, then the euphoria began to wear off and we saw the ugly side of addiction. We found that the higher our drugs took us, the lower they brought us. We faced two choices: either we suffered the pain of withdrawal or took more drugs.

For all of us, the day came when there was no longer a choice; we had to use. Having given our will and lives to our addiction, in utter desperation, we looked for another way. In Narcotics Anonymous, we decide to turn our will and our lives over to the care of God as we understand Him. This is a giant step. We don't have to be religious; anyone can take this step. All that is required is willingness. All that is essential is that we open the door to a Power greater than ourselves.

Our concept of God comes not from dogma but from what we believe and from what works for us. Many of us understand God to be simply whatever force keeps us clean. The right to a God of your understanding is total and without any catches. Because we have this right, it is necessary to be honest about our belief if we are to grow spiritually.

We found that all we needed to do was try. When we gave our best effort, the program worked for us as it has worked for countless others. The Third Step does not say, "We turned our will and our lives over to the care of God." It says, "*We made a decision to turn our will and our lives over to the care of God* as we understood Him." We made the decision; it was not made for us by the drugs, our families, a probation officer, judge, therapist or doctor. We made it! For the first time since that first high, we have made a decision for ourselves.

The word decision implies action. This decision is based on faith. We have only to believe that the miracle that we see working in the lives of clean addicts can happen to any addict with the desire to change. We simply realize there is a force for spiritual growth that can help us become more tolerant, patient, and useful in helping others. Many of us have said, "Take my will and my life. Guide me in my recovery. Show me how to live." The relief of "letting go and letting God" helps us develop a life that is worth living.

Surrendering to the will of our Higher Power gets easier with daily practice. When we honestly try, it works. Many of us start our day with a simple request for guidance from our Higher Power.

Although we know that "turning it over" works, we may still take our will and life back. We may even get angry because God permits it. At times during our recovery, the decision to ask for God's help is our greatest source of strength and courage. We cannot make this decision often enough. We surrender quietly, and let the God of our understanding take care of us.

At first, our heads reeled with the questions: "What will happen when I turn my life over? Will I become 'perfect'?" We may have been more realistic than this. Some of us had to turn to an experienced NA member and ask, "What was it like for you?" The answer will vary from member to member. Most of us feel open-mindedness, willingness and surrender are the keys to this step.

We have surrendered our will and our lives to the care of a Power greater than ourselves. If we are thorough and sincere, we will notice a change for the better. Our fears are lessened, and faith begins to grow as we learn the true meaning of surrender. We are no longer fighting fear, anger, guilt, self-pity or depression. We realize that the Power that brought us to this program is still with us and will continue to guide us if we allow It. We are slowly beginning to lose the paralyzing fear of hopelessness. The proof of this step is shown in the way we live.

We have come to enjoy living clean and want more of the good things that the NA Fellowship holds for us. We know now that we cannot pause in our spiritual program; we want all that we can get.

We are now ready for our first honest self-appraisal, and we begin with Step Four.

Step Four

"We made a searching and fearless moral inventory of ourselves."

The purpose of a searching and fearless moral inventory is to sort through the confusion and the contradiction of our lives, so that we can find out who we really are. We are starting a new way of life and need to be rid of the burdens and traps that controlled us and prevented our growth.

As we approach this step, most of us are afraid that there is a monster inside of us that, if released, will destroy us. This fear can cause us to put off our inventory or may even prevent us from taking this crucial step at all. We have found that fear is a lack of faith, and we have found a loving, personal God to whom we can turn. We no longer need to be afraid.

We have been experts at self-deception and rationalization. By writing our inventory, we can overcome these obstacles. A written inventory will unlock parts of our subconscious that remain hidden when we simply think about or talk about who we are. Once it is all down on paper, it is much easier to see, and much harder to deny our true nature. Honest self-assessment is one of the keys to our new way of life.

Let's face it; when we were using, we were not honest with ourselves. We are becoming honest with ourselves when we admit that addiction has defeated us and that we need help. It took a long time to admit that we were beaten. We found that we do not recover physically, mentally or spiritually overnight. Step Four will help us toward our recovery. Most of us find that we were neither as terrible, nor as wonderful, as we supposed. We are surprised to find that we have good points in our inventory. Anyone who has some time in the program and has worked this step will tell you that the Fourth Step was a turning point in their life.

Some of us make the mistake of approaching the Fourth Step as if it were a confession of how horrible we are—what a bad person we have been. In this new way of life, a binge of emotional sorrow can be dangerous. This is not the purpose of the Fourth Step. We are trying to free ourselves of living in old, useless patterns. We take the Fourth Step to grow and to gain strength and insight. We may approach the Fourth Step in a number of ways.

To have the faith and courage to write a fearless inventory, Steps One, Two and Three are the necessary preparation. It is advisable that before we start, we go over the first three steps with a sponsor. We get comfortable with our understanding of these steps. We allow ourselves the privilege of feeling good about what we are doing. We have been thrashing about for a long time and have gotten nowhere. Now we start the Fourth Step and let go of fear. We simply put it on paper, to the best of our present ability.

We must be done with the past, not cling to it. We want to look our past in the face, see it for what it really was and release it so we can live today. The past, for most of us, has been a ghost in the closet. We have been afraid to open that closet for fear of what that ghost may do to us. We do not have to look at the past alone. Our wills and our lives are now in the hands of our Higher Power.

Writing a thorough and honest inventory seemed impossible. It was, as long as we were operating under our own power. We take a few quiet moments before writing and ask for the strength to be fearless and thorough.

In Step Four, we begin to get in touch with ourselves. We write about our liabilities such as guilt, shame, remorse, self-pity, resentment, anger, depression, frustration, confusion, loneliness, anxiety, betrayal, hopelessness, failure, fear and denial.

We write about the things that bother us here and now. We have a tendency to think negatively, so putting it on paper gives us a chance to look more positively at what is happening.

Assets must also be considered, if we are to get an accurate and complete picture of ourselves. This is very difficult for most of us, because it is hard to accept that we have good qualities. However, we all have assets, many of them newly found in the program, such as being clean, open-mindedness, God-awareness, honesty with others, acceptance, positive action, sharing, willingness, courage, faith, caring, gratitude, kindness and generosity. Also, our inventories usually include material on relationships.

We review our past performance and our present behavior to see what we want to keep and what we want to discard. No one is forcing us to give up our misery. This step has the reputation of being difficult; in reality, it is quite simple.

We write our inventory without considering the Fifth Step. We work Step Four as if there were no Step Five. We can write alone or near other people; whatever is more comfortable to the writer is fine. We can write as long or as short as needed.

Someone with experience can help. The important thing is to write a moral inventory. If the word moral bothers us, we may call it a positive/negative inventory.

The way to write an inventory is to write it! Thinking about an inventory, talking about it, theorizing about the inventory will not get it written. We sit down with a notebook, ask for guidance, pick up our pen and start writing. Anything we think about is inventory material. When we realize how little we have to lose, and how much we have to gain, we begin this step.

A basic rule of thumb is that we can write too little, yet we can never write too much. The inventory will fit the individual. Perhaps this seems difficult or painful. It may appear impossible. We may fear that being in touch with our feelings will trigger an overwhelming chain reaction of pain and panic. We may feel like avoiding an inventory because of a fear of failure. When we ignore our feelings, the tension becomes too much for us. The fear of impending doom is so great that it overrides our fear of failure.

An inventory becomes a relief, because the pain of doing it is less than the pain of not doing it. We learn that pain can be a motivating factor in recovery. Thus, facing it becomes unavoidable. Every topic of step meetings seems to be on the Fourth Step or doing a daily inventory. Through the inventory process, we are able to deal with all the things that can build up. The more we live our program, the more God seems to put us in positions where issues surface. When issues surface, we write about them. We begin enjoying our recovery, because we have a way to resolve shame, guilt, or resentment.

The stress once trapped inside of us is released. Writing will lift the lid off of our pressure cooker. We decide whether we want to serve it up, put the lid back on it, or throw it out. We no longer have to stew in it.

We sit down with paper and pen and ask for our God's help in revealing the defects that are causing pain and suffering. We pray for the courage to be fearless and thorough and that this inventory may help us to put our lives in order. When we pray and take action, it always goes better for us.

We are not going to be perfect. If we were perfect, we would not be human. The important thing is that we do our best. We use the tools available to us, and we develop the ability to survive our emotions. We do not want to lose any of what we have gained; we want to continue in the program. It is our experience that no matter how searching and thorough, no inventory is of any lasting effect unless it is promptly followed by an equally thorough Fifth Step.

Step Five

"We admitted to God, to ourselves, and to another human being the exact nature of our wrongs."

The Fifth Step is the key to freedom. It allows us to live clean in the present. Sharing the exact nature of our wrongs sets us free to live. After taking a thorough Fourth Step, we deal with the contents of our inventory. We are told that if we keep these defects inside us, they will lead us back to using. Holding on to our past would eventually sicken us and keep us from taking part in our new way of life. If we are not honest when we take a Fifth Step, we will have the same negative results that dishonesty brought us in the past.

Step Five suggests that we admit to God, to ourselves, and to another human being the exact nature of our wrongs. We looked at our wrongs, examined our behavior patterns, and started to see the deeper aspects of our disease. Now we sit with another person and share our inventory out loud.

Our Higher Power will be with us during our Fifth Step. We will receive help and be free to face ourselves and another human being. It seemed unnecessary to admit the exact nature of our wrongs to our Higher Power. "God already knows that stuff," we rationalized. Although He already knows, the admission must come from our own lips to be truly effective. Step Five is not simply a reading of Step Four.

For years, we avoided seeing ourselves as we really were. We were ashamed of ourselves and felt isolated from the rest of the world. Now that we have the shameful part of our past trapped, we can sweep it out of our lives if we face and admit it. It would be tragic to write it all down and then shove it in a drawer. These defects grow in the dark, and die in the light of exposure.

Before coming to Narcotics Anonymous, we felt that no one could understand the things that we had done. We feared that if we ever revealed ourselves as we were, we would surely be rejected. Most addicts are uncomfortable about this. We recognize that we have been unrealistic in feeling this way. Our fellow members do understand us.

We must carefully choose the person who is to hear our Fifth Step. We must make sure that they know what we are doing and why we are doing it. Although there is no hard rule about the person of our choice, it is important that we trust the person. Only complete confidence in the person's integrity and discretion can make us willing to be thorough in this step. Some of us take our Fifth Step with a total stranger, although some of us feel more comfortable choosing a member of Narcotics Anonymous. We know that another addict would be less likely to judge us with malice or misunderstanding.

Once we make a choice and are actually alone with that person, we proceed with their encouragement. We want to be definite, honest and thorough, realizing that this is a life and death matter.

Some of us tried to hide part of our past in an attempt to find an easier way of dealing with our inner feelings. We may think that we have done enough by writing about our past. We cannot afford this mistake. This step will expose our motives and our actions. We cannot expect these things to reveal themselves.

Our embarrassment is eventually overcome, and we can avoid future guilt.

We do not procrastinate. We must be exact. We want to tell the simple truth, cut and dried, as quickly as possible. There is always a danger that we will exaggerate our wrongs. It is equally dangerous to minimize or rationalize our part in past situations. After all, we still want to sound good.

Addicts tend to live secret lives. For many years, we covered low self-esteem by hiding behind phony images that we hoped would fool people. Unfortunately, we fooled ourselves more than anyone. Although we often appeared attractive and confident on the outside, we were really hiding a shaky, insecure person on the inside. The masks have to go. We share our inventory as it is written, skipping nothing. We continue to approach this step with honesty and thoroughness until we finish. It is a great relief to get rid of all our secrets and to share the burden of our past.

Usually, as we share this step, the listener will share some of his or her story too. We find that we are not unique. We see, by the acceptance of our confidant, that we can be accepted just the way we are.

We may never be able to remember all of our past mistakes. We do, however, give it our best and most complete effort. We begin to experience real personal feelings of a spiritual nature. Where once we had spiritual theories, we now begin to awaken to spiritual reality. This initial examination of ourselves usually reveals some behavior patterns that we don't particularly like. However, facing these patterns and bringing them out in the open makes it possible for us to deal with them constructively. We cannot make these changes alone. We will need the help of God, as we understand Him, and the Fellowship of Narcotics Anonymous.

Step Six

"We were entirely ready to have God remove all these defects of character."

Why ask for something before we are ready for it? This would be asking for trouble. So many times addicts have sought the rewards of hard work without the labor. Willingness is what we strive for in Step Six. How sincerely we work this step will be proportionate to our desire for change.

Do we really want to be rid of our resentments, our anger, our fear? Many of us cling to our fears, doubts, self-loathing or hatred because there is a certain distorted security in familiar pain. It seems safer to embrace what we know than to let go of it for the unknown.

Letting go of character defects should be done decisively. We suffer because their demands weaken us. Where we were proud, we now find that we cannot get away with arrogance. If we are not humble, we are humiliated. If we are greedy, we find that we are never satisfied. Before taking Steps Four and Five, we could indulge in fear, anger, dishonesty or self-pity. Now indulgence in these character defects clouds our ability to think logically. Selfishness becomes an intolerable, destructive chain that ties us to our bad habits. Our defects drain us of all our time and energy.

We examine the Fourth Step inventory and get a good look at what these defects are doing to our lives. We begin to long for freedom from these defects. We pray or otherwise become willing, ready and able to let God remove these destructive traits. We need a personality change, if we are to stay clean. We want to change.

We should approach old defects with an open mind. We are aware of them and yet we still make the same mistakes and are unable to break the bad habits. We look to the Fellowship for the kind of life that we want for ourselves. We ask our friends, "Did you let go?" Almost without exception the answer is, "Yes, to the best of my ability." When we see how our defects exist in our lives and accept them, we can let go of them and get on with our new life. We learn that we are growing when we make new mistakes instead of repeating old ones.

When we are working Step Six, it is important to remember that we are human and should not place unrealistic expectations on ourselves. This is a step of willingness. Willingness is the spiritual principle of Step Six. Step Six helps us move in a spiritual direction. Being human we will wander off course.

Rebellion is a character defect that spoils us here. We need not lose faith when we become rebellious. Rebellion can produce indifference or intolerance which can be overcome by persistent effort. We keep asking for willingness. We may be doubtful that God will see fit to relieve us or that something will go wrong. We ask another member who says, "You're right where you're supposed to be." We renew our readiness to have our defects removed. We surrender to the simple suggestions that the program offers us. Even though we are not entirely ready, we are headed in the right direction.

Eventually faith, humility and acceptance replace pride and rebellion. We come to know ourselves. We find ourselves growing into mature consciousness. We begin to feel better, as willingness grows into hope. Perhaps for the first time, we see a vision of our new life. With this in sight, we put our willingness into action by moving on to Step Seven.

Step Seven

"We humbly asked Him to remove our shortcomings."

Character defects or shortcomings are those things that cause pain and misery all of our lives. If they contributed to our health and happiness, we would not have come to such a state of desperation. We had to become ready to have God, as we understood Him, remove these defects.

Having decided that we want God to relieve us of the useless or destructive aspects of our personalities, we have arrived at the Seventh Step. We couldn't handle the ordeal of life all by ourselves. It wasn't until we made a real mess of our lives that we realized we couldn't do it alone. By admitting this, we achieved a glimpse of humility. This is the main ingredient of Step Seven. Humility is a result of getting honest with ourselves. We have practiced being honest since Step One. We accepted our addiction and powerlessness. We found a strength beyond ourselves and learned to rely on it. We examined our lives and discovered who we really are. To be truly humble is to accept and honestly try to be ourselves. None of us is perfectly good or perfectly bad. We are people who have assets and liabilities. Most importantly, we are human.

Humility is as much a part of staying clean as food and water are to staying alive. As our addiction progressed, we devoted our energy toward satisfying our material desires. All other needs were beyond our reach. We always wanted gratification of our basic desires.

The Seventh Step is an action step, and it is time to ask God for help and relief. We have to understand that our way of thinking is not the only way; other people can give us direction. When someone points out a shortcoming, our first reaction may be defensive. We must realize that we are not perfect. There will always be room for growth. If we truly want to be free, we will take a good look at input from fellow addicts. If the shortcomings we discover are real, and we have a chance to be rid of them, we will surely experience a sense of well-being.

Some will want to get on their knees for this step. Some will be very quiet, and others will put forth a great emotional effort to show intense willingness. The word humble applies because we approach this Power greater than ourselves to ask for the freedom to live without the limitations of our past ways. Many of us are willing to work this step without reservations, on pure blind faith, because we are sick of what we have been doing and how we are feeling. Whatever works, we go all the way.

This is our road to spiritual growth. We change every day. We gradually and carefully pull ourselves out of the isolation and loneliness of addiction and into the mainstream of life. This growth is not the result of wishing, but of action and prayer. The main objective of Step Seven is to get out of ourselves and strive to achieve the will of our Higher Power.

If we are careless and fail to grasp the spiritual meaning of this step, we may have difficulties and stir up old troubles. One danger is in being too hard on ourselves.

Sharing with other recovering addicts will help us to avoid becoming morbidly serious about ourselves. Accepting the defects of others can help us become humble and pave the way for our own defects to be relieved. God often works through those who care enough about recovery to help make us aware of our shortcomings.

We have noticed that humility plays a big part in this program and our new way of life. We take our inventory; we become ready to let God remove our defects of character; we humbly ask Him to remove our shortcomings. This is our road to spiritual growth, and we will want to continue. We are ready for Step Eight.

Step Eight

"We made a list of all persons we had harmed, and became willing to make amends to them all."

Step Eight is the test of our newfound humility. Our purpose is to achieve freedom from the guilt that we have carried. We want to look the world in the eye with neither aggressiveness nor fear.

Are we willing to make a list of all persons we had harmed to clear away the fear and guilt that our past holds for us? Our experience tells us that we must become willing before this step will have any effect.

The Eighth Step is not easy; it demands a new kind of honesty about our relations with other people. The Eighth Step starts the process of forgiveness: We forgive others; possibly we are forgiven; and finally we forgive ourselves and learn how to live in the world. By the time we reach this step, we have become ready to understand rather than to be understood. We can live and let live easier when we know the areas in which we owe amends. It seems hard now, but once we have done it, we will wonder why we did not do it long ago.

We need some real honesty before we can make an accurate list. In preparing to make the Eighth Step list, it is helpful to define harm. One definition of harm is physical or mental damage. Another definition of harm is inflicting pain, suffering or loss. The damage may be caused by something that is said, done or left undone. Harm can result from words or actions, either intentional or unintentional. The degree of harm can range from making someone feel mentally uncomfortable to inflicting bodily injury or even death.

The Eighth Step presents us with a problem. Many of us have difficulty admitting that we caused harm for others, because we thought we were victims of our addiction. Avoiding this rationalization is crucial to the Eighth Step. We must separate what was done to us from what we did to others. We cut away our justifications and our ideas of being a victim. We often feel that we only harmed ourselves, yet we usually list ourselves last, if at all. This step is doing the legwork to repair the wreckage of our lives.

It will not make us better people to judge the faults of another. It will make us feel better to clean up our lives by relieving ourselves of guilt. By writing our list, we can no longer deny that we caused harm. We admit that we hurt others, directly or indirectly, through some action, lie, broken promise or neglect.

We make our list, or take it from our Fourth Step, and add additional people as we think of them. We face this list honestly, and openly examine our faults so we can become willing to make amends.

In some cases, we may not know the persons that we have wronged. While using, anyone that we contacted was at risk. Many members mention their parents, spouses, children, friends, lovers, other addicts, casual acquaintances, co-workers, employers, teachers, landlords and total strangers. We may also place ourselves on the list, because while practicing our addiction, we have slowly been killing ourselves. We may find it beneficial to make a separate list of people to whom we owe financial amends.

As with each step, we must be thorough. Most of us fall short of our goals more often than we exceed them. At the same time, we cannot put off completion of this step just because we are not sure that our list is complete. We are never finished.

The final difficulty in working the Eighth Step is separating it from the Ninth Step. Projections about actually making amends can be a major obstacle both in making the list and in becoming willing. We do this step as if there were no Ninth Step. We do not even think about making the amends but just concentrate on exactly what the Eighth Step says: make a list and become willing. The main thing this step does for us is to help build awareness that, little by little, we are gaining new attitudes about ourselves and how we deal with other people.

Listening carefully to other members share their experience regarding this step can relieve any confusion that we may have about writing our list. Also, our sponsors may share with us how Step Eight worked for them. Asking a question during a meeting can give us the benefit of group conscience.

The Eighth Step offers a big change from a life dominated by guilt and remorse. Our futures are changed, because we don't have to avoid those who we have harmed. As a result of this step, we receive a new freedom that can end isolation. As we realize our need to be forgiven, we tend to be more forgiving. At least, we know that we are no longer intentionally making life miserable for people.

The Eighth Step is an action step. Like all the steps, it offers immediate benefits. We are now free to begin our amends in Step Nine.

Step Nine

"We made direct amends to such people wherever possible, except when to do so would injure them or others."

This step should not be avoided. If we do, we are reserving a place in our program for relapse. Pride, fear and procrastination often seem an impossible barrier; they stand in the way of progress and growth. The important thing is to take action and to be ready to accept the reactions of those persons we have harmed. We make amends to the best of our ability.

Timing is an essential part of this step. We should make amends when the opportunity presents itself, except when to do so will cause more harm. Sometimes we cannot actually make the amends; it is neither possible nor practical. In some cases, amends may be beyond our means. We find that willingness can serve in the place of action where we are unable to contact the person that we have harmed. However, we should never fail to contact anyone because of embarrassment, fear or procrastination.

We want to be free of our guilt, but we don't wish to do so at the expense of anyone else. We might run the risk of involving a third person or some companion from our using days who does not wish to be exposed. We do not have the right or the need to endanger another person. It is often necessary to take guidance from others in these matters.

We recommend turning our legal problems over to lawyers and our financial or medical problems to professionals. Part of learning how to live successfully is learning when we need help.

In some old relationships, an unresolved conflict may still exist. We do our part to resolve old conflicts by making our amends. We want to step away from further antagonisms and ongoing resentments. In many instances, we can only go to the person and humbly ask for understanding of past wrongs. Sometimes this will be a joyous occasion when old friends or relatives prove willing to let go of their bitterness. Contacting someone who is still hurting from the burn of our misdeeds can be dangerous. Indirect amends may be necessary where direct ones would be unsafe or endanger other people. We make our amends to the best of our ability. We try to remember that when we make amends, we are doing it for ourselves. Instead of feeling guilty and remorseful, we feel relieved about our past.

We accept that it was our actions that caused our negative attitude. Step Nine helps us with our guilt and helps others with their anger. Sometimes, the only amend we can make is to stay clean. We owe it to ourselves and to our loved ones. We are no longer making a mess in society as a result of our using. Sometimes the only way we can make amends is to contribute to society. Now, we are helping ourselves and other addicts to recover. This is a tremendous amend to the whole community.

In the process of our recovery, we are restored to sanity and part of sanity is effectively relating to others. We less often view people as a threat to our security. Real security will replace the physical ache and mental confusion that we have experienced in the past. We approach those we have harmed with humility and patience. Many of our sincere well-wishers may be reluctant to accept our recovery as real. We must remember the pain that they have known. In time, many miracles will occur. Many of us who were separated from our families succeed in establishing relationships with them. Eventually it becomes easier for them to accept the change in us. Clean time speaks for itself. Patience is an important part of our recovery. The unconditional love we experience will rejuvenate our will to live, and each positive move on our part will be matched by an unexpected opportunity. A lot of courage and faith goes into making an amend, and a lot of spiritual growth results.

We are achieving freedom from the wreckage of our past. We will want to keep our house in order by practicing a continuous personal inventory in Step Ten.

Step Ten

"We continued to take personal inventory and when we were wrong promptly admitted it."

Step Ten frees us from the wreckage of our present. If we do not stay aware of our defects, they can drive us into a corner that we can't get out of clean.

One of the first things we learn in Narcotics Anonymous is that if we use, we lose. By the same token, we won't experience as much pain if we can avoid the things that cause us pain. Continuing to take a personal inventory means that we form a habit of looking at ourselves, our actions, attitudes and relationships on a regular basis.

We are creatures of habit and are vulnerable to our old ways of thinking and reacting. At times it seems easier to continue in the old rut of self-destruction than to attempt a new and seemingly dangerous route. We don't have to be trapped by our old patterns. Today, we have a choice.

The Tenth Step can help us correct our living problems and prevent their recurrence. We examine our actions during the day. Some of us write about our feelings, explaining how we felt and what part we might have played in any problems which occurred. Did we cause someone harm? Do we need to admit that we were wrong? If we find difficulties, we make an effort to take care of them. When these things are left undone, they have a way of festering.

This step can be a defense against the old insanity. We can ask ourselves if we are being drawn into old patterns of anger, resentment or fear. Do we feel trapped? Are we setting ourselves up for trouble? Are we too hungry, angry, lonely or tired? Are we taking ourselves too seriously? Are we judging our insides by the outside appearances of others? Do we suffer from some physical problem? The answers to these questions can help us deal with the difficulties of the moment. We no longer have to live with the feeling that we have a "hole in the gut." A lot of our chief concerns and major difficulties come from our inexperience with living without drugs. Often when we ask an oldtimer what to do, we are amazed at the simplicity of the answer.

The Tenth Step can be a pressure relief valve. We work this step while the day's ups and downs are still fresh in our minds. We list what we have done and try not to rationalize our actions. This may be done in writing at the end of the day. The first thing we do is stop! Then we take the time to allow ourselves the privilege of thinking. We examine our actions, reactions, and motives. We often find that we've been doing better than we've been feeling. This allows us to examine our actions and admit fault, before things get any worse. We need to avoid rationalizing. We promptly admit our faults, not explain them.

We work this step continuously. This is a preventive action. The more we work this step the less we will need the corrective part of this step. This step is a great tool for avoiding grief before we bring it on ourselves. We monitor our feelings, emotions, fantasies and actions. By constantly looking at ourselves, we are able to avoid repeating the actions that make us feel bad.

We need this step even when we're feeling good and when things are going well. Good feelings are new to us, and we need to nurture them. In times of trouble, we can try the things that worked during the good times. We have the right to feel good. We have a choice. The good times can also be a trap; the danger is that we may forget that our first priority is to stay clean. For us, recovery is more than just pleasure.

We need to remember that everyone makes mistakes. We will never be perfect. However, we can accept ourselves by using Step Ten. By continuing a personal inventory, we are set free, in the here and now, from ourselves and the past. We no longer justify our existence. This step allows us to be ourselves.

Step Eleven

"We sought through prayer and meditation to improve our conscious contact with God as we understood Him, praying only for knowledge of His will for us and the power to carry that out."

The first ten steps have set the stage for us to improve our conscious contact with the God of our understanding. They give us the foundation to achieve our long-sought, positive goals. Having entered this phase of our spiritual program through practicing the previous ten steps, most of us welcome the exercise of prayer and meditation. Our spiritual condition is the basis for a successful recovery that offers unlimited growth.

Many of us really begin to appreciate our recovery when we get to the Eleventh Step. In the Eleventh Step, our lives take on a deeper meaning. By surrendering control, we gain a far greater power.

The nature of our belief will determine the manner of our prayers and meditations. We need only make sure that we have a system of belief that works for us. Results count in recovery. As has been noted elsewhere, our prayers seemed to work as soon as we entered the Program of Narcotics Anonymous and we surrendered to our disease. The conscious contact described in this step is the direct result of living the steps. We use this step to improve and maintain our spiritual condition.

When we first came into the program, we received help from a Power greater than ourselves. This was set in motion by our surrender to the program. The purpose of the Eleventh Step is to increase our awareness of that Power and to improve our ability to use it as a source of strength in our new lives.

The more we improve our conscious contact with our God through prayer and meditation, the easier it is to say, "Your will, not mine, be done." We can ask for God's help when we need it, and our lives get better. The experiences that some people talk about regarding meditation and individual religious beliefs don't always apply to us. Ours is a spiritual, not a religious program. By the time we get to the Eleventh Step, character defects that caused problems in the past have been addressed by working the preceding ten steps. The image of the kind of person that we would like to be is a fleeting glimpse of God's will for us. Often our outlook is so limited that we can only see our immediate wants and needs.

It is easy to slip back into our old ways. To ensure our continued growth and recovery, we have to learn to maintain our lives on a spiritually sound basis. God will not force His goodness on us, but we will receive it if we ask. We usually feel something is different in the moment, but don't see the change in our lives till later. When we finally get our own selfish motives out of the way, we begin to find a peace that we never imagined possible. Enforced morality lacks the power that comes to us when we choose to live a spiritual life. Most of us pray when we are hurting. We learn that if we pray regularly we won't be hurting as often, or as intensely.

Outside of Narcotics Anonymous, there are any number of different groups practicing meditation. Nearly all of these groups are connected with a particular religion or philosophy. An endorsement of any one of these methods would be a violation of our traditions and a restriction on the individual's right to have a God of his understanding. Meditation allows us to develop spiritually in our own way. Some of the things that didn't work for us in the past, might work today. We take a fresh look at each day with an open mind. We know that if we pray for God's will, we will receive what is best for us, regardless of what we think. This knowledge is based on our belief and experience as recovering addicts.

Prayer is communicating our concerns to a Power greater than ourselves. Sometimes when we pray, a remarkable thing happens; we find the means, ways and energies to perform tasks far beyond our capacities. We grasp the limitless strength provided for us through our daily prayer and surrender, as long as we keep faith and renew it.

For some, prayer is asking for God's help; meditation is listening for God's answer. We learn to be careful of praying for specific things. We pray that God will show us His will, and that He will help us carry that out. In some cases, he makes His will so obvious to us that we have little difficulty seeing it. In others, our egos are so self-centered that we won't accept God's will for us without another struggle and surrender. If we pray for God to remove any distracting influences, the quality of our prayers usually improves and we feel the difference. Prayer takes practice, and we should remind ourselves that skilled people were not born with their skills. It took lots of effort on their part to develop them. Through prayer, we seek conscious contact with our God. In meditation, we achieve this contact, and the Eleventh Step helps us to maintain it.

We may have been exposed to many religions and meditative disciplines before coming to Narcotics Anonymous. Some of us were devastated and completely confused by these practices. We were sure that it was God's will for us to use drugs to reach higher consciousness. Many of us found ourselves in very strange states as a result of these practices. We never suspected the damaging effects of our addiction as the root of our difficulty and pursued to the end whatever path offered hope.

In quiet moments of meditation, God's will can become evident to us. Quieting the mind through meditation brings an inner peace that brings us into contact with the God within us. A basic premise of meditation is that it is difficult, if not impossible, to obtain conscious contact unless our mind is still. The usual, never-ending succession of thoughts has to cease for progress to be made. So our preliminary practice is aimed at stilling the mind, and letting the thoughts that arise die a natural death. We leave our thoughts behind as the meditation part of the Eleventh Step becomes a reality for us.

Emotional balance is one of the first results of meditation, and our experience bears this out. Some of us came into the program broken, and hung around for awhile, only to find God or salvation in one kind of religious cult or another. It is easy to float back out the door on a cloud of religious zeal and forget that we are addicts with an incurable disease.

It is said that for meditation to be of value, the results must show in our daily lives. This fact is implicit in the Eleventh Step: "...His will for us and the power to carry it out." For those of us who do not pray, meditation is our only way of working this step.

We find ourselves praying, because it brings us peace and restores our confidence and courage. It helps us to live a life that is free of fear and distrust. When we remove our selfish motives and pray for guidance, we find feelings of peace and serenity. We begin to experience an awareness and an empathy with other people that was not possible before working this step.

As we seek our personal contact with God, we begin to open up as a flower in the sun. We begin to see that God's love has been·present all the time, just waiting for us to accept it. We do the footwork and accept what's being given to us freely on a daily basis. We find relying on God becomes more comfortable for us.

When we first come to the program, we usually ask for a lot of things that seem to be important wants and needs. As we grow spiritually and find a Power greater than ourselves, we begin to realize that as long as our spiritual needs are met, our living problems are reduced to a point of comfort. When we forget where our real strength lies, we quickly become subject to the same patterns of thinking and action that got us to the program in the first place. We eventually redefine our beliefs and understanding to the point where we see that our greatest need is for knowledge of God's will for us and the strength to carry that out. We are able to set aside some of our personal preference, because we learn that God's will for us consists of the very things we most value. God's will for us becomes our own true will for ourselves. This happens in an intuitive manner that cannot be adequately explained in words.

We become willing to let other people be who they are without having to pass judgment on them. The urgency to take care of things isn't there anymore. We couldn't comprehend acceptance in the beginning; today we can.

We know that whatever the day brings, God has given us everything we need for our spiritual well-being. It is all right for us to admit powerlessness, because God is powerful enough to help us stay clean and to enjoy spiritual progress. God is helping us to get our house in order.

We begin to see more clearly what is real. Through constant contact with our Higher Power, the answers that we seek come to us. We gain the ability to do what we once could not. We respect the beliefs of others. We encourage you to seek strength and guidance according to your belief.

We are thankful for this step, because we begin to get what is best for us. Sometimes we prayed for our wants and got trapped once we got them. We could pray and get something, then have to pray for its removal, because we couldn't handle it.

Hopefully, having learned the power of prayer and the responsibility prayer brings with it, we can use the Eleventh Step as a guideline for our daily program.

We begin to pray only for God's will for us. This way we are getting only what we are capable of handling. We are able to respond to it and handle it, because God helps us prepare for it. Some of us simply use our words to give thanks for God's grace.

In an attitude of surrender and humility, we approach this step again and again to receive the gift of knowledge and strength from the God of our understanding. The Tenth Step clears away the errors of the present so we may work the Eleventh Step. Without this step, it is unlikely that we could experience a spiritual awakening, practice spiritual principles in our lives or carry a sufficient message to attract others to recovery. There is a spiritual principle of giving away what we have been given in Narcotics Anonymous in order to keep it. By helping others to stay clean, we enjoy the benefit of the spiritual wealth that we have found. We must give freely and gratefully that which has been freely and gratefully given to us.

Step Twelve

"Having had a spiritual awakening as a result of these steps, we tried to carry this message to addicts, and to practice these principles in all our affairs."

We came to Narcotics Anonymous as the result of the wreckage of our past. The last thing we expected was an awakening of the spirit. We just wanted to stop hurting.

The steps lead to an awakening of a spiritual nature. This awakening is evidenced by changes in our lives. These changes make us better able to live by spiritual principles and to carry our message of recovery and hope to the addict who still suffers. The message, however, is meaningless unless we LIVE it. As we live it, our lives and actions give it more meaning than our words and literature ever could.

The idea of a spiritual awakening takes many different forms in the different personalities that we find in the Fellowship.

However, all spiritual awakenings have some things in common. Common elements include an end to loneliness and a sense of direction in our lives. Many of us believe that a spiritual awakening is meaningless unless accompanied by an increase in peace of mind and a concern for others. In order to maintain peace of mind, we strive to live in the here and now.

Those of us who have worked these steps to the best of our ability received many benefits. We believe that these benefits are a direct result of living this program.

When we first begin to enjoy relief from our addiction, we run the risk of assuming control of our lives again. We forget the agony and pain that we have known. Our disease controlled our lives when we were using. It is ready and waiting to take over again. We quickly forget that all our past efforts at controlling our lives failed.

By this time, most of us realize that the only way that we can keep what was given to us is by sharing this new gift of life with the still-suffering addict. This is our best insurance against relapse to the torturous existence of using. We call it carrying the message, and we do it in a number of ways.

In the Twelfth Step, we practice the spiritual principles of giving the NA message of recovery in order to keep it. Even a member with one day in the NA Fellowship can carry the message that this program works.

When we share with someone new, we may ask to be used as a spiritual instrument of our Higher Power. We don't set ourselves up as gods. We often ask for the help of another recovering addict when sharing with a new person. It is a privilege to respond to a cry for help. We, who have been in the pits of despair, feel fortunate to help others find recovery.

We help new people learn the principles of Narcotics Anonymous. We try to make them feel welcome and help them learn what the program has to offer. We share our experience, strength and hope. Whenever possible, we accompany newcomers to a meeting.

The selfless service of this work is the very principle of Step Twelve. We received our recovery from the God of our understanding. We now make ourselves available as His tool to share recovery with those who seek it. Most of us learn that we can only carry our message to someone who is asking for help. Sometimes, the only message necessary to make the suffering addict reach out is the power of example. An addict may be suffering but unwilling to ask for help. We can make ourselves available to these people, so when they ask, someone will be there.

Learning to help others is a benefit of the Narcotics Anonymous Program. Remarkably, working the Twelve Steps guides us from humiliation and despair to acting as instruments of our Higher Power. We are given the ability to help a fellow addict when no one else can. We see it happening among us every day. This miraculous turnabout is evidence of spiritual awakening. We share from our own personal experience what it has been like for us. The temptation to give advice is great, but when we do so we lose the respect of newcomers. This clouds our message. A simple, honest message of recovery from addiction rings true.

We attend meetings and make ourselves visible and available to serve the Fellowship. We give freely and gratefully of our time, service, and what we have found here. The service we speak of in Narcotics Anonymous is the primary purpose of our groups. Service work is carrying the message to the addict who still suffers. The more eagerly we wade in and work, the richer our spiritual awakening will be.

The first way that we carry the message speaks for itself. People see us on the street and remember us as devious, frightened loners. They notice the fear leaving our faces. They see us gradually come alive.

Once we find the NA way, boredom and complacency have no place in our new life. By staying clean, we begin to practice spiritual principles such as hope, surrender, acceptance, honesty, open-mindedness, willingness, faith, tolerance, patience, humility, unconditional love, sharing and caring. As our recovery progresses, spiritual principles touch every area of our lives, because we simply try to live this program in the here and now.

We find joy as we start to learn how to live by the principles of recovery. It is the joy of watching as a person two days clean says to a person with one day clean, "An addict alone is in bad company." It is the joy of watching a person who was struggling to make it suddenly, in the middle of helping another addict to stay clean, become able to find the words needed to carry the message of recovery.

We feel that our lives have become worthwhile. Spiritually refreshed, we are glad to be alive. When we were using, our lives became an exercise in survival. Now we are doing much more living than surviving. Realizing that the bottom line is staying clean, we can enjoy life. We like being clean and enjoy carrying the message of recovery to the addict who still suffers. Going to meetings really works.

Practicing spiritual principles in our daily lives leads us to a new image of ourselves. Honesty, humility and open-mindedness help us to treat our associates fairly. Our decisions become tempered with tolerance. We learn to respect ourselves.

The lessons we learn in our recovery are sometimes bitter and painful. By helping others we find the reward of self-respect, as we are able to share these lessons with other members of Narcotics Anonymous. We cannot deny other addicts their pain, but we can carry the message of hope that was given to us by fellow addicts in recovery. We share the principles of recovery, as they have worked in our lives. God helps us as we help each other. Life takes on a new meaning, a new joy, and a quality of being and feeling worthwhile. We become spiritually refreshed and are glad to be alive. One aspect of our spiritual awakening comes through the new understanding of our Higher Power that we develop by sharing another addict's recovery.

Yes, we are a vision of hope. We are examples of the program working. The joy that we have in living clean is an attraction to the addict who still suffers.

We do recover to live clean and happy lives. Welcome to NA. The steps do not end here. The steps are a new beginning!

Chapter Five

What Can I Do?

Begin your own program by taking Step One from the previous chapter, How It Works. When we fully concede to our innermost selves that we are powerless over our addiction, we have taken a big step in our recovery. Many of us have had some reservations at this point, so give yourself a break and be as thorough as possible from the start. Go on to Step Two, and so forth, and as you go on you will come to an understanding of the program for yourself. If you are in an institution of any kind and have stopped using for the present, you can with a clear mind try this way of life.

Upon release, continue your daily program and contact a member of NA. Do this by mail, by phone, or in person. Better yet, come to our meetings. Here, you will find answers to some of the things that may be disturbing you now.

If you are not in an institution, the same holds true. Stop using for today. Most of us can do for eight or twelve hours what seems impossible for a longer period of time. If the obsession or compulsion becomes too great, put yourself on a five minute basis of not using. Minutes will grow to hours, and hours to days, so you will break the habit and gain some peace of mind. The real miracle happens when you realize that the need for drugs has in some way been lifted from you. You have stopped using and have started to live.

The first step to recovery is to stop using. We cannot expect the program to work for us if our minds and bodies are still clouded by drugs. We can do this anywhere, even in prison or an institution. We do it anyway we can, cold turkey or in a detox, just as long as we get clean.

Developing the concept of God as we understand Him is a project that we can undertake. We can also use the steps to improve our attitudes. Our best thinking got us into trouble. We recognize the need for change. Our disease involved much more than just using drugs, so our recovery must involve much more than simple abstinence. Recovery is an active change in our ideas and attitudes.

The ability to face problems is necessary to stay clean. If we had problems in the past, it is unlikely that simple abstinence will solve these problems. Guilt and worry can keep us from living in the here and now. Denial of our disease and other reservations keep us sick. Many of us feel that we cannot possibly have a happy life without drugs. We suffer from fear and insanity and feel that there is no escape from using. We may fear rejection from our friends if we get clean. These feelings are common to the addict seeking recovery. We could be suffering from an overly sensitive ego. Some of the most common excuses for using are loneliness, self-pity, and fear. Dishonesty, close-mindedness, and unwillingness are three of our greatest enemies. Self-obsession is the core of our disease.

We have learned that old ideas and old ways won't help us to stay clean or to live a better life. If we allow ourselves to stagnate and cling to terminal hipness and fatal cool, we are giving into the symptoms of our disease. One of the problems is that we found it easier to change our perception of reality than to change reality. We must give up this old concept and face the fact that reality and life go on, whether we choose to accept them or not. We can only change the way we react and the way we see ourselves. This is necessary for us to accept that change is gradual and recovery is an ongoing process.

A meeting a day for at least the first ninety days of recovery is a good idea. There is a special feeling for addicts when they discover that there are other people who share their difficulties, past and present. At first we can do little more than attend meetings. Probably we cannot remember a single word, person or thought from our first meeting. In time, we can relax and enjoy the atmosphere of recovery. Meetings strengthen our recovery. We may be scared at first because we don't know anyone. Some of us think that we don't need meetings. However, when we hurt, we go to a meeting and find relief. Meetings keep us in touch with where we've been, but more importantly with where we could go in our recovery. As we go to meetings regularly, we learn the value of talking with other addicts who share our problems and goals. We have to open up and accept the love and understanding that we need in order to change. When we become acquainted with the Fellowship and its principles and begin to put them into action, we start to grow. We apply effort to our most obvious problems and let go of the rest. We do the job at hand, and as we progress, new opportunities for improvement present themselves.

Our new friends in the Fellowship will help us. Our common effort is recovery. Clean, we face the world together. We no longer have to feel backed into a corner, at the mercy of events and circumstances. It makes a difference to have friends who care if we hurt. We find our place in the Fellowship, and we join a group whose meetings help us in our recovery. We have been untrustworthy for so long that most of our friends and families will doubt our recovery. They think it won't last. We need people who understand our disease and the recovery process. At meetings we can share with other addicts, ask questions and learn about our disease. We learn new ways to live. We are no longer limited to our old ideas.

Gradually, we replace old habits with new ways of living. We become willing to change. We go to meetings regularly, get and use telephone numbers, read literature, and most importantly, we don't use. We learn to share with others. If we don't tell someone we are hurting, they will seldom see it. When we reach out for help, we can receive it.

Another tool for the newcomer is involvement with the Fellowship. As we become involved we learn to keep the program first and take it easy in other matters. We begin by asking for help and trying out the recommendations of people at the meetings. It is beneficial to allow others in the group to help us. In time, we will be able to pass on what we have been given. We learn that service to others will get us out of ourselves. Our work can begin with simple actions: emptying ashtrays, making coffee, cleaning up, setting up for a meeting, opening the door, chairing a meeting, and passing out literature. Doing these things helps us feel a part of the Fellowship.

We have found it helpful to have a sponsor and to use this sponsor. Sponsorship is a two-way street. It helps both the newcomer and the sponsor. The sponsor's clean time and experience may well depend on the availability of sponsors in a locality. Sponsorship for newcomers is also the responsibility of the group. It is implied and informal in its approach, but it is the heart of the NA way of recovery from addiction—one addict helping another.

One of the most profound changes in our lives is in the realm of personal relationships. Our earliest involvements with others often begin with our sponsor. As newcomers, we find it easier if we have someone whose judgement we trust and in whom we can confide. We find that trusting others with more experience is a strength rather than a weakness. Our experience reveals that working the steps is our best guarantee against relapse. Our sponsors and friends can advise us on how to work the steps. We can talk over what the steps mean. They can help us to prepare for the spiritual experience of living the steps. Asking God as we understand Him for help improves our understanding of the steps. When we are prepared, we must try out our newly found way of life. We learn that the program won't work when we try to adapt it to our life. We must learn to adapt our life to the program.

Today, we seek solutions, not problems. We try what we have learned on an experimental basis. We keep what we need and leave the rest. We find that by working the steps, communicating with our Higher Power, talking to our sponsors, and sharing with newcomers, we are able to grow spiritually.

The Twelve Steps are used as a program of recovery. We learn that we can go to our Higher Power for help in solving problems. When we find ourselves sharing difficulties that used to have us on the run, we experience good feelings that give us the strength to begin seeking God's will for us.

We believe that our Higher Power will take care of us. If we honestly try to do God's will, to the best of our ability, we can handle anything that happens. Seeking our Higher Power's will is a spiritual principle found in the steps. Working the steps and practicing the principles simplifies our lives and changes our old attitudes. When we admit that our lives have become unmanageable, we don't have to argue our point of view. We have to accept ourselves as we are. We no longer have to be right all the time. When we give ourselves this freedom, we can allow others to be wrong. Freedom to change seems to come after acceptance of ourselves.

Sharing with fellow addicts is a basic tool in our program. This help can only come from another addict. It is this help that says, "I have had something like that happen to me, and I did this ..." For anyone who wants our way of life, we share experience, strength, and hope instead of preaching and judging. If sharing the experience of our pain helps just one person, it was worth the suffering. We strengthen our own recovery when we share it with others who ask for help. If we keep what we have to share, we lose it. Words mean nothing until we put them into action.

We recognize our spiritual growth when we are able to reach out and help others. We help others when we participate in service work and try to carry the message of recovery to the addict who still suffers. We learn that we keep what we have only by giving it away. Also, our experience shows that many personal problems are resolved when we get out of ourselves and offer to help those in need. We recognize that one addict can best understand and help another addict. No matter how much we give, there is always another addict seeking help.

We cannot afford to lose sight of the importance of sponsorship and of taking a special interest in a confused addict who wants to stop using. Experience shows clearly that those who get the most out of the Narcotics Anonymous Program are those to whom sponsorship is important. Sponsorship responsibilities are welcomed by us and accepted as opportunities to enrich our personal NA experience.

Working with others is only the beginning of service work. NA service allows us to spend much of our time directly helping suffering addicts, as well as ensuring that Narcotics Anonymous itself survives. This way we keep what we have by giving it away.

Chapter Six

The Twelve Traditions
of Narcotics Anonymous

*We keep what we have only with vigilance, and just as freedom
for the individual comes from the Twelve Steps, so freedom for
the group springs from our Traditions.*

*As long as the ties that bind us together are stronger than
those that would tear us apart, all will be well.*

1. *Our common welfare should come first; personal recovery
   depends on NA unity.*

2. *For our group purpose there is but one ultimate
   authority—a loving God as He may express Himself
   in our group conscience. Our leaders are but trusted
   servants; they do not govern.*

3. *The only requirement for membership is a desire to stop
   using.*

4. *Each group should be autonomous except in matters
   affecting other groups or NA as a whole.*

5. *Each group has but one primary purpose—to carry the
   message to the addict who still suffers.*

6. *An NA group ought never endorse, finance, or lend the
   NA name to any related facility or outside enterprise, lest
   problems of money, property or prestige divert us from our
   primary purpose.*

7. *Every NA group ought to be fully self-supporting,
   declining outside contributions.*

8. *Narcotics Anonymous should remain forever
   nonprofessional, but our service centers may employ
   special workers.*

9. *NA, as such, ought never be organized, but we may create service boards or committees directly responsible to those they serve.*

10. *Narcotics Anonymous has no opinion on outside issues; hence the NA name ought never be drawn into public controversy.*

11. *Our public relations policy is based on attraction rather than promotion; we need always maintain personal anonymity at the level of press, radio, and films.*

12. *Anonymity is the spiritual foundation of all our Traditions, ever reminding us to place principles before personalities.*

Understanding these Traditions comes slowly over a period of time. We pick up information as we talk to members and visit various groups. It usually isn't until we get involved with service that someone points out that "personal recovery depends on NA unity," and that unity depends on how well we follow our Traditions. The Twelve Traditions of NA are not negotiable. They are the guidelines that keep our Fellowship alive and free.

By following these guidelines in our dealings with others, and society at large, we avoid many problems. That is not to say that our Traditions eliminate all problems. We still have to face difficulties as they arise: communication problems, differences of opinion, internal controversies, and troubles with individuals and groups outside the Fellowship. However, when we apply these principles, we avoid some of the pitfalls.

Many of our problems are like those that our predecessors had to face. Their hard won experience gave birth to the Traditions, and our own experience has shown that these principles are just as valid today as they were when these Traditions were formulated. Our Traditions protect us from the internal and external forces that could destroy us. They are truly the ties that bind us together. It is only through understanding and application that they work.

Tradition One

"Our common welfare should come first; personal recovery depends on NA unity."

Our First Tradition concerns unity and our common welfare. One of the most important things about our new way of life is being a part of a group of addicts seeking recovery. Our survival is directly related to the survival of the group and the Fellowship. To maintain unity within Narcotics Anonymous, it is imperative that the group remain stable, or the entire Fellowship perishes and the individual dies.

It wasn't until we came to Narcotics Anonymous that recovery became possible. This program can do for us what we could not do for ourselves. We became part of a group and found that we could recover. We learned that those who did not continue to be an active part of the Fellowship faced a rough road. The individual is precious to the group, and the group is precious to the individual. We never experienced the kind of attention and personal care that we found in the program. We are accepted and loved for who we are, not in spite of who we are. No one can revoke our membership or make us do anything that we do not choose to do. We follow this way of life by example rather than direction. We share our experience and learn from each other. In our addiction, we consistently placed our personal desires before anything else. In Narcotics Anonymous we find that what is best for the group is usually good for us.

Our personal experiences while using differed from one another. As a group, however, we have found many common themes in our addiction. One of these was the need to prove self-sufficiency. We had convinced ourselves that we could make it alone and proceeded to live life on that basis. The results were disastrous and, in the end, each of us had to admit that self-sufficiency was a lie. This admission was the starting point of our recovery and is a primary point of unity for the Fellowship. We had common themes in our addiction, and we find that in our recovery we have much in common. We share a common desire to stay clean. We have learned to depend on a Power greater than ourselves. Our purpose is to carry the message to the addict who still suffers. Our Traditions are the guidelines that protect us from ourselves. They are our unity.

Unity is a must in Narcotics Anonymous. This is not to say that we do not have our disagreements and conflicts; we do. Whenever people get together there are differences of opinions. However, we can disagree without being disagreeable. Time and time again, in crises we have set aside our differences and worked for the common good. We have seen two members, who usually do not get along, work together with a newcomer. We have seen a group doing menial tasks to pay rent for their meeting hall. We have seen members drive hundreds of miles to help support a new group. These activities and many others are commonplace in our Fellowship. Without these actions NA could not survive.

We must live and work together as a group to ensure that in a storm our ship does not sink and our members do not perish. With faith in a Power greater than ourselves, hard work, and unity we will survive and continue to carry the message to the addict who still suffers.

Tradition Two

"For our group purpose there is but one ultimate authority—
a loving God as He may express Himself in our group
conscience. Our leaders are but trusted servants; they do
not govern."

In Narcotics Anonymous, we are concerned with protecting ourselves from ourselves. Our Second Tradition is an example of this. By nature, we are strong-willed, self-centered people, who are thrust together in NA. We are mismanagers and not one of us is capable of consistently making good decisions.

In Narcotics Anonymous, we rely on a loving God as He expresses Himself in our group conscience, rather than on personal opinion or ego. By working the steps, we learn to depend on a Power greater than ourselves, and to use this Power for our group purposes. We must be constantly on guard that our decisions are truly an expression of God's will. There is often a vast difference between group conscience and group opinion, as dictated by powerful personalities or popularity. Some of our most painful growing experiences have come as a result of decisions made in the name of group conscience. True spiritual principles are never in conflict; they complement each other. The spiritual conscience of a group will never contradict any of our Traditions.

The Second Tradition concerns the nature of leadership in NA. We have learned that for our Fellowship, leadership by example and by selfless service works. Direction and manipulation fail. We choose not to have presidents, masters, or directors. Instead we have secretaries, treasurers and representatives. These titles imply service rather than control. Our experience shows that if a group becomes an extension of the personality of a leader or member, it loses its effectiveness. An atmosphere of recovery in our groups is one of our most valued assets, and we must guard it carefully, lest we lose it to politics and personalities.

Those of us who have been involved in service or in getting a group started sometimes have a hard time letting go. Egos, unfounded pride, and self-will destroy a group if given authority. We must remember that offices have been placed in trust, that we are trusted servants, and that at no time do any of us govern. Narcotics Anonymous is a God-given program, and we can maintain our group in dignity only with group conscience and God's love.

Some will resist. However, many will become the role models for the newcomers. The self-seekers soon find that they are on the outside, causing dissension and eventually disaster for themselves. Many of them change; they learn that we can only be governed by a loving God as expressed in our group conscience.

Tradition Three

"The only requirement for membership is a desire to stop using."

This tradition is important for both the individual and the group. Desire is the key word; desire is the basis of our recovery. In our stories and in our experience of trying to carry the message of recovery to the addict who still suffers, one painful fact of life has emerged again and again. An addict who does not want to stop using will not stop using. They can be analyzed, counseled, reasoned with, prayed over, threatened, beaten, or locked up, but they will not stop until they want to stop. The only thing we ask of our members is that they have this desire. Without it they are doomed, but with it miracles will happen.

Desire is our only requirement. Addiction does not discriminate. This tradition is to ensure that any addict, regardless of drugs used, race, religious beliefs, sex, sexual preference, or financial condition is free to practice the NA way of life. With "… a desire to stop using" as the only requirement for membership, one addict is never superior to another. All addicted persons are welcome and equal in obtaining the relief that they are seeking from their addiction; every addict can recover in this program on an equal basis. This tradition guarantees our freedom to recover.

Membership in Narcotics Anonymous is not automatic when someone walks in the door or when the newcomer decides to stop using. The decision to become a part of our Fellowship rests with the individual. Any addict who has a desire to stop using can become a member of NA. We are addicts, and our problem is addiction.

The choice of membership rests with the individual. We feel that the ideal state for our Fellowship exists when addicts can come freely and openly to an NA meeting, whenever and wherever they choose, and leave just as freely. We realize that recovery is a reality and that life without drugs is better than we ever imagined. We open our doors to other addicts, hoping that they can find what we have found. But we know that only those who have a desire to stop using and want what we have to offer will join us in our way of life.

Tradition Four

"Each group should be autonomous except in matters affecting other groups or NA as a whole."

The autonomy of our groups is necessary for our survival. A dictionary defines autonomous as "having the right or power of self-government...undertaken or carried on without outside control." This means our groups are self-governing, and not subject to outside control. Every group has had to stand and grow on its own.

One might ask, "Are we truly autonomous? Don't we have service committees, offices, activities, hot lines, and other activities in NA?" They are services we use to help us in our recovery and to further the primary purpose of our groups. Narcotics Anonymous is a Fellowship of men and women, addicts meeting in groups and using a given set of spiritual principles to find freedom from addiction and a new way to live. The services that we mentioned are the result of members who care enough to reach out and offer help and experience so that our road might be easier.

A Narcotics Anonymous group is any group that meets regularly, at a specified place and time, for the purpose of recovery, provided that it follows the Twelve Steps and Twelve Traditions of Narcotics Anonymous. There are two basic types of meetings: those open to the general public and those closed to the public (for addicts only). Meeting formats vary widely from group to group; some are participation meetings, some speakers, some are question and answer, and some focus on special problems discussion.

Whatever the type or format a group uses for its meetings, the function of a group is always the same; to provide a suitable and reliable environment for personal recovery and to promote such recovery. These Traditions are part of a set of spiritual principles of Narcotics Anonymous, and without them NA does not exist.

Autonomy gives our groups the freedom to act on their own to establish an atmosphere of recovery, serve their members and fulfill their primary purpose. It is for these reasons that we guard our autonomy so carefully.

It would seem that we, in our groups, can do whatever we decide, regardless of what anyone says. This is partly true. Each group does have complete freedom, except when their actions affect other groups or NA as a whole. Like group conscience, autonomy can be a two-edged sword. Group autonomy has been used to justify violation of the Traditions. If a contradiction exists, we have slipped away from our principles. If we check to make sure that our actions are clearly within the bounds of our traditions; if we do not dictate to other groups, or force anything upon them; and if we consider the consequences of our action ahead of time, then all will be well.

Tradition Five

"Each group has but one primary purpose—to carry the message to the addict who still suffers."

"You mean to say that our primary purpose is to carry the message? I thought we were here to get clean. I thought that our primary purpose was to recover from drug addiction." For the individual, this is certainly true; our members are here to find freedom from addiction and a new way of life. However, groups aren't addicted and don't recover. All our groups can do is plant the seed for recovery and bring addicts together so that the magic of empathy, honesty, caring, sharing, and service can do their work. The purpose of this tradition is to ensure that this atmosphere of recovery is maintained. This can only be achieved by keeping our groups recovery-oriented. The fact that we, each and every group, focus on carrying the message provides consistency; addicts can count on us. Unity of action and purpose makes possible what seemed impossible for us—recovery.

The Twelfth Step of our personal program also says that we carry the message to the addict who still suffers. Working with others is a powerful tool. "The therapeutic value of one addict helping another is without parallel." For the newcomers, this is how they found Narcotics Anonymous and learned to stay clean. For the members, this reaffirms their commitment to recovery. The group is the most powerful vehicle we have for carrying the message. When a member carries the message, he is somewhat bound by interpretation and personality. The problem with literature is language. The feelings, the intensity, and the strengths are sometimes lost. In our group, with many different personalities, the message of recovery is a recurring theme.

What would happen if our groups had another primary purpose? We feel our message would be diluted and then lost. If we concentrated on making money, many might get rich. If we were a social club, we could find many friends and lovers. If we specialized in education, we'd end up with many smart addicts. If our specialty was medical help, many would get healthy. If our group purpose were anything other than to carry the message, many would die and few would find recovery.

What is our message? The message is that an addict, any addict, can stop using drugs, lose the desire to use, and find a new way to live. Our message is hope and the promise of freedom. When all is said and done, our primary purpose can only be to carry the message to the addict who still suffers because that is all we have to give.

Tradition Six

"An NA group ought never endorse, finance, or lend the NA name to any related facility or outside enterprise, lest problems of money, property or prestige divert us from our primary purpose."

Our Sixth Tradition tells us some of the things that we must do to preserve and protect our primary purpose. This tradition is the basis for our policy of non-affiliation and is extremely important to the continuation and growth of Narcotics Anonymous.

Let's take a look at what this tradition says. The first thing a group ought never do is endorse. To endorse is to sanction, approve or recommend. Endorsements can be either direct or implied. We see direct endorsements every day in television commercials. An implied endorsement is one that is not specifically stated.

Many other organizations wish to ride on the NA name. To allow them to do so would be an implied endorsement and a violation of this tradition. Hospitals, drug recovery houses, probation and parole offices are some of the facilities we deal with in carrying the NA message. While these organizations are sincere and we hold NA meetings in their establishments, we cannot endorse, finance or allow them to use the NA name to further their growth. However, we are willing to carry the NA principles into these institutions, to the addicts who still suffer so that they can make the choice.

The next thing we ought never do is finance. This is more obvious. To finance means to supply funds or to help support financially.

The third thing warned against in this tradition is lending the NA name to fulfill the purposes of other programs. For example, several times other programs have tried to use Narcotics Anonymous as part of their services offered, to help justify funding.

Further the tradition tells us that a related facility is any place involving NA members. It might be a halfway house, a detox center, a counseling center, or a clubhouse. People are easily confused by what is NA and what are the related facilities. Recovery houses that have been started or staffed by NA members have to take care that the differentiation is clear. Perhaps the most confusion exists when it involves a clubhouse. Newcomers and older members often identify the clubhouse with Narcotics Anonymous. We should make a special effort to let these people know that these facilities and NA are not the same. An outside enterprise is any agency, business venture, religion, society, organization, related activity, or any other fellowship. Most of these are easy to identify, except for the other fellowships. Narcotics Anonymous is a separate and distinct fellowship in its own right. Our problem is addiction. The other Twelve Step Fellowships specialize in other problems, and our relationship with them is one of cooperation, not affiliation. The use of literature, speakers, and announcements from other fellowships in our meetings constitutes an implied endorsement of an outside enterprise.

The Sixth Tradition goes on to warn us what may happen: "lest problems of money, property or prestige divert us from our primary purpose." These problems often become obsessions and shut us off from our spiritual aim. For the individual, this type of abuse can be devastating; for the group, it can be disastrous. When we, as a group, waiver from our primary purpose, addicts who might have found recovery die.

Tradition Seven

"Every NA group ought to be fully self-supporting, declining outside contributions."

Being self-supporting is an important part of our new way of life. For the individual, this is usually quite a change. In our addiction, we were dependent on people, places, and things. We looked to them to support us and supply the things that we found lacking in ourselves. As recovering addicts, we find that we are still dependent, but our dependence has shifted from the things around us to a loving God and the inner strength we get in our relationship with Him. We, who were unable to function as human beings, now find that anything is possible of us. Dreams that we gave up long ago can now become realities. Addicts as a group have been a burden to society. In NA, our groups not only stand on their own, but demand the right to do so.

Money has always been a problem for us. We could never find enough to support ourselves and our habits. We worked, stole, conned, begged and sold ourselves; there was never enough money to fill the emptiness inside. In our recovery, money is often still a problem.

We need money to run our group; there is rent to pay, supplies and literature to buy. We take a collection in our meetings to cover these expenses and whatever is left goes to support our services and to further our primary purpose. Unfortunately, there is little left once a group pays its way. Sometimes members who can afford it give a little extra to help. Sometimes a committee is formed to put on an activity to raise funds. These efforts help and without them, we could not have come this far. NA services remain in need of money, and even though it is sometimes frustrating, we really would not have it any other way; we know the price would be too high. We all have to pull together, and in pulling together we learn that we really are part of something greater than ourselves.

Our policy concerning money is clearly stated: We decline any outside contributions; our Fellowship is completely self-supporting. We accept no funding, endowments, loans, and/or gifts. Everything has its price, regardless of intent. Whether the price is money, promises, concessions, special recognition, endorsements, or favors, it's too high for us. Even if those who would help us could guarantee no strings, we still would not accept their aid. We cannot afford to let our members contribute more than their fair share. We have found that the price paid by our groups is disunity and controversy. We will not put our freedom on the line.

Tradition Eight

"Narcotics Anonymous should remain forever nonprofessional, but our service centers may employ special workers."

The Eighth Tradition is vital to the stability of NA as a whole. In order to understand this tradition we need to define "nonprofessional service centers" and "special workers." With an understanding of these terms, this important tradition is self-explanatory.

In this tradition we say that we have no professionals. By this, we mean we have no staff psychiatrists, doctors, lawyers, or counselors. Our program works by one addict helping another. If we employed professionals in NA groups, we would destroy our unity. We are simply addicts of equal status freely helping one another.

We recognize and admire the professionals. Many of our members are professionals in their own right, but there is no room for professionalism in NA.

A service center is defined as a place where NA service committees operate. The World Service Office or local, regional, and area offices are examples of service centers. A clubhouse or halfway house, or similar facility, is not an NA service center and is not affiliated with NA. A service center is, very simply, a place where NA services are offered on a continuing basis.

The tradition states, "Service centers may employ special workers." This statement means that service centers may employ workers for special skills such as phone answering, clerical work, or printing. Such employees are directly responsible to a service committee. As NA grows, the demand for these workers will grow. Special workers are necessary to ensure efficiency in an ever-expanding fellowship.

The difference between professionals and special workers should be defined for clarity. Professionals work in specific professions that do not directly service NA, but are for personal gain. Professionals do not follow the NA Traditions. Our special workers, on the other hand, work within our Traditions and are always directly responsible to those they serve, to the Fellowship.

In our Eighth Tradition, we do not single out our members as professional. By not placing professional status on any member, we ensure that we remain "forever nonprofessional."

Tradition Nine

"NA, as such, ought never be organized, but we may create service boards or committees directly responsible to those they serve."

This tradition defines the way that our Fellowship functions. We must first understand what NA is. Narcotics Anonymous is addicts who have the desire to stop using, and have joined together to do so. Our meetings are a gathering of members for the purpose of staying clean and carrying the message of recovery. Our steps and traditions are set down in a specific order. They are numbered, they are not random and unstructured. They are organized, but this is not the type of organization referred to in the Ninth Tradition. In this tradition, "organized" means having management and control. On this basis, the meaning of Tradition Nine is clear. Without this tradition, our Fellowship would be in opposition to spiritual principles. A loving God, as He may express Himself in our group conscience, is our ultimate authority.

The Ninth Tradition goes on to define the nature of the things that we can do to help NA. It says that we may create service boards or committees to serve the needs of the Fellowship. They exist solely to serve the Fellowship. This is the nature of our service structure as it has evolved and been defined in the NA service manual.

Tradition Ten

"Narcotics Anonymous has no opinion on outside issues; hence the NA name ought never be drawn into public controversy."

In order to achieve our spiritual aim, Narcotics Anonymous must be known and respected. Nowhere is this more obvious than in our history. NA was founded in 1953. For twenty years, our Fellowship remained small and obscure. In the 1970's, society realized that addiction had become a worldwide epidemic and began to look for answers. Along with this came change in the way people thought of the addict. This change allowed addicts to seek help more openly. NA groups sprang up in many places where we were never tolerated before. Recovering addicts paved the way for more groups and more recovery. Today NA is a worldwide Fellowship. We are known and respected everywhere.

If an addict has never heard of us, he cannot seek us out. If those who work with addicts are unaware of our existence, they cannot refer them to us. One of the most important things we can do to further our primary purpose is to let people know who, what and where we are. If we do this and keep our good reputation, we will surely grow.

Our recovery speaks for itself. Our Tenth Tradition specifically helps protect our reputation. This tradition says that NA has no opinion on outside issues. We don't take sides. We don't have any recommendations. NA, as a Fellowship, does not participate in politics; to do so would invite controversy. It would jeopardize our Fellowship. Those who agree with our opinions might commend us for taking a stand, but some would always disagree. With a price this high, is it any wonder we choose not to take sides in society's problems? For our own survival, we have no opinion on outside issues.

Tradition Eleven

"Our public relations policy is based on attraction rather than promotion; we need always maintain personal anonymity at the level of press, radio, and films."

This tradition deals with our relationship to those outside the Fellowship. It tells us how to conduct our efforts at the public level. Our public image consists of what we have to offer, a successful proven way of maintaining a drug-free lifestyle. While it is important to reach as many people as possible, it is imperative for our protection that we are careful about advertisements, circulars and any literature that may reach the public's hands.

Our attraction is that we are successes in our own right. As groups, we offer recovery. We have found that the success of our program speaks for itself; this is our promotion.

This tradition goes on to tell us that we need to maintain personal anonymity at the level of press, radio, and films. This is to protect the membership and the reputation of Narcotics Anonymous. We do not give our last names nor appear in the media as a member of Narcotics Anonymous. No individual inside or outside the Fellowship represents Narcotics Anonymous.

Tradition Twelve

"Anonymity is the spiritual foundation of all our Traditions, ever reminding us to place principles before personalities."

A dictionary definition of anonymity is "a state of bearing no name." In keeping with Tradition Twelve, the "I" becomes "we." The spiritual foundation becomes more important than any one group or individual.

As we find ourselves growing closer together, the awakening of humility occurs. Humility is a by-product that allows us to grow and develop in an atmosphere of freedom, and removes the fear of becoming known by our employers, families or friends as addicts. Therefore, we attempt to rigorously adhere to the principle that "what is said in meetings stays in meetings."

Throughout our Traditions, we speak in terms of "we" and "our" rather than "me" and "mine." By working together for our common welfare, we achieve the true spirit of anonymity.

We have heard the phrase "principles before personalities" so often that it is like a cliche. While we may disagree as individuals, the spiritual principle of anonymity makes us all equal as members of the group. No member is greater or lesser than any other member. The drive for personal gain in the areas of sex, property and social position, which brought so much pain in the past, falls by the wayside if we adhere to the principle of anonymity. Anonymity is one of the basic elements of our recovery and it pervades our Traditions and our Fellowship. It protects us from our own defects of character and renders personalities and their differences powerless. Anonymity in action makes it impossible for personalities to come before principles.

Chapter Seven

Recovery and Relapse

Many people think that recovery is simply a matter of not using drugs. They consider a relapse a sign of complete failure, and long periods of abstinence a sign of complete success. We in the recovery program of Narcotics Anonymous have found that this perception is too simplistic. After a member has had some involvement in our Fellowship, a relapse may be the jarring experience that brings about a more rigorous application of the program. By the same token we have observed some members who remain abstinent for long periods of time whose dishonesty and self-deceit still prevent them from enjoying complete recovery and acceptance within society. Complete and continuous abstinence, however, in close association and identification with others in NA groups, is still the best ground for growth.

Although all addicts are basically the same in kind, we do, as individuals, differ in degree of sickness and rate of recovery. There may be times when a relapse lays the groundwork for complete freedom. At other times that freedom can only be achieved by a grim and obstinate willfulness to hang on to abstinence come hell or high water until a crisis passes. An addict, who by any means can lose, even for a time, the need or desire to use, and has free choice over impulsive thinking and compulsive action, has reached a turning point that may be the decisive factor in his recovery. The feeling of true independence and freedom hangs here at times in the balance. To step out alone and run our own lives again draws us, yet we seem to know that what we have has come from dependence on a Power greater than ourselves and from the giving and receiving of help from others in acts of empathy. Many times in our recovery the old bugaboos will haunt us. Life may again become meaningless, monotonous and boring. We may tire mentally in repeating our new ideas and tire physically in our new activities, yet we know that if we fail to repeat them we will surely take up our old practices. We suspect that if we do not use what we have, we will lose what we have. These times are often the periods of our greatest growth. Our minds and bodies seem tired of it all, yet the dynamic forces of change or true conversion, deep within, may be working to give us the answers that alter our inner motivations and change our lives.

Recovery as experienced through our Twelve Steps is our goal, not mere physical abstinence. To improve ourselves takes effort, and since there is no way in the world to graft a new idea on a closed mind, an opening must be made somehow. Since we can do this only for ourselves, we need to recognize two of our seemingly inherent enemies, apathy and procrastination. Our resistance to change seems built in, and only a nuclear blast of some kind will bring about any alteration or initiate another course of action. A relapse, if we survive it, may provide the charge for the demolition process. A relapse and sometimes subsequent death of someone close to us can do the job of awakening us to the necessity for vigorous personal action.

We have seen addicts come to our Fellowship, try our program and stay clean for a period of time. Over time some addicts lost contact with other recovering addicts and eventually returned to active addiction. They forgot that it is really the first drug that starts the deadly cycle all over again. They tried to control it, to use in moderation, or to use just certain drugs. None of these control methods work for addicts.

Relapse is a reality. It can and does happen. Experience shows that those who do not work our program of recovery on a daily basis may relapse. We see them come back seeking recovery. Maybe they were clean for years before their relapse. If they are lucky enough to make it back, they are shaken badly. They tell us that the relapse was more horrible than earlier use. We have never seen a person who lives the Narcotics Anonymous Program relapse.

Relapses are often fatal. We have attended funerals of loved ones who died from a relapse. They died in various ways. Often we see relapsers lost for years, living in misery. Those who make it to jail or institutions may survive and perhaps have a reintroduction to NA.

In our daily lives, we are subject to emotional and spiritual lapses, causing us to become defenseless against the physical relapse of drug use. Because addiction is an incurable disease, addicts are subject to relapse.

We are never forced into relapse. We are given a choice. Relapse is never an accident. Relapse is a sign that we have a reservation in our program. We begin to slight our program and leave loopholes in our daily lives. Unaware of the pitfalls ahead, we stumble blindly in the belief that we can make it on our own. Sooner or later we fall into the illusions that drugs make life easier. We believe that drugs can change us, and we forget that these changes are lethal. When we believe that drugs will solve our problems and forget what they can do to us, we are in real trouble. Unless the illusions that we can continue to use or stop using on our own are shattered, we most certainly sign our own death warrant. For some reason, not taking care of our personal affairs lowers our self-esteem and establishes a pattern that repeats itself in all areas of our lives. If we begin to avoid our new responsibilities by missing meetings, neglecting Twelfth Step work, or not getting involved, our program stops. These are the kinds of things that lead to relapse. We may sense a change coming over us. Our ability to remain open-minded disappears. We may become angry and resentful toward anyone or anything.

We may begin to reject those who were close to us. We isolate ourselves. We become sick of ourselves in a short time. We revert back to our sickest behavior patterns without even having to use drugs.

When a resentment or any other emotional upheaval occurs, failure to practice the steps can result in a relapse.

Obsessive behavior is a common denominator for addictive people. We have times when we try to fill ourselves up until we are satisfied, only to discover that there is no way to satisfy us. Part of our addictive pattern is that we can never get enough. Sometimes we forget, and we think that if we can just get enough food or enough sex, or enough money we'll be satisfied, and everything will be all right. Self-will still leads us to make decisions based on manipulation, ego, lust or false pride. We don't like to be wrong. Our egos tell us that we can do it on our own, but loneliness and paranoia quickly return. We find that we cannot really do it alone; when we try, things get worse. We need to be reminded of where we came from and that our disease will get progressively worse if we use. This is when we need the Fellowship.

We don't recover overnight. When we realize that we have made a bad decision or bad judgment, our inclination is to rationalize it. We often become extreme in our self-obsessive attempt to cover our tracks. We forget that we have a choice today. We get sicker.

There is something in our self-destructive personalities that cries for failure. Most of us feel that we do not deserve to succeed. This is a common theme with addicts. Self-pity is one of the most destructive of defects; it will drain us of all positive energy. We focus on anything that isn't going our way and ignore all the beauty in our lives. With no real desire to improve our lives, or even to live, we just keep going further and further down. Some of us never make it back.

We must relearn many things that we have forgotten and develop a new approach to life if we are to survive. This is what Narcotics Anonymous is all about. It is about people who care about desperate, dying addicts and who can, in time, teach them how to live without drugs. Many of us had difficulty coming into the Fellowship, because we did not understand that we have the disease of addiction. We sometimes see our past behavior as part of ourselves and not part of our disease.

We take the First Step. We admit that we are powerless over our addiction, that our lives have become unmanageable. Slowly things get better, and we start getting our confidence back. Our ego tells us that we can do it on our own. Things are getting better, and we think we really don't need this program. Cockiness is a red light indicator. The loneliness and paranoia will come back. We find out that we can't do it on our own and things get worse. We really take the First Step, this time internally. There will be times, however, when we really feel like using. We want to run, and we feel lousy. We need to be reminded of where we came from and that it will be worse this time. This is when we need the program the most. We realize we must do something.

When we forget the effort and the work that it took us to get a period of freedom in our lives, a lack of gratitude sinks in, and self-destruction begins again. Unless action is taken immediately, we run the risk of a relapse that threatens our very existence. Keeping our illusion of reality, rather than using the tools of the program, will return us to isolation. Loneliness will kill us inside and the drugs that almost always come next may do the job completely. The symptoms and the feelings that we experienced at the end of our using will come back even stronger than before. This impact is sure to destroy us if we don't surrender ourselves to the NA Program.

Relapse can be the destructive force that kills us or leads us to the realization of who and what we really are. The eventual misery of using is not worth the temporary escape it might give us. For us, to use is to die, often in more ways than one.

One of the biggest stumbling blocks to recovery seems to be placing unrealistic expectations on ourselves or others. Relationships can be a terribly painful area. We tend to fantasize and project what will happen. We get angry and resentful if our fantasies are not fulfilled. We forget that we are powerless over other people. The old thoughts and feelings of loneliness, despair, helplessness and self-pity creep in. Thoughts of sponsors, meetings, literature and all other positive input leave our consciousness. We have to keep our recovery first and our priorities in order.

Writing about what we want, what we are asking for, what we get, and sharing this with our sponsor or another trusted person helps us to work through negative feelings. Letting others share their experience with us gives us hope that it does get better. It seems that being powerless is a huge stumbling block. When a need arises for us to admit our powerlessness, we may first look for ways to exert power against it. After exhausting these ways, we begin sharing with others, and we find hope. Attending meetings daily, living a day at a time, and reading literature seems to send our mental attitude back toward the positive. Willingness to try what has worked for others is vital. Even when we feel that we don't want to attend, meetings are a source of strength and hope for us.

It is important to share our feelings of wanting to use drugs. It is amazing how often newcomers think that it is really abnormal for a drug addict to want to use. When we feel the old urges come over us, we think there must be something wrong with us, and that other people in Narcotics Anonymous couldn't possibly understand.

It is important to remember that the desire to use will pass. We never have to use again, no matter how we feel. All feelings will eventually pass.

The progression of recovery is a continuous, uphill journey. Without effort we start the downhill run again. The progression of the disease is an ongoing process, even during abstinence.

We come here powerless, and the power that we seek comes to us through other people in Narcotics Anonymous, but we must reach out for it. Now clean and in the Fellowship, we need to keep ourselves surrounded by others who know us well. We need each other. Narcotics Anonymous is a Fellowship of survival, and one of its advantages is that it places us in intimate, regular contact with the very people who can best understand and help us in our recovery. Good ideas and good intentions do not help if we fail to put them into action. Reaching out is the beginning of the struggle that will set us free. It will break down the walls that imprison us. A symptom of our disease is alienation, and honest sharing will free us to recover.

We are grateful that we were made so welcome at meetings that we felt comfortable. Without staying clean and coming to those meetings, we would surely have a rougher time with the steps. Any use of drugs will interrupt the process of recovery.

We all find that the feeling we get from helping others motivates us to do better in our own lives. If we are hurting, and most of us do from time to time, we learn to ask for help. We find that pain shared is pain lessened. Members of the Fellowship are willing to help a relapser recover and have insight and useful suggestions to offer when asked. Recovery found in Narcotics Anonymous must come from within, and no one stays clean for anyone but themselves.

In our disease, we are dealing with a destructive, violent power greater than ourselves that can lead to relapse. If we have relapsed, it is important to keep in mind that we must get back to meetings as soon as possible. Otherwise, we may have only months, days, or hours before we reach a threshold where we are gone beyond recall. Our disease is so cunning that it can get us into impossible situations. When it does, we come back to the program if we can, while we can. Once we use, we are under the control of our disease.

We can never fully recover, no matter how long we stay clean. Complacency is the enemy of members with substantial clean time. If we remain complacent for long, the recovery process ceases. The disease will manifest apparent symptoms in us. Denial returns, along with obsession and compulsion. Guilt, remorse, fear, and pride may become unbearable. Soon we reach a place where our backs are against the wall. Denial and the First Step conflict in our minds. If we let the obsession of using overcome us, we are doomed. Only a complete and total acceptance of the First Step can save us. We must totally surrender ourselves to the program.

The first thing to do is to stay clean. This makes the other stages of recovery possible. As long as we stay clean, no matter what, we have the greatest possible advantage over our disease. For this we are grateful.

Many of us get clean in a protected environment, such as a rehabilitation center or recovery house. When we re-enter the world, we feel lost, confused and vulnerable. Going to meetings as often as possible will reduce the shock of change. Meetings provide a safe place to share with others. We begin to live the program; we learn to apply spiritual principles in our lives. We must use what we learn or we will lose it in a relapse.

Many of us would have had nowhere else to go, if we could not have trusted NA groups and members. At first, we were both captivated and intimidated by the fellowship. No longer comfortable with our using friends, we were not yet at home in the meetings. We began to lose our fear through the experience of sharing. The more we shared, the more our fears slipped away. We shared for this reason. Growth means change. Spiritual maintenance means ongoing recovery. Isolation is dangerous to spiritual growth.

Those of us who find the Fellowship and begin to live the steps develop relationships with others. As we grow, we learn to overcome the tendency to run and hide from ourselves and our feelings. Being honest about our feelings helps others to identify with us. We find that when we communicate honestly, we reach others. Honesty takes practice, and none of us claims to be perfect. When we feel trapped or pressured, it takes great spiritual and emotional strength to be honest. Sharing with others keeps us from feeling isolated and alone. This process is a creative action of the spirit.

When we work the program, we are living the steps daily. This gives us experience in applying spiritual principles. The experience that we gain with time helps our ongoing recovery. We must use what we learn or we will lose it, no matter how long we have been clean. Eventually we are shown that we must get honest, or we will use again. We pray for willingness and humility and finally get honest about our mistaken judgments or bad decisions. We tell those we have harmed that we were to blame and make whatever amends are necessary. Now we are in the solution again. We are working the program. It becomes easier to work the program now. We know that the steps help prevent relapse.

Relapsers may also fall into another trap. We may doubt that we can stop using and stay clean. We can never stay clean on our own. Frustrated, we cry, "I cannot do it!" We beat ourselves as we come back into the program. We imagine that our fellow members will not respect the courage it takes to come back. We have learned the utmost respect for that type of courage. We applaud heartily. It is not shameful to relapse—the shame is in not coming back. We must smash the illusion that we can do it alone.

Another type of relapse happens when being clean is not the top priority. Staying clean must always come first. At times, we all experience difficulty in our recovery. Emotional lapses result when we don't practice what we have learned. Those who make it through these times show a courage not their own. After coming through one of these periods, we can readily agree that it is always darkest before the dawn. Once we get through a difficult time clean, we are given a tool of recovery that we can use again and again.

If we relapse, we may feel guilt and embarrassment. Our relapse is embarrassing, but we cannot save our face and our ass at the same time. We find that it is best to get back on the program as soon as possible. It is better to swallow our pride than to die or to go permanently insane.

As long as we maintain an attitude of thankfulness for being clean, we find it is easier to remain clean. The best way to express gratitude is by carrying the message of our experience, strength and hope to the still-suffering addict. We are ready to work with any suffering addict.

Living the program on a daily basis provides many valuable experiences. If we are plagued by an obsession to use, experience has taught us to call a fellow recovering addict and get to a meeting.

Using addicts are self-centered, angry, frightened and lonely people. In recovery, we experience spiritual growth. While using, we were dishonest, self-seeking and often institutionalized. The program allows us to become responsible and productive members of society.

As we begin to function in society, our creative freedom helps us sort our priorities and do the basic things first. Daily practice of our Twelve Step Program enables us to change from what we were to people guided by a Higher Power. With the help of our sponsor or spiritual advisor, gradually we learn to trust and depend on our Higher Power.

Chapter Eight

We Do Recover

Although "Politics makes strange bedfellows," as the old saying goes, addiction makes us one of a kind. Our personal stories may vary in individual pattern but in the end we all have the same thing in common. This common illness or disorder is addiction. We know well the two things that make up true addiction: obsession and compulsion. Obsession—that fixed idea that takes us back time and time again to our particular drug, or some substitute, to recapture the ease and comfort we once knew.

Compulsion—once having started the process with one fix, one pill, or one drink we cannot stop through our own power of will. Because of our physical sensitivity to drugs, we are completely in the grip of a destructive power greater than ourselves.

When at the end of the road we find that we can no longer function as a human being, either with or without drugs, we all face the same dilemma. What is there left to do? There seems to be this alternative: either go on as best we can to the bitter ends—jails, institutions or death—or find a new way to live. In years gone by, very few addicts ever had this last choice. Those who are addicted today are more fortunate. For the first time in man's entire history, a simple way has been proving itself in the lives of many addicts. It is available to us all. This is a simple spiritual—not religious—program, known as Narcotics Anonymous.

When my addiction brought me to the point of complete powerlessness, uselessness and surrender some fifteen years ago,[2] there was no NA. I found A.A., and in that Fellowship

---

[2] Written in 1965

87

*met addicts who had also found that program to be the answer
to their problem. However, we knew that many were still going
down the road of disillusion, degradation and death, because
they were unable to identify with the alcoholic in A.A. Their
identification was at the level of apparent symptoms and not at
the deeper level of emotions or feelings, where empathy becomes
a healing therapy for all addicted people. With several other
addicts and some members of A.A. who had great faith in us and
the program, we formed, in July of 1953, what we now know as
Narcotics Anonymous. We felt that now the addict would find
from the start as much identification as each needed to convince
himself that he could stay clean, by the example of others who
had recovered for many years.*

*That this was what was principally needed has proved itself
in these passing years. That wordless language of recognition,
belief and faith, which we call empathy, created the atmosphere
in which we could feel time, touch reality and recognize spiritual
values long lost to many of us. In our program of recovery we
are growing in numbers and in strength. Never before have so
many clean addicts, of their own choice and in free society, been
able to meet where they please, to maintain their recovery in
complete creative freedom.*

*Even addicts said it could not be done the way we had it
planned. We believed in openly scheduled meetings—no more
hiding as other groups had tried. We believed this differed from
all other methods tried before by those who advocated long
withdrawal from society. We felt that the sooner the addict could
face his problem in everyday living, just that much faster would
he become a real productive citizen. We eventually have to stand
on our own feet and face life on its own terms, so why not from
the start.*

*Because of this, of course, many relapsed and many were lost
completely. However, many stayed and some came back after
their setback. The brighter part is the fact that of those who are*

*now our members, many have long terms of complete abstinence
and are better able to help the newcomer. Their attitude, based on
the spiritual values of our steps and traditions, is the dynamic
force that is bringing increase and unity to our program. Now
we know that the time has come when that tired old lie, "Once
an addict, always an addict," will no longer be tolerated by
either society or the addict himself. We do recover.*

Recovery begins with surrender. From that point, each of us
is reminded that a day clean is a day won. In Narcotics Anonymous, our attitudes, thoughts and reactions change. We come to
realize that we are not alien and begin to understand and accept
who we are.

As long as there have been people, addiction has existed. For
us, addiction is an obsession to use the drugs that are destroying
us, followed by a compulsion that forces us to continue. Complete
abstinence is the foundation for our new way of life.

In the past, there was no hope for an addict. In Narcotics
Anonymous, we learn to share the loneliness, anger and fear
that addicts have in common and cannot control. Our old ideas
are what got us into trouble. We weren't oriented toward fulfillment; we focused on the emptiness and worthlessness of it all.
We could not deal with success, so failure became a way of life.
In recovery, failures are only temporary setbacks rather than
links in an unbreakable chain. Honesty, open-mindedness and
willingness to change are all new attitudes that help us to admit
our faults and to ask for help. We are no longer compelled to
act against our true nature and to do things that we don't really
want to do.

Most addicts resist recovery, and the program we share with
them interferes with their using. If newcomers tell us that they
can continue to use drugs in any form and suffer no ill effects,
there are two ways we can look at it. The first possibility is
that they are not addicts. The other is that their disease has not

become apparent to them and that they are still denying their addiction. Addiction and withdrawal distort rational thought, and newcomers usually focus on differences rather than similarities. They look for ways to disprove the evidence of addiction or disqualify themselves from recovery.

Many of us did the same thing when we were new, so when we work with others we try not to do or say anything that will give them the excuse to continue using. We know that honesty and empathy are essential. Complete surrender is the key to recovery, and total abstinence is the only thing that has ever worked for us. In our experience, no addict who has completely surrendered to this program has ever failed to find recovery.

Narcotics Anonymous is a spiritual, not religious program. Any clean addict is a miracle, and keeping the miracle alive is an ongoing process of awareness, surrender and growth. For an addict, not using is an abnormal state. We learn to live clean. We learn to be honest with ourselves and to think of both sides of things. Decision making is rough at first. Before we got clean, most of our actions were guided by impulse. Today, we are not locked into this type of thinking. We are free.

In our recovery, we find it essential to accept reality. Once we can do this, we do not find it necessary to use drugs in an attempt to change our perceptions. Without drugs, we have a chance to begin functioning as useful human beings, if we accept ourselves and the world exactly as it is. We learn that conflicts are a part of reality, and we learn new ways to resolve them instead of running from them. They are a part of the real world. We learn not to become emotionally involved with problems. We deal with what is at hand and try not to force solutions. We have learned that if a solution isn't practical, it isn't spiritual. In the past, we made simple situations into problems; we made mountains out of molehills. Our best ideas got us here. In recovery, we learn to depend on a Power greater than ourselves. We don't have all the answers or solutions, but we can learn to live without drugs.

We can stay clean and enjoy life, if we remember to live "Just for Today."

We are not responsible for our disease, only for our recovery. As we begin to apply what we have learned, our lives begin to change for the better. We seek help from addicts who are enjoying lives free from the obsession to use drugs. We do not have to understand this program for it to work. All we have to do is to follow direction.

We get relief through the Twelve Steps, which are essential to the recovery process, because they are a new, spiritual way of life that allows us to participate in our own recovery.

From the first day, the Twelve Steps become a part of our lives. At first, we may be filled with negativity, and only allow the First Step to take hold. Later, we have less fear and can use these tools more fully and to our greater advantage. We realize that old feelings and fears are symptoms of our disease. Real freedom is now possible.

As we recover, we gain a new outlook on being clean. We enjoy a feeling of release and freedom from the desire to use. We find that everyone we meet eventually has something to offer. We become able to receive as well as to give. Life can become a new adventure for us. We come to know happiness, joy and freedom.

There is no model of the recovering addict. When the drugs go and the addict works the program, wonderful things happen. Lost dreams awaken and new possibilities arise. Our willingness to grow spiritually keeps us buoyant. When we take the actions indicated in the steps, the results are a change in our personality. It is our actions that are important. We leave the results to our Higher Power.

Recovery becomes a contact process; we lose the fear of touching and of being touched. We learn that a simple, loving hug can make all the difference in the world when we feel alone. We experience real love and real friendship.

We know that we are powerless over a disease that is incurable, progressive and fatal. If not arrested, it gets worse until we die. We cannot deal with the obsession and compulsion. The only alternative is to stop using and start learning how to live. When we are willing to follow this course of action and take advantage of the help available to us, a whole new life is possible. In this way, we do recover.

Today, secure in the love of the Fellowship, we can finally look another human being in the eye and be grateful for who we are.

Chapter Nine

Just for Today— Living the Program

Tell yourself:

JUST FOR TODAY *my thoughts will be on my recovery, living and enjoying life without the use of drugs.*

JUST FOR TODAY *I will have faith in someone in NA who believes in me and wants to help me in my recovery.*

JUST FOR TODAY *I will have a program. I will try to follow it to the best of my ability.*

JUST FOR TODAY *through NA I will try to get a better perspective on my life.*

JUST FOR TODAY *I will be unafraid, my thoughts will be on my new associations, people who are not using and who have found a new way of life. So long as I follow that way, I have nothing to fear.*

We admit that our lives have been unmanageable, but sometimes we have a problem admitting our need for help. Our own self-will leads to many problems in our recovery. We want and demand that things always go our way. We should know from our past experience that our way of doing things did not work. The principle of surrender guides us into a way of life in which we draw our strength from a Power greater than ourselves. Our daily surrender to our Higher Power provides the help we need. As addicts, we have trouble with acceptance, which is critical to our recovery. When we refuse to practice acceptance, we are, in effect, still denying our faith in a Higher Power. Worrying is a lack of faith.

Surrendering our will puts us in contact with a Higher Power who fills the empty place inside that nothing could ever fill. We learned to trust God for help daily. Living just for today relieves the burden of the past and the fear of the future. We learned to take whatever actions are necessary and to leave the results in the hands of our Higher Power.

The Narcotics Anonymous Program is spiritual. We strongly suggest that members make an attempt to find a Higher Power of their understanding. Some of us have profound spiritual experiences, dramatic and inspirational in nature. For others, the awakening is more subtle. We recover in an atmosphere of acceptance and respect for one another's beliefs. We try to avoid the self-deception of arrogance and self-righteousness. As we develop faith in our daily lives, we find that our Higher Power supplies us with the strength and guidance that we need.

Each of us is free to work out our own concept of a Higher Power. Many of us were suspicious and skeptical because of disappointments that we have had with religion. As new members, the talk of God we heard in meetings repelled us. Until we sought our own answers in this area, we were trapped in the ideas gathered from our past. Agnostics and atheists sometimes start by just talking to "whatever's there." There is a spirit or an energy that can be felt in the meetings. This is sometimes the newcomer's first concept of a Higher Power. Ideas from the past are often incomplete and unsatisfactory. Everything we know is subject to revision, especially what we know about the truth. We re-evaluate our old ideas, so we can become acquainted with the new ideas that lead to a new way of life. We recognize that we are human with a physical, mental and spiritual sickness. When we accept that our addiction caused our own hell and that there is a power available to help us, we begin to make progress in solving our problems.

Lack of daily maintenance can show up in many ways. Through open-minded effort, we come to rely on a daily relationship with God as we understand Him. Each day most of us ask our Higher Power to help us stay clean, and each night we give thanks for the gift of recovery. As our lives become more comfortable, many of us lapse into spiritual complacency, and risking relapse, we find ourselves in the same horror and loss of purpose from which we have been given only a daily reprieve. This is, hopefully, when our pain motivates us to renew our daily spiritual maintenance. One way that we can continue a conscious contact, especially in hard times, is to list the things for which we are grateful.

Many of us have found that setting aside quiet time for ourselves is helpful in making conscious contact with our Higher Power. By quieting the mind, meditation can lead us to calmness and serenity. This quieting of the mind can be done in any place, time, or manner, according to the individual.

Our Higher Power is accessible to us at all times. We receive guidance when we ask for knowledge of God's will for us. Gradually, as we become more God-centered than self-centered, our despair turns to hope. Change also involves the great source of fear, the unknown. Our Higher Power is the source of courage that we need to face this fear.

Some things we must accept, others we can change. The wisdom to know the difference comes with growth in our spiritual program. If we maintain our spiritual condition daily, we find it easier to deal with the pain and confusion. This is the emotional stability that we so badly need. With the help of our Higher Power, we never have to use again.

Any clean addict is a miracle. We keep this miracle alive in ongoing recovery with positive attitudes. If, after a period of time, we find ourselves in trouble with our recovery, we have probably stopped doing one or more of the things that helped us in the earlier stages of our recovery.

Three basic spiritual principles are honesty, open-mindedness, and willingness. These are the HOW of our program. The initial honesty that we express is the desire to stop using. Next we honestly admit our powerlessness and the unmanageability of our lives.

Rigorous honesty is the most important tool in learning to live for today. Although honesty is difficult to practice, it is most rewarding. Honesty is the antidote to our diseased thinking. Our newly found faith serves as a firm foundation for courage in the future.

What we knew about living before we came to NA almost killed us. Managing our own lives got us to the Narcotics Anonymous Program. We came to NA knowing very little about how to be happy and enjoy life. A new idea cannot be grafted onto a closed mind. Being open-minded allows us to hear something that might save our lives. It allows us to listen to opposing points of view, and come to conclusions of our own. Open-mindedness leads us to the very insights that have eluded us during our lives. It is this principle that allows us to participate in a discussion without jumping to conclusions or predetermining right and wrong. We no longer need to make fools of ourselves by standing up for nonexistent virtues. We have learned that it is okay to not know all the answers, for then we are teachable and can learn to live our new life successfully.

Open-mindedness without willingness, however, will get us nowhere. We must be willing to do whatever is necessary to recover. We never know when the time will come when we must put forth all the effort and strength we have just to stay clean.

Honesty, open-mindedness, and willingness work hand in hand. The lack of one of these principles in our personal program can lead to relapse, and will certainly make recovery difficult and painful when it could be simple. This program is a vital part of our everyday living. If it were not for this program, most of us would be dead or institutionalized. Our viewpoint changes from that of a loner to that of a member. We emphasize setting our house in order, because it brings us relief. We trust in our Higher Power for the strength to meet our needs.

One way to practice the principles of HOW is by taking a daily inventory. Our inventory allows us to recognize our daily growth. We shouldn't forget about our assets while striving to eliminate our defects. The old self-deception and self-centeredness can be replaced with spiritual principles.

Staying clean is the first step in facing life. When we practice acceptance, our lives are simplified. When problems arise, we hope to be well-equipped with the tools of the program. We honestly have to surrender our own self-centeredness and self-destructiveness. In the past, we believed desperation would give us the strength to survive. Now we accept responsibility for our problems and see that we're equally responsible for our solutions.

As recovering addicts, we come to know gratitude. As our defects are removed, we are free to become all that we can. We emerge as new individuals with an awareness of ourselves and the ability to take our places in the world.

In living the steps, we begin to let go of our self-obsession. We ask a Higher Power to remove our fear of facing ourselves and life. We redefine ourselves by working the steps and using the tools of recovery. We see ourselves differently. Our personalities change. We become feeling people, capable of responding appropriately to life. We put spiritual living first and learn to use patience, tolerance and humility in our daily affairs.

Other people in our lives help us to develop trust and loving attitudes, we demand less and give more. We are slower to anger and quicker to forgive. We learn about the love that we receive in our Fellowship. We begin to feel lovable which is a feeling totally alien to our old egocentric selves.

Ego used to control us in all sorts of subtle ways. Anger is our reaction to our present reality. Resentments are reliving past experiences again and again, and fear is our response to the future.

We need to become willing to let God remove these defects that burden our spiritual growth.

New ideas are available to us through the sharing of our living experience. By rigorously practicing the few simple guidelines in this chapter, we recover daily. The principles of the program shape our personalities.

From the isolation of our addiction, we find a fellowship of people with a common bond of recovery. NA is like a lifeboat in a sea of isolation, hopelessness and destructive chaos. Our faith, strength and hope come from people sharing their recovery and from our relationship with the God of our own understanding. At first it feels awkward to share feelings. Part of the pain of addiction is being cut off from this sharing experience. If we find ourselves in a bad place or we sense trouble coming, we call someone or go to a meeting. We learn to seek help before making difficult decisions. By humbling ourselves and asking for help, we can get through the toughest of times. I can't, we can! In this way we find the strength that we need. We form a mutual bond, as we share our spiritual and mental resources.

Sharing in regularly scheduled meetings and one-on-one with recovering addicts helps us stay clean. Attending meetings reminds us of what it is like to be new and of the progressive nature of our disease. Attending our home group provides encouragement from the people that we get to know. This sustains our recovery and helps us in our daily living. When we honestly tell our own story, someone else may identify with us. Serving the needs of our members and making our message available gives us a feeling of joy. Service gives us opportunities to grow in ways that touch all parts of our lives. Our experience in recovery may help them deal with their problems, what worked for us might work for them. Most addicts are able to accept this type of sharing, even from the very beginning. The get-togethers after our meetings are good opportunities to share things that we didn't get to discuss during the meeting. This is also a good time to talk one-on-one with our sponsors. Things we need to hear will surface and become clear to us.

By sharing the experience of our recovery with newcomers, we help ourselves stay clean. We share comfort and encouragement with others. Today we have people in our lives who stand with us. Getting away from our self-centeredness gives us a better perspective on life. By asking for help, we can change. Sharing is risky at times, but by becoming vulnerable we are able to grow.

Some will come to Narcotics Anonymous still trying to use people to help them continue their habit. Their closed mind is a barrier against change. A spirit of open-mindedness, coupled with an admission of powerlessness, is a key that will unlock the door to recovery. If someone with a drug problem comes to us seeking recovery, and is willing, we gladly share with them how we stay clean.

We develop self-esteem as we help others find a new way of life. When we honestly evaluate what we have, we can learn to appreciate it. We begin to feel worthwhile by being members of NA. We can carry the gifts of recovery with us everywhere. The Twelve Steps of Narcotics Anonymous are a progressive recovery process established in our daily living. Ongoing recovery is dependent on our relationship with a loving God who cares for us and will do for us what we find impossible to do for ourselves.

During our recovery, each of us comes to our own understanding of the program. If we have difficulties, we trust our groups, our sponsors and our Higher Power to guide us. Thus, recovery, as found in Narcotics Anonymous, comes both from within and without.

We live a day at a time but also from moment to moment. When we stop living in the here and now, our problems become magnified unreasonably. Patience isn't a strong point with us. That's why we need our slogans and our NA friends to remind us to live the program just for today.

Tell yourself:

JUST FOR TODAY my thoughts will be on my recovery, living and enjoying life without the use of drugs.

JUST FOR TODAY I will have faith in someone in NA who believes in me and wants to help me in my recovery.

JUST FOR TODAY I will have a program. I will try to follow it to the best of my ability.

JUST FOR TODAY through NA I will try to get a better perspective on my life.

JUST FOR TODAY I will be unafraid, my thoughts will be on my new associations, people who are not using and who have found a new way of life. So long as I follow that way, I have nothing to fear.

Chapter Ten

More Will Be Revealed

As our recovery progressed, we became increasingly aware of ourselves and the world around us. Our needs and wants, our assets and liabilities were revealed to us. We came to realize that we had no power to change the outside world, we could only change ourselves. The Program of Narcotics Anonymous provides an opportunity for us to ease the pain of living through spiritual principles.

We are very fortunate to have had this program. Before, very few people recognized that addiction was a disease. Recovery was only a dream.

The responsible, productive, drug-free lives of thousands of members illustrate the effectiveness of our program. Recovery is a reality for us today. By working the steps, we are rebuilding our fractured personalities. Narcotics Anonymous is a healthy environment for growth. As a fellowship, we love and cherish one another, supporting our new way of life together.

As we grow, we come to understand humility as acceptance of both our assets and our liabilities. What we want most is to feel good about ourselves. Today we have real feelings of love, joy, hope, sadness, excitement. Our feelings are not our old drug-induced feelings.

Sometimes we find ourselves caught up in old ideas, even with time in the program. The basics are always important to recovery. We need to avoid old thinking patterns, both the old ideas and the tendency toward complacency. We cannot afford to become complacent, because our disease is with us twenty-four hours a day. If, while practicing these principles, we allow ourselves to feel superior or inferior, we isolate ourselves. We are headed for trouble if we feel apart from other addicts. Separation from the atmosphere of recovery and from the spirit of service to others slows our spiritual growth. Complacency keeps us from good will, love and compassion.

If we are unwilling to listen to others, we will deny the need for improvement. We learn to become flexible and to admit when others are right and we are wrong. As new things are revealed, we feel renewed. We need to stay open-minded and willing to do that one extra thing, go to one extra meeting, stay on the phone one extra minute, and help a newcomer stay clean one extra day. This extra effort is vital to our recovery.

We come to know ourselves for the first time. We experience new sensations: to love, to be loved, to know that people care about us and to have concern and compassion for others. We find ourselves doing and enjoying things that we never thought we would be doing. We make mistakes, and we accept and learn from them. We experience failure, and we learn how to succeed. Often we have to face some type of crisis during our recovery, such as the death of a loved one, financial difficulties or divorce. These are realities of life, and they don't go away just because we get clean. Some of us, even after years of recovery, found ourselves jobless, homeless or penniless. We entertained the thought that staying clean was not paying off, and the old think-ing stirred up self-pity, resentment and anger. No matter how painful life's tragedies can be for us, one thing is clear, we must not use, no matter what!

This is a program of total abstinence. There are times, however, such as in cases of health problems involving surgery and/or ex-treme physical injury, when medication may be valid. This does not constitute a license to use. There is no safe use of drugs for us. Our bodies don't know the difference between the drugs pre-scribed by a physician for pain and the drugs prescribed by our-selves to get high. As addicts, our skill at self-deception will be at its peak in such a situation. Often our minds will manufacture additional pain as an excuse to use. Turning it over to our Higher Power and getting the support of our sponsor and other members can prevent us from becoming our own worst enemies. Being alone during such times would give our disease an opportunity to take over. Honest sharing can dispel our fears of relapse.

Serious illness or surgery can present particular problems for us. Physicians should have specific knowledge of our addiction. Remember that we, not our doctors, are ultimately responsible for our recovery and our decisions. To minimize the danger, there are a few specific options that we may consider. Using local anesthesia, avoiding our drug of choice, stopping drug use while we are still hurting, and spending extra days in the hospital in case withdrawal occurs are some of our options.

Whatever pain we experience will pass. Through prayer, meditation and sharing, we keep our minds off our discomfort and have the strength to keep our priorities in order. It is imperative to keep NA members close to us at all times, if possible. It is amazing how our minds will go back to our old ways and old thinking. You'd be surprised how much pain we can handle without medication. In this program of total abstinence, however, we need to feel no guilt after having taken a minimum amount of medication prescribed by an informed professional for extreme physical pain.

We grow through pain in recovery and often find that such a crisis is a gift, an opportunity to experience growth by living clean. Before recovery, we were unable to even conceive of the thought that problems brought gifts. This gift may be finding strength within ourselves or regaining the feeling of self-respect that we had lost.

Spiritual growth, love, and compassion are idle potentials until shared with a fellow addict. By giving unconditional love in the Fellowship, we become more loving, and by sharing spiritual growth we become more spiritual.

By carrying this message to another addict, we are reminded of our own beginnings. Having had an opportunity to remember old feelings and behaviors, we are able to see our own personal and spiritual growth. In the process of answering the questions of another, our own thinking becomes clearer. Newer members are a constant source of hope, ever reminding us that the program works. We have the opportunity to live the knowledge acquired by staying clean, when we work with newcomers.

We have learned to value the respect of others. We are pleased when people depend on us. For the first time in our lives, we may be asked to serve in positions of responsibility in community organizations outside of NA. Our opinions are sought and valued by non-addicts in areas other than addiction and recovery. We can enjoy our families in a new way and may become a credit to them instead of an embarrassment or a burden. They can be proud of us today. Our individual interests can broaden to include social or even political issues. Hobbies and recreation give us new pleasure. It gives us good feelings to know that aside from our value to others as recovering addicts, we are also of value as human beings.

The reinforcement received by sponsorship is limitless. We spent years taking from others in every conceivable way. Words cannot describe the sense of spiritual awareness that we receive when we have given something, no matter how small, to another person.

We are each other's eyes and ears. When we do something wrong, our fellow addicts help us by showing us what we cannot see. We sometimes find ourselves caught up in old ideas. We need to constantly review our feelings and thoughts if we are to stay enthusiastic and grow spiritually. This enthusiasm will aid our ongoing recovery.

Today we have the freedom of choice. As we work the program to the best of our ability, the obsession with self is removed. Much of our loneliness and fear is replaced by the love and security of the Fellowship. Helping a suffering addict is one of the greatest experiences life has to offer. We are willing to help. We have had similar experiences and understand fellow addicts as no one else can. We offer hope, for we know that a better way of life is now real for us, and we give love because it was given so freely to us. New frontiers are open to us as we learn how to love. Love can be the flow of life energy from one person to another. By caring, sharing, and praying for others, we become a part of them. Through empathy, we allow addicts to become part of us.

As we do this, we undergo a vital spiritual experience and are changed. On a practical level, changes occur because what's appropriate to one phase of recovery may not be for another. We constantly let go of what has served its purpose, and let God guide us through the current phase with what works here and now.

As we become more God-reliant and gain more self-respect, we realize that we don't need to feel superior or inferior to anyone. Our real value is in being ourselves. Our egos, once so large and dominant, now take a back seat because we are in harmony with a loving God. We find that we lead richer, happier and much fuller lives when we lose self-will.

We become able to make wise and loving decisions, based on principles and ideals that have real value in our lives. By shaping our thoughts with spiritual ideals, we are freed to become who we want to be. What we had feared, we can now overcome through our dependence on a loving God. Faith has replaced our fear and given us freedom from ourselves.

In recovery, we also strive for gratitude. We feel grateful for ongoing God-consciousness. Whenever we confront a difficulty that we do not think we can handle, we ask God to do for us what we cannot do for ourselves.

A spiritual awakening is an ongoing process. We experience a wider view of reality as we grow spiritually. An opening of our minds to new spiritual and physical experiences is the key to better awareness. As we grow spiritually we become attuned to our feelings and our purpose in life.

By loving ourselves, we become able to truly love others. This is a spiritual awakening that comes as a result of living this program. We find ourselves daring to care and love!

Higher mental and emotional functions, such as conscience and the ability to love, were sharply affected by our drug use. Living skills were reduced to the animal level. Our spirit was broken. The capacity to feel human was lost. This seems extreme, but many of us have been in this state.

In time, through recovery, our dreams come true. We don't mean that we necessarily become rich or famous. However, by realizing the will of our Higher Power, dreams do come true in recovery.

One of the continuing miracles of recovery is becoming a productive, responsible member of society. We need to tread carefully into areas that expose us to ego-inflating experience, prestige and manipulation that may be difficult for us. We have found that the way to remain a productive, responsible member of society is to put our recovery first. NA can survive without us, but we cannot survive without NA.

Narcotics Anonymous offers only one promise and that is freedom from active addiction, the solution that eluded us for so long. We will be freed from our self-made prisons.

Living just for today, we have no way of knowing what will happen to us. We are often amazed at how things work out for us. We are recovering in the here and now and the future becomes an exciting journey. If we had written down our list of expectations when we came to the program, we would have been cheating ourselves. Hopeless living problems have become joyously changed. Our disease has been arrested, and now anything is possible.

We become increasingly open-minded and open to new ideas in all areas of our lives. Through active listening, we hear things that work for us. This ability to listen is a gift and grows as we grow spiritually. Life takes on a new meaning when we open ourselves to this gift. In order to receive, we must be willing to give.

In recovery, our ideas of fun change. We are now free to enjoy the simple things in life, like fellowship and living in harmony with nature. We now have become free to develop a new understanding of life. As we look back, we are grateful for our new life. It is so unlike the events that brought us here.

While using, we thought that we had fun and that non-users were deprived of it. Spirituality enables us to live life to its fullest, feeling grateful for who we are and for what we have done in life. Since the beginning of our recovery, we have found that joy doesn't come from material things, but from within ourselves. We find that when we lose self-obsession, we are able to understand what it means to be happy, joyous, and free. Indescribable joy comes from sharing from the heart, we no longer need to lie to gain acceptance.

Narcotics Anonymous offers addicts a program of recovery that is more than just a life without drugs. Not only is this way of life better than the hell we lived, it is better than any life that we have ever known.

We have found a way out, and we see it work for others. Each day more will be revealed.

OUR MEMBERS SHARE

"My gratitude speaks,
When I care and
When I share with others
the NA way."

Introduction to
Our Members Share

In our meetings, our lives, and our literature, we help each other by sharing our experience and the tools we use to live clean and recover. The Basic Text is an expression of this desire to carry our message. The first ten chapters contain our collective wisdom describing the program, and now we turn to our individual experiences living the program. Our members' lives depend on our program; our program comes to life through the voices of our members.

Our First Tradition teaches us to look past our differences for our common welfare. The concept of unity described in this tradition is not the same thing as uniformity. Over time we find that those differences are precisely the things that enrich us. In the particulars of our stories the truth of our message comes through and we see how alike we really are. This can seem like a contradiction in NA: Our development as individuals and as a fellowship is about fostering our common bonds and common identity; at the same time, we cultivate and cherish the things that make each of us who we are. To stay strong and grow, we need both of these points of view.

Since our Basic Text was first published, we have grown and changed as a fellowship. Our membership has broadened, and our experience has deepened. Today we are truly worldwide, and each of our local NA communities contains worlds as well. Together we made a decision to revise this part of the book to embrace and reflect these changes. In the pages that follow, our members share their experiences getting clean, staying clean, and living clean.

The experience shared here is as diverse as we are. Our members write about going back to school, losing people they love, struggling with health problems, making amends, coming to terms with their sexuality, raising children, serving the fellowship we all love, and countless other successes and challenges. You may read about choices that are contrary to your beliefs or to the customs of your NA community. The individual paths our members choose to walk do not necessarily reflect the views of NA as a whole, and it is important to keep in mind that these are all personal experiences. It would be impossible, in one collection, to fully reflect the diversity in who our members are or what we have gone through, but here we have gathered some of that richness.

Each individual piece is very briefly summarized at the beginning and in the Table of Contents. If you are looking for something specific (like someone confronted with illness, or someone who got clean young) you may be able to find it more quickly.

We have organized the collection into four sections, each of which begins with an assortment of brief reflections from our members. The first section, "Beginnings," consists of six stories from previous editions of the Basic Text. The pieces have been chosen, in part, for their historical significance and are not edited for publication here. These voices of some of our early members act as a window on our formative years.

After "Beginnings," the text is divided into three more sections. In the "Coming Home" section, members share about finding NA, or in some cases, starting NA in their part of the world. Our readings tell us that anyone can find a home in NA "regardless of age, race, sexual identity, creed, religion, or lack of religion." In the "Regardless of..." section, members talk about their journey to find acceptance in NA, and to make NA a place where all of us can feel safe and welcome. The final section, "Life on Life's Terms," focuses on practicing the principles in the face of all that life offers: Fully awake and alive, we confront joy and tragedy and the simple pleasures of day-to-day life.

You may not relate to everything you read here—just as you might not identify with everyone who shares in an NA meeting— but we hope that at least some of these voices will touch and inspire you. In NA we learn that as addicts we are not unique, but as people we are individuals, and our experience matters. Collectively we are so much more than the sum of our parts. Each of us, regardless of our clean time or where we came from, has something to contribute by sharing openly and honestly, and something to gain when we listen with an open heart.

Beginnings

This sample of stories from early members gives some glimpses of NA in the late seventies and early eighties. They have been chosen in part for their historical significance and, as such, have not been edited. Over time we have learned to be clear in our language and identification; these stories, however, are reproduced exactly as they were published in the Fifth Edition Basic Text (1988).

The short passages that begin this section are excerpted from stories in previous editions of the Basic Text.

Reflections

It was suggested to me that I start an NA meeting in my area. I was frightened and didn't think I had enough clean time. My friends told me that I could be miserable as long as I wanted to be. With the help of God and other addicts, that meeting began and continues to thrive.

I want to keep what has been given to me, so I actively share through loving service to NA, wherever and however I am asked. The spirit of this Fellowship is in me today. I have come to know unconditional love.

I was 5'5" tall, and weighed 282 pounds.[3] I ate compulsively to try and handle my feelings and emotions and to make me feel better. As a matter of fact, this is how I originally got into using heavy drugs. I wanted to lose weight so desperately that I became willing to use heroin. I thought I would be smart enough not to get hooked, that I could use and lose my appetite, feel good and outsmart the game. I bounced around the country and ended up in penitentiaries and jails. This was the beginning of the end; not only was I a compulsive overeater and remained fat, but I was also addicted to the drugs I was using.

When I came to this program, I found something that I had never experienced before—total acceptance for who and what I was. I was invited to keep coming back to a Fellowship that told me there were no fees or dues—that I had already paid my dues via my past life—and that if I kept coming back, I would find total freedom and a new way of life.

---

[3] 1.65 meters; 128 kilograms

117

There is no question about it, I owe my life to the Narcotics Anonymous Fellowship and God.

So much had been going really good. I had a diploma, a brand new car, a driver's license and a good relationship with my parents. My girlfriend was seeing a therapist who told her we should get involved in something together, like starting an NA meeting in our area. The closest NA meeting was over an hour away, and there were only two a month at that. After we started the meeting, she got high and moved out. My best friend had been getting high for a while and they started going out together, and that really ripped me up inside. I had a dog who I cried to every night and he couldn't even stand it and ran away.

Since I had started this NA meeting, I continued to go and the meeting grew. Here I was with two years, crying in the meeting, feeling sorry for myself and depressed and having newcomers with thirty days clean telling me it would be better, be grateful for what you have, and keep coming back. People who were new in the Fellowship would come over to my house and Twelfth Step me. They kept me coming back. They told me that they loved me. I was depressed for two months like that and during that time two more meetings started. I was making three meetings a week and I started working the steps. I was getting involved in our area service and started being grateful for everything I had. I was so grateful to be alive and I believed that that was because of the NA Fellowship.

I remember feeling like I didn't belong in NA because pot was really my problem although I had used other drugs. I read the little white pamphlet *Narcotics Anonymous*. It said an addict was someone who "lived to use and used to live" and that our lives and thinking were centered on getting and using drugs. That sounded like me. Then it said they didn't care what drug I used and the only requirement for membership was the honest desire to stop using. I thought, "Well, maybe, just maybe they would let me stay." I started going to a meeting every day or I talked with another addict. The members told me they needed me and I began to feel a part of! I attended regularly and tried to support new meetings. I learned about the steps and I tried to work them. I didn't use, I took inventories, I made amends, and I prayed. That's one of the things I'm grateful for is having the freedom to have a God as I understood Him. One day I realized I was being freed from my addiction. The obsession and the compulsion were no longer the dominating force in my life; growing spiritually was.

A year before I came to Narcotics Anonymous I found myself hopelessly addicted to cough syrup, drinking five or six four-ounce bottles a day. I needed help so I went to a doctor; he prescribed dexedrine and would give me a shot that made me feel good. I found myself going to him practically every day.

This continued for about eight months and I was very happy with my new found legal addiction. I was also getting codeine from a different doctor. I now became insanely afraid and began drinking too. This went on around the clock for a month and I ended up in a mental institution. After being released from the hospital, I thought I was free from narcotics and now I could drink socially. I soon found out I could not. It was then that I sought help from NA.

Here I learned that my real problem did not lie in the drugs that I had been using, but in a distorted personality that had developed over the years of my using and even before that. In NA I was able to help myself with the help of others in the Fellowship. I find I am making progress in facing reality and I'm growing a day at a time. I find new interests now that mean something, and realize that that was one of the things which I was looking for in drugs.

I had a job and was working steadily, but my life wasn't working; I was still drug dependent. This was the beginning of the end, the start of my recovery. I was in a state of hopeless desperation; I just wanted to lay down and die.

I looked for a methadone program, but none were available. My boss asked me the next day what was wrong with me. Before I knew it, I was telling him the truth. I said I was a drug addict. He asked me if I wanted help. I told him, "yes."

This was the first of many spiritual awakenings. I went to a hospital in Louisiana and from there to a halfway house. This is where I found Narcotics Anonymous. NA was the tribe I never had. I found the same type of people that I had run with on the streets. There was something different about them. They had a peace I wanted.

Today, I can look in the mirror and laugh at myself. I won't say that I have a good self image today, but it's better than it used to be. When I was using, I mastered the art of fight or flee. I would either run from a situation or fight it out, but never face it. Most of the time, it was me I was running from. The words serenity and surrender were foreign to my vocabulary. I am learning that I usually have as much serenity as I have surrendered.

For half my life I have been careening wildly through the sea of chaos and destruction. The Program of Narcotics Anonymous has shown me serenity and direction. I am growing to realize that my experience can benefit those who still suffer. The freedom that I have always sought I have found in the steps of the program.

*When he was using he went from one "mother"
to another—from his mother's house to the military
to marriage—until his wife tired of the insanity and found
the only NA meeting in the world. In his story from our First
Edition, this addict admits that it took him time but finally
he learned to take action and be responsible for himself.*

I Found the Only NA Meeting in the World

My name is Bob B. from Los Angeles. On the subject of people, places and things, my story is not much different from the executive, it's just on the opposite end of the stick.

I grew up on the wrong side of the tracks, poor, deprived, during the depression, in a broken home. The words of love were never spoken in my household. There were a lot of kids in my house.

Most of the things I remember about my life are recalled in retrospect. While they were happening, I didn't know anything about it. I just remember going through life feeling different, feeling deprived. I never felt quite comfortable wherever I was, with whatever I had at any given time. I grew up in a fantasy world. Things on the other side of the fence always looked better. My grass was never green enough. My head was always out to lunch. I learned all the short cuts in order to make it through school.

I always had a dream of leaving home. It was not the place to be. My great fantasy was that there was going to be something good out there somewhere.

I started using drugs fairly late in life, I was eighteen years old. I say late in comparison with the age kids are doing it today.

My mother ruled her house with a big stick. That was her method. The constant way I gained attention was by getting my butt whipped on a daily basis. I found another way to get attention

121

was to get sick. When I got sick I got the things I felt were necessary, love and attention.

I blamed my mother because she didn't make better choices in her life so that I could have been happy growing up.

I went into the military because it was a place to run. I stayed in the military for a long time because they afforded me the same opportunities I had at home; three hots, a cot, and no responsibility. I can say I was a responsible person because I had rank and did this or that, but it was only because they gave me advance directions on what to do, when to do it, and how much to do.

My first drug was alcohol. I found that there were two personalities. When under the influence of alcohol and, later other narcotics, there was a personality change.

I found out later, however, that this personality change went back even farther. I was two people before I even started using. I had learned how to steal early. I had learned how to lie early. I had learned how to cheat early. I used these processes successfully. I was addicted to stealing long before I was addicted to drugs because it made me feel good. If I had some of your goodies to spread around, I felt good. I had a thing about stealing. I couldn't go into a place unless I took something.

I was so naive, I knew nothing about drugs. Drugs were not something that were talked about in the 1930's and 1940's. It is not that drugs have changed, they just didn't talk about them before. They didn't talk about sex, or drugs, or religion, or discuss or explain them. It just wasn't one of those things that was talked about.

I first experienced my drug of choice, heroin, in the Far East. I heard about opium and tried that. I found that you could cook up heroin and put it in a spike. There were a great variety of drugs in other countries that you could get by just walking into a drug store and asking for them. So I stayed out of the country for nine years. That way I wasn't confronted with the attitudes and restrictions in the United States.

I knew nothing about the progression of my disease. I knew nothing about addiction. I ran around in the ignorance of addiction for a lot of years, not knowing, just not knowing.

No one explained to me that when you use drugs over a year's time you can get hooked. No one told me about withdrawal from drugs. The only thing anyone told me was, "Don't get sick," and the way to do that was to keep on using.

One of the problems I found in the military was that they give you orders, ship you out, and they don't send your connection with you. You get sick. You try to back that up the next time by trying to get a big enough supply, and your month's supply lasts a week, or two or three days.

I knew nothing about progression of the disease nor the consequences of my actions. The progression of my disease caught up with me, as far as the military was concerned, when I started transporting and smuggling. Also, when you use drugs to the extent that you can't be there for duty, they frown on it. The next thing they do is take you away and lock you up. Then the military did a cruel thing, they put me out on the streets.

I was ill equipped to take care of myself. I had gone from one mama to another mother. They had taken care of me, then I found myself on the street with no one to take care of me. I knew nothing of paying rent, working or being responsible. So I had to give that responsibility to whoever I could give it to. I ran through a lot of mothers.

I had to learn how to hustle on the street. You have to realize that the military has a lot of equipment that can be sold and I used to sell it, because I liked to steal. I had to learn other processes, like running through stores winging steaks and cigarettes under my arm, jumping from second story windows, and running from policemen.

I think there is a certain excitement that goes along with drug addiction. It was a lot like my childhood games of cops and robbers. I found out that there are more policemen than drug addicts. They were standing around watching you. I could never understand how they could go into a crowd of people and pick me out, and say, "Let's get in the car, let's go." Nine times out of ten they had me dirty.

During the process of finding mothers, one mother found me. I thought I should hem this one up and get papers on her, then she couldn't run away.

I chose correctly, I chose someone who wasn't using. I knew about the ones that were using. They were never there when I got locked up. They never had bail money. They could never visit because they were too busy taking care of their own habits.

So I found one of those unsuspecting ones. She was in school and working and she had a place to stay. She had one shortcoming, she didn't know she needed someone to take care of. I was a prime candidate. I wanted to be taken care of. She was going to help me get my act together. She proposed to me in jail and I said, "Yes, I do. Just go down and pay the bail."

For the next three years I ran her crazy trying to keep up with me. Then she went out and found the only Narcotics Anonymous meeting in the world. How she did that, I don't know. At that time, there was only one meeting in the whole world, and she went out and found it, and I sent her off to the meeting. I had her go check it out.

You have to realize that in those days, drug addicts were very unpopular. To just intimate that two drug addicts were going to congregate anywhere would constitute a police stakeout. That's the way they treated drug addicts at the time. There was very little understanding about addiction. I was very leery about anything to do about helping drug addicts. I knew what they did with drug addicts; they locked them up, period! There was no program to go to, except in Ft. Worth and Lexington.

I always had a sad story to justify my using. One day, after one of those six month trips to go get a loaf of bread at the corner grocery, I came home and my bags were sitting by the door.

She had told me fifty times or a thousand times, "You got to go." This time was different. There was something in her voice this time. So I took my bags and went to the only place there was to go, the streets.

I had become accustomed to living in the streets. I knew how to live in the back of old cars, old laundry rooms, any old empty building, your house or my house. Of course, I never had my house. I couldn't pay the rent. I never knew how to pay rent. If I had three dollars in my pocket, that three dollars was going for drugs before a place to stay. It was that simple. I think I paid rent one time while I was using drugs and living on the streets, that was just to move in. It was called "catch me if you can" from then on. It usually didn't make any difference, because I was a ward of the state much of the time anyway. I just ran in the streets until they locked me up, then I had a place to stay. I could rest up, and get my health back in order to go back out and do it again.

I came to Narcotics Anonymous nearly 21 years ago.[4] But I didn't come for me. I came just to keep her mouth shut. I went to meetings loaded.

I didn't have a driver's license. I was unemployable. I had no place to stay. I was the wrong color. I had no money. I didn't have a car. I didn't have an old lady, or I needed a new one. I took them all these problems and they would tell me, "Keep coming back." And they said, "Work the steps." I used to read the steps and thought that that was working them. I found out years later that even though I read the steps, I didn't know what I had read. I did not understand what I read.

They told me in many places that I was an addict. I had been labeled an addict. From the military, to the jails, and right on down the line, I had been labeled. I accepted that, but I didn't understand it. I had to go out and do some more experimenting before I got back to the program.

One of the things I had to learn to do was to understand what the program was all about. I had to become willing to find out

---

[4] Written in 1981

what the program was about. Only after standing at the gates of death did I want to understand. I think death is the counsel permanent. I had overdosed a number of times, but that was kind of like the place where I always wanted to be. It was just before going over the brink and everything seemed okay. When I came out of it, I could say, "Wow, give me some more." That's insanity!

The final case for me was that I was about to be shot off a fence, and not by my own doing. I didn't like that. Playing cops and robbers is dangerous out there. They have guns, and I don't like being used for target practice. There were more and more cases of policemen sticking guns in my mouth and upside my head, and telling me to lay upside a wall.

My last day of narcotics use or drugs of any type, I had just fixed and two policemen got me spread-eagled on a chainlink fence that I was trying to get over. I became sober and clean immediately. Everything became very clear and I didn't want to die that way. Something clicked on in my mind and I thought, "It doesn't have to be this way."

After that last rest and recuperation, I found out that I could work these steps. The sum total of my life has changed as a direct result. I got involved in working the steps, trying to understand what they were talking about, to really understand what they were talking about. I found there is a certain amount of action that goes with every step. I had to get into action about how the steps applied to me. I always thought the steps applied to you, not me.

It got down to talking about God and spirituality. I had canned God a long time ago, then I put that in church, and I didn't have anything to do with church. I found out that God and spirituality have nothing to do with church.

I had to learn to get involved. It has been one hell of an adventure. My life has changed to such an extent that it is almost unbelievable that I was ever there. However, I know from where

I came. I have constant reminders. I need that constant reminder of newcomers and talking with others.

This program has become a part of me. It has become a part of life and living for me. I understand more clearly the things that are happening in my life today. I no longer fight the process.

I came to meetings of Narcotics Anonymous in order to take care of the responsibilities that have been given to me. Today, I care. I am addicted to the loving and caring and sharing that goes on in NA. I look forward to more of these things in my life.

My problem is addiction, it has something to do with drugs being the means of not coping with life, it has something to do with that within, that compulsion and that obsession. I now have the tools to do something about it. The Twelve Steps of recovery are the tools.

He lived in a place that many call paradise, but in his story from our First Edition, this beachcomber shares that for an addict, "skid row is in the mind." Through NA, he has found a sense of peace and a new way of life.

Mid-Pacific Serenity

I am a happy, grateful drug addict, clean by the grace of God and the Twelve Steps of Narcotics Anonymous. Life today is fulfilling and there is joy in my heart.

It wasn't always this way. I drank and used drugs for twelve years, on a daily basis for ten of them. I was an addict of the hopeless variety. It really seems to me that I was born this way.

I was born and raised in Southern California, in a loving middle class family. Both my sister and I were wanted, loved children and were shown that in every way. As far back as I can remember, I have felt separate from this family and all of life. Of course, I am talking of an intense fear of life. I cannot remember feeling the simplicity of being a child.

I had the addict's personality growing up, self will run riot. I always wanted my own way, and if I didn't get it, I sure let everyone know.

Growing up in Southern California, I seemed to get into all the normal things, going to the beach, getting into sports, yet always the fears and feelings of inadequacy never let me live up to my potential.

I was an average student throughout school, had lots of friends yet I withdrew, dominated by the fear. I guess I was about fifteen when I tried my first drug, alcohol. From the first drink it was oblivion. Finally I had found freedom from fear, or so I thought. From the beginning I identified with the rejects, the people who slept on the beach, under the piers.

As I look back over these twelve years, I see how I loved each new drug I tried. Alcohol was only the beginning; if it got you

128

loaded, I wanted to try it and I always wanted more. It didn't matter if it was sniffing glue or shooting the best coke or heroin. I wasn't a rich, choosy addict, I just needed to stay high and all my energy was put into that direction.

I quit school in the twelfth grade. Surfing had become part of my life, so it was off to Hawaii. My parents were very confused about their son who didn't do a very good job of hiding his desperation. To all who were sane and living life, I appeared very lost and unhappy. You see, it was a very short time after I started using, that the alcohol and drugs quit doing for me what they did in the beginning. The fear had returned, only much worse than before.

My first trip to Hawaii in 1962 was only the beginning of many more to come, always trying to run from myself. Hawaii was, and is, a paradise, but I only saw it through the eyes of being loaded. Thanks to the warm weather, it was easy to pursue the only life I knew, the way of life was to wander the streets and sleep in parked cars or other available shelters. At the age of nineteen, I was back in Hawaii for the third time, a full-blown addict and so lost and confused I only knew I had to drink and use drugs and there was no other way.

Returning to California at the end of the summer of 1963, I found myself joining the Navy. Being lost, that seemed to be the easiest thing to do, just sign my name. It was easier than looking for a job. I was so burned out already and wanted something different, yet didn't know how to ask for help. The Navy, of course, was not the answer. The drugs continued and after two years I was discharged. The psychiatrist said my mind had become disordered from the use of marijuana and LSD, plus I had jumped overboard in rage at the Navy.

I convinced myself that once I got out of the Navy things would be different, no one would be telling me what to do, but I met a new friend at this point, the world of fixing. This was in

1965 and the next six years were the worst years of my life. As I see it today, those years got me into the program.

After getting out of the Navy, I got married. How and why this woman married me is a mystery even today. On our wedding night, I shot some dope and slept on Venice Beach with my dogs. This is the type of behavior a selfish, self-centered addict has, concerned only with himself and getting loaded. The way I was able to stay loaded was by dealing, always being the middle man. The house where we lived was being watched, it was on the Venice canal in Venice, California.

My parents knew what was going on, so with my wife four months pregnant they helped us get out of there, and it was back to Hawaii. We lived on the north shore, it was a more isolated part of Oahu, lots of young people lived there. This was the year 1967 and at this time, LSD was really popular and everyone was into the spiritual thing; Eastern religion and gurus. There were two Harvard professors who were taking LSD and saying that you could find God, so I thought all that love, peace, and joy sounded good. I wanted out of the feelings that I was having. Fear dominated my life. I had been shooting a lot of speed in California the past year. I decided to clean up my life in Hawaii, so I took psychedelics, smoked hashish and tried to meditate.

Somewhere I had read that when the student was ready, the teacher would appear. Little did I know that the Program of Narcotics Anonymous was about to be introduced to me, and that it would become my teacher.

I was able to stay away from shooting dope that year. My wife and I had a baby girl and were on welfare, living in the country. I seemed to be fitting right into the movement of the time; flower children, the everything is beautiful consciousness. Yet still, inside, everything wasn't beautiful.

There was a four bedroom house next door to us for rent, and one day this woman appeared and told us that God had told her that she was supposed to live there. She was in her fifties, had long gray hair to her waist and wore a bikini most of the time. She had no money, but said she was led to this house.

This woman seemed to radiate a feeling of love and joy that I had never felt from anyone else before. Immediately upon meeting her, I felt as if I had known her forever. Something in me was drawn to her. Little did I know that she was to become my sponsor, and play such a big part in my life! This was the beginning of a journey that even today amazes me. It is a way of life, a way of learning complete trust in a Higher Power. Through a series of miracles, which I now have come to see as quite normal to my life, this woman ended up in this house with the rent paid every month. Needless to say, this house became a program house.

A meeting was started at this house. It was called the Beachcombers Spiritual Progress Traveling Group and through the years it has traveled throughout the United States, from Hawaii to the East coast, and through Europe twice, always attracting the addict who still suffers, offering a way up and out.

I remember my first meeting at this house in 1968. For the first time, I felt as if I really belonged. Not so much because I heard people talk of using drugs as I had, but because they spoke of what was going on inside. For the first time, I found out that other people had fears also. Yet with all the hope this meeting brought me, it was only the beginning of a three year period that I would not want to live through again.

I identified from that first meeting and wanted a new way of life. I would stay clean for a short period, and then I would use again. First I would just pick up a beer or smoke a joint, but I would always end up shooting dope again. I couldn't understand it then, today I realize that I still had reservations. There was still that thought that I could use.

In the year 1970 I stayed clean for three months two different times. The last time was right before Christmas, I smoked two joints and went into convulsions. After that, I took two downs once and that was it. For almost an entire year I didn't know what it was to be clean again. I drank, took pills, and shot cocaine and heroin daily.

Living on the North Shore made it easy to stay out of trouble. There weren't many police in that area. I stayed loaded, my wife left and I knew that I would never stay clean again. One time I ran out of dope and I shot several hundred milligrams of caffeine tablets and went into the shakes for hours. I seemed to be so desperate to die. Although I never woke up in the gutter or on skid row, I woke up on the beach, under a palm tree, with my face in the sand. The feelings were the same, skid row is in the mind.

I really feel that it doesn't matter what or how much we use, where we live or how much money we have, it's what is going on inside that counts. For me, I knew I was dying but still couldn't stop. I'd given up on NA, everyone I knew in the program had left. My sponsor and a group of clean addicts were in Europe and one of the clean addicts was living on another island and would call every so often to see if I was still alive.

On the morning of October 20, 1971, I woke up with dope in the house and for some reason I walked out to the beach and didn't get loaded the moment I opened my eyes. I remember it was a gray, overcast day and I was feeling hopeless. I just sat on the beach crying, just wanting to die; I couldn't go on. A feeling went through me that I never experienced before in my life. I felt warm and peaceful inside. A voice said, "It's over, you never have to use again." I felt a peace I had never felt before.

I returned to the house, packed some stuff and headed for the airport. I was going to the island of Maui, where my clean friend was. My recovery started with miracles. I had no money, yet I was led to the right places at the right times and I got to Maui. I walked in and told him that I was ready to go to any lengths to stay clean. Staying clean today goes a long way beyond not taking that first fix, pill or drink; it is a way of life, a life that I call an adventure.

I have an outline for living, it is the Twelve Steps of NA. I either practice and live these steps or I die! I really believe that a person who stays clean for any amount of time is staying clean through periods when it seems to make no sense to stay clean. I feel we all have felt like that at one time or another.

I've stayed clean by the grace of God. The steps have become my life. I've had to take many inventories, the Fourth and Fifth Steps, and I will continue to have to write down what is going on inside me and give it away.

For me, this is the way it works; keep giving away the old and making room for the new. For me, it never gets really easy to do, usually I have to be backed up against the wall and humiliated and then I share. They say that this is a program of action, that you can't keep it without giving it away; how true it is. In the beginning, I thought I had to say all the right things and save everyone. Today I realize I only have what's in my heart to share. Today, I can walk into a meeting and if I am full of the Father's love, then I share it, yet there are times that I walk into a meeting and want to throw the coffee pot through the window. Yet I have to stay honest, for that's the way I stay clean.

I know today that staying clean and having a relationship with God as I understand Him is the most important thing in my life. When I do that and carry the message to the ones who still suffer, than all else is provided in my life. I really believe that I don't have to prove anything to anybody. I carry the message by letting the newcomer know who I am inside and sharing how I work the steps one day at a time.

Since getting clean in 1971, life has been anything but boring. I have traveled all over. My sponsor was an able example of following your heart, and that wherever we went, NA was alive. Our houses were always open, with a coffee pot going. We started meetings wherever we arrived. Sometimes we had no money, but we went out to do our primary purpose and God always showed us the way.

My sponsor died three years ago with eighteen years clean. Most of the group has family now, and we're scattered around the United States, learning different lessons, yet NA always comes first. Today, I am married and pursue different things than during the first seven years of my recovery, yet I know that the only way I can have any outside gifts is to put this program and God first. We really have found a way up and out, and so long as we keep giving it away, no matter if it is love and joy or tears and fears, it will be all right.

Today I live because people are there who care and will listen. I really believe in magic, for my life is full of it. God is loving us now.

After a lifetime of using, this "southern gentleman" learned that the most gracious thing he could do was open the doors to an NA meeting. In this story from our First Edition, he recalls that the first time a man told him he loved him was in Narcotics Anonymous.

If You Want What We Have

My name is Bill, and I'm a junkie and a juicer. For many years of my life I felt that the world had dealt me a cruel hand, which left me with many inadequate feelings. Fear ate a hole in me that I was never able to fill with drugs and alcohol.

I was born in Alabama in 1933. My father's job required constant moving, which meant new schools and new faces. I was small and sickly and my insecurities and inadequacies around people increased. I fought these feelings verbally and with my fists. Punishment in some fashion followed me everywhere.

My father died when I was seven, and I remember the hate that I felt because he had left an only child to fend for himself. A grandmother, aunt and mother spoiled me rotten. Every time the church door was open, I was there. At the age of ten, everyone in the family thought baptism was in order. I didn't feel any different when I got up than when I knelt down. Control was the name of the game. I tried to control everyone in our little family and outside, including the nun who caught me stealing cold drinks in a convent.

Another form of punishment that I felt was rejection. My mother married a man who later proved to be an addict. We moved to another city, and the war within me intensified. Continuous fighting at home created more fear and insecurities. When I was away, I hated my home and resented the people in it. Drawing upon different concepts, I began another way of living. It did not matter to me to what lengths I had to go in order to gain love and approval from everyone. Up went the false front with more dishonesty and deceptions. I was to spend many years of my life trying to be something that I was not.

Relief came at the ripe old age of sixteen in the form of alcohol at a dance. Immediately my fear of girls was gone. My two left feet disappeared, and I knew exactly when and where to lay my newfound wisdom of people. The effect left, and I was back at war with me.

I believed rules were made to be broken. Society's laws were not for me. They hampered my way of living, and I began to deal with reality the only way I knew, and that was using the drug alcohol. This is the only drug I was aware of in the late forties, and I used it to ease the pain. At the time, it was the best way to cope with them. Anyone could punch my buttons if I thought that it was needed for their approval of me.

After a small skirmish with school officials and city authorities, private school was necessary to finish high school. Two years of college proved even further that this world, and everything in it, was full of crap.

I cared for no one at this stage of the game. However, I met a young lady who met all of my requirements. She was from an old family, very regal in appearance and possessed all of the social graces. We ran off and got married. I entered into a new relationship that I was not mature enough to handle.

I fancied myself in the future as the old southern gentleman, broad brim hat, bow string tie, overlooking his vast domain with a mint julep in one hand and a gold cane in the other. Material things were the basis for happiness in my life at this time. I looked either up or down to people, depending on their seeming net worth. After attaining a lot of these things, happiness and peace of mind did not come. My salary as purchasing agent at a large hospital was not enough. Stealing to support my materialistic ambitions was necessary. The salesmen soon found my vulnerable spot: wine, women and song. They began to supply my demand. Drinking and partying every night soon made a

physical wreck out of me. In the latter part of 1954, I was introduced to a little goodie called codeine by a salesman to draw a
clean breath. Something was cruising in me every moment of
every day.

I was twenty-one years old and a full-blown addict. Routine
encounters of addicts and alcoholics treated at the hospital convinced me that I was unique. I would never become like they
were.

The standards and expectations I set for myself and others
were too high to be met. Negative thinking and escapism became
my total personality. Greediness compelled me to study drugs
and experiment. This may have saved my life while I was using.
I feared certain combinations in trying to get off.

The sixties came along, and I decided I needed a change. I left
the hospital for what I thought were greener pastures and began
to travel. Life was still hell. That old nest of negativism followed
me everywhere that I went. Jobs came and went, then they came
no more. The jails and hospital stays were more frequent and
longer.

In 1973, I came into a mental ward; I was chained like an animal. My psychiatrists, who I constantly conned over the years,
knew of my alcohol problem, but not of my other addictions. It
was suggested that I try a Twelve Step Program. My family was
willing to try anything, so off I went for all the wrong reasons.
People were kind and helpful to me, so I began to use them as
I had others all my life. They had never seen me clean and dry,
so how were they to know if I was using. I was very careful not
to talk about too much of anything lest they become suspicious.
Deception and denial were the games that I played and they almost killed me. At this time I had gotten off the hard stuff and on
to downers, uppers and mood elevators. People seemed happy
and sober, and I wondered what they were using. I do not believe
there was a fragment of honesty in me at the time. Willingness
to change never crossed my mind. Gambling, women and using

were my bag. For over three years I lived in hopelessness and despair going back to using, and going back to the program.

After hearing the Higher Power concept and about a spiritual way of life, I knew drugs were not for me. I had at one time a God graciously given to me by my environment, whom I did not understand. I knew this God did not want anything to do with someone like me.

There were times when I tried to relate, but there seemed to be something missing. I sincerely think that even though my feelings seemed to be the same as others, there seemed a lack of deeper understanding that I needed. God bless them they tried. There were no recovering addicts in the area and no NA. I looked for people with other drug dependencies and finally found one lady in the group. She had spent ten years in and out without any success.

Things did get a little better. There were no arrests and no stays in the hospitals for a period of two years. Then, in the fall of 1975, everything went to pieces. Back to the hospital I went. Exchanging the alcohol for pills, I was back in the old paradox again. Then, a series of events began that changed my life. There was talk of committing me to the state institution. My family no longer wanted me like I was. Two program members came one afternoon to see me and they both told me the same thing; that I wasn't crazy, to come back, don't use, and ask for help.

My sponsor, who had fired herself several times from my case, picked me up and took me to a meeting. The girl who rode with us spoke that night. She talked about God of her understanding. Sitting next to my wife that night I began to see where I had missed the boat. I went back to that dark room and thanked God for those people, because somehow I knew they cared. Even though they did not understand many things about me, they gave me time out of their lives and asked for nothing back. I remembered the Eleventh Step in the program and I thought maybe, just maybe, if I asked for knowledge of His will for me and the power to carry it out, He might help. I got a little brave, I knew that I wasn't honest, I added, "P.S., Please help me get honest." It would be great to say that I left that hospital and never used again, but it didn't happen that way. It was almost like all the other confinements I had experienced. I came out of that hospital with exactly what I went in with: me!

Thanksgiving, Christmas, and New Year's passed just like a wink, blink and a nod, and I was still praying. Everything got worse. My family kicked me out the day after New Year's. I knew it was hopeless, but I was still asking for honesty. On or around the fifth of January, I began to ease off the pills I was using. It wasn't any fun, but I know today that all the suffering was necessary. Praying and tapering off had become my obsessions. I felt that this was my last chance.

I took my last pill, shot, etc., in March. By God's grace I was clean! People began to tell me, look what you have done, and I began to believe them. I got to looking so good to me that I just invited me out for a drink. What a rude awakening. I came off that drunk cold turkey, no pills, nothing, for the first time in over twenty-one years. For five days I shook and I mean shook. On the fifth day, I wanted no more. I sat down in my little V.W., bowed my head and told God, "If this is all in life for me, I want life no longer. Death would be far more merciful. It doesn't make any difference any longer." I felt a peace come into me that I had never felt. I don't know how long this lasted, and it doesn't matter. It happened and that is the important part. Since then, I have experienced the same feeling from time to time. It was like being brought forward from darkness to light. God doesn't let me stay in the sunlight too long, but He will help me if I choose to stay in the twilight. I walked away from that car a free man. I did not realize this for a long time. Since that day, I have not had a desire to use.

A God of my understanding had sent me enough honesty to get started down the right path. I went back to the program and again I made another mistake. I kept my mouth shut with the intention of letting the winners teach me how to become clean. Today I know that for me I walked a different path through addiction, and I had to walk a different path through this program. I had to learn about me. For almost two years in the program, I saw people come and go with addictions other than alcohol. One night in Birmingham, I was sharing with a group and also talking about drugs when a man approached me with tears in his eyes. He told me of his son and daughter somewhere hooked on drugs. He said, "Surely God must have some program for people like them." All the way back home that night I talked to a girl using drugs, a schoolmate of my wife. The telephone gave us the answer through some new friends from Georgia and Tennessee in Narcotics Anonymous. A visit to share in Chattanooga proved to be a blessing. Several people came up from Atlanta, including one guy from Marietta who kept telling people that he loved them. I was forty-four years of age at the time, that was the first time a man had ever told me that he loved me. For some unexplainable reason, I also felt his love. A couple of months later, we went to Atlanta and found a repetition of our first trip. I wanted so much to give and feel as these people did. At the close of the dance that night, I overheard something that went like this, "If you want what we have, you have got to take the steps."

I came back to Alabama and began to take the steps. I learned about me and found a God of my understanding. Trust God, Clean House, Help Others, explains it as simply as I can. I spent many years looking for something around the corner, or someone coming down the street who would give me happiness and peace of mind. Today, through the steps and the people in NA, I have found a solution. I have to stay honest with me, stay open-minded enough to change and be willing to accept God's love for me through the members of NA.

I am very grateful to our brothers and sisters in Georgia for their tolerance and support during our first year or so in the program in Alabama. They more or less sponsored me in those early days. Just knowing they were there was very comforting. Many times I called my friend in Marietta, despondent over the way things were going. He always seemed to have the answer. Keep the doors open and God will do the rest.

NA groups now have sprung up in several cities and now those people are sponsoring me through their growth in NA and God's grace. I finally got it all together, but without God's help I forget where I put it.

There is one thing that I feel I can give to every addict to use. I love each and every one of you, and most importantly, God loves you too! I found this love in the wonderful Program of NA, through God's grace and you people. Come join us; it works!

In this story originally published in our Little White Book and added to the Basic Text at the Second Edition, a mother learns that she can come out of the paralyzing fear of addiction and turn her whole life around. She claims her seat as a woman in NA and hopes that one day more women will find recovery.

Fearful Mother

I thought an addict was a person who was using hard drugs, someone who was on the streets or in jail. My pattern was different—I got my drugs from a doctor. I knew something was wrong yet I tried to do right—at work, in my marriage and in raising my children. I really tried hard. I would be doing well and then I'd fail. It went on like this and each time it seemed like forever; it seemed like nothing would ever change. I wanted to be a good mother. I wanted to be a good wife. I wanted to be involved in society yet never felt a part of it.

I went through years of telling my children "I'm sorry but this time it will be different." I went from one doctor to another asking for help. I went for counseling feeling everything will be all right now, but the inside was still saying, "What is wrong?" I was changing jobs, changing doctors, changing drugs, trying different books, religions and hair colors. I moved from one area to another, changed friends and moved furniture. I went on vacations and also remained hidden in my home—so many things through the years—constantly feeling, I'm wrong, I'm different, I'm a failure.

When I had my first child I liked it when they knocked me out; I liked the feeling of the drugs they gave me. It was a feeling that whatever is going on around me, I don't know and I don't care, really. Through the years the tranquilizers gave me the feeling that nothing is really that important. Toward the end, things became so mixed up I was not sure what was and what was not important. I was shaking inside and out. Drugs would not help.

I was still trying, but very little. I had quit work and was trying to go back but I couldn't. I would be on the couch afraid of everything. I was 103 pounds and had sores on my lips and in my nose. I had diabetes and shook so that I had a hard time putting a spoon to my mouth. I felt I was out to kill myself and people around me were out to hurt me. Physically and mentally I had a breakdown. I had just become a grandmother and I could not even communicate with a small child. I was almost a vegetable. I wanted to be a part of living but did not know how. Part of me said I'd be better off dead and part of me said there has to be a better way of living.

When I started on the Program of NA, there were a lot of people who suggested just everyday things for me to do, like eating, taking a bath, getting dressed, going for a walk, going to meetings. They told me, "Don't be afraid, we have all gone through this." I went to a lot of meetings through the years. One thing has stuck with me, one thing they said from the beginning, "Betty, you can stop running and you can be whatever you want to be and do whatever you want to do."

Since being on the program I have listened and watched many people and have seen them go through many ups and downs. I have used the teachings I felt were best for me. My work area has had to change and I have been going to school. I have had to relearn all the way back to the grammar school level. It has been slow for me but very rewarding.

I also decided that I need to know me better before I can have a meaningful relationship with a man. I am learning to communicate with my daughters. I am trying many things which I wanted to do for years. I am able to remember many things that I had pushed out of my mind. I have found that Betty is not that big pile of nothing but is someone and something that I never really stopped to look at or listen to. April 1, will be my fifth NA birthday. How's that for April Fool's day!

I have been asked to update my story. This April 1, will be my tenth year birthday.[5] I think, "Where have I been and have I really grown?" I know that I have gotten married. I would like to say I love my husband very dearly, and at times this is hard for me to say. Expressing a deep feeling for any person has been very hard for me. I have felt like it would be taken away, or that he would hurt me or laugh at me. That has happened at times, but I have still loved him and it has not been that big and crushing a deal. I am learning not to put him or myself on a pedestal. If I am expecting too much of him that means I had better look a little closer at myself. There are times when we can talk, and there are times it takes time before we can talk. How boring if we both thought alike and everything went smoothly or if we fought constantly.

I still get feelings of running away from home, and maybe going back to the Islands or Michigan. I have been living in the same place for almost four years. I think that is a record for me. I am still moving furniture around. I love it and would like to put everything on rollers, it would be a lot easier.

I still do not understand men. Every once in a while I tell my husband that I am a woman and I need to be taken to a movie or somewhere. I am learning to verbalize my needs to another person. I also go to the show alone once in a while.

I graduated from high school two years ago. I would love to graduate from college, maybe some time in the future. Everyone needs something to look forward to. My daughter, son-in-law and granddaughter gave me a violin for Christmas. When I was in grammar school I took lessons for a very short time. The school stopped giving lessons and took back their violin and I never forgot that. I started out this year by slowly taking lessons and I became obsessed. I was going to two teachers and studying out of three different books. I found myself looking at one of my books and saying, "Where am I?" So now I am back to one teacher and one book.

---

[5] Written in 1981

I had a breast operated on and they removed part of it. I will not say this was a whiz because it wasn't, but I was luckier than some. I had the NA Program and people to walk through it with me. I cannot say my life has been like tiptoeing through the tulips, because that is not reality. I can say that my life is now getting better and I am more open to looking and walking in reality. With the world in such a turmoil, I feel I have been blessed to be where I am.

I look at how NA has grown. We are in Germany, Australia, England, Scotland, Italy, Brazil, etc. Maybe some day we will reach the countries that are so damn hard to reach.

I have been told there are not many women with a lot of time on the program. I am surprised when I hear this. I just assume there are and maybe they have moved to other cities and states. Maybe even to some of these countries that are so damn hard to reach. When a woman wants something bad enough, look out, she can move heaven and hell. One of the first things said to me was, "No one else in this world knows what you want, but you. If you want to survive in this world you had better do what is right for you, because no one else is going to do it." I get bumps and bruises and I suck my thumb once in awhile, but I sure get stronger each time.

I have a dog named Baba Wawa, she was very tiny when my daughter gave her to me. My daughter said, "Mom, here is a little dog and she will never grow very large." Well, she has grown very big and she surprises me every once in a while. Last night she tried to fight a big dog right through a chain link fence. I thought she was still a puppy, but she can stand her own. I guess it's like me. I have grown more than I realized and, unlike Baba Wawa, I have been known to climb the fence and go after whatever I want. I have also been known to knock those fences down. I feel like there is more to say, but who can put all of ten years down on paper? I would rather spend my time living it than writing it.

I have been active in NA answering phones, typing, and working in different areas of NA. I go to meetings and talk and still feel funny and awkward. Sometimes I am a kid, all hyper, other times it goes so smoothly that I can't remember what happened or what I said, but I feel good. What I am trying to say is, "Thank Heaven nothing is as bad as it used to be and there is so much more of what there should be in my life."

This addict found freedom behind bars through the Fellowship of Narcotics Anonymous. This is a story from our First Edition.

Jails, Institutions, and Recovery

I first came to Narcotics Anonymous in a state prison. It was my third term in prison over a seven year period, with only a few months at any one time in the streets.

One night in this prison I heard of a meeting going on about something to do with drugs. Well, I could relate to this, so I decided to check it out. Besides, it would get me away from the cell for a while.

I can remember how confused I was leaving the first meeting. Back in my cell, I dwelled on all those years in and out of jails and all the things that I'd been through just to get loaded. Most of all, I began thinking of how tired I was of living this kind of life. This group called Narcotics Anonymous seemed then to be a little too much for me. I told myself that I wasn't a hardcore dope fiend, but just a guy who liked to get loaded every day and a thief who could not stay out of jail. Although in those first meetings I did not see NA as a solution to my craziness, I did hear some things I could relate to. So, I kept going back. I heard the people in NA say that they didn't take drugs anymore, not even grass. I listened. Sure I wanted to stop all the insane situations in my life, but I didn't think I had to give up drugs altogether to do it. I thought that I needed to learn how to handle drugs better.

Some of the NA members, who came into the prison to share at these meetings, had been inmates themselves. They attributed the change in their lives to the support of Narcotics Anonymous; one addict sharing and helping another addict. I enjoyed hearing these people tell how it was and how it is today and soon felt a real kinship in the pain that we had all been through. I began respecting these people in NA who talked about how they found a way to live without drugs, alcohol, and jails.

I continued to get stoned in the institution whenever and whatever way I could while still attending NA meetings regularly. The members told me to keep coming back no matter what, so I did. Besides, it sure beat talking that talk in the yard.

Soon I was to be transferred for pre-release to a much looser security prison. I had been there before and had been busted for smoking grass, for which I was sent to a more maximum prison. Now, as I was packing my property for this transfer, I remembered a lot of trouble I had gotten into at this institution, just to use drugs. The Man knew me there, and I was pretty nervous now, thinking about being eye-balled from the time I stepped off that bus. I was already thinking hard about getting loaded when I could and scared stiff inside knowing what would happen if I got caught again.

So I smoked a joint that morning before the long bus ride. I didn't know it then, but it was to be my last. Back in the beginning, when I was attending these NA meetings, I would wonder why it wasn't working for me like it did for others. I was tired of this drug and institutional life, but at that point I guess I wasn't tired enough, because I was still using when I was going to the meetings. I had a decision to make on that bus ride which was paid for by the Department of Corrections. The decision I made that day was mostly out of fear and some things I heard in those first NA meetings.

I remember being in that bus, moving down the highway with chains wrapped around my waist and shackles on my feet, uncomfortably looking up at a resentful guard behind a cage with a shotgun. Staring out the window as the miles of freedom passed me by, I wondered why I couldn't be a part of that world. Getting loaded did not feel right anymore. Yet thinking about not taking anything sure felt strange. What a relief, when later I learned that it was easier by doing it just one day at a time.

Upon arrival at this other prison I was met by an inmate who was an NA member. I knew him from meetings that we both attended at another prison. It really made a difference to see his face when I drove up because, again, I knew I had the support that would help me make it. I continued in the fellowship at this prison and became active in the service part of the program in the institution.

During these last six months I had to do on my sentence, I would wake up in the morning and say, "Just for today, I won't take anything," and I hung with NA people in the institution to keep myself away from temptation. There were plenty of opportunities, so it wasn't easy, but I now had the support of the NA Fellowship. Once I was let out to attend an outside meeting, which made me want the Fellowship on the outside even more. I started going to the meetings clean for the first time and something happened. The program began to work.

Today I know what makes NA work. One really starts understanding why it can work only when totally abstaining from all mind-altering chemicals.

I also was beginning to understand what caring means; by helping each other, we can make it. I felt that the only one who really understood me was another addict. And the only one who could help was a clean addict.

I was so proud to stand before the group in prison and announce that I had ninety days clean. Feeling proud was not part of my life before NA. It was such a relief, not having to hustle drugs out on the yard, and do the crazy things that I did to get high. I had never done time like this and it sure felt great.

I made another decision through the advice the NA members gave me, which was the second most important decision I had ever made in my life. This decision was to have someone from the NA Program at the gate to pick me up when I was released. A person that I knew understood what I needed my first day out, because I sure didn't at this point.

When I go back into prisons today to carry the message of Narcotics Anonymous, I suggest that inmates have an NA member at that gate when they get out. I heard so many say, "Oh, I'll check it out, but I've gotta do this first, or be here first." Don't kid yourself; you might die first if you are an addict like me.

That first day out was so righteous. I was taken to a home where NA members were expecting me. This one member gave me a new address book with NA phone numbers in it and said, "Give me your old address book, you don't need those old numbers of your connections anymore." Another member took me to his closet, and gave me some clothes. I went to a bunch of meetings that day, and sure received the love and care I needed, which seemed to make up for all the attention I missed while locked up over the years.

Recently, one of the many benefits, for me, was being able to stand before the judge of the Superior Court and receive my Certificate of Rehabilitation. I never thought I would be standing in front of any judge for this reason. I am so grateful today to say that I have been able to go beyond the Fellowship for the support I need. I'm speaking about God. I mean a God I can understand and talk to when I need a Higher Strength, the God I found in Narcotics Anonymous.

So, if you are in a cell reading this, my message goes to you. If you are wondering whether drugs or booze, or both are screwing up your life, find out where an NA meeting is in your facility and check it out. You might be saving your own life, and learning a better way. If one addict can make it, so can another. We help each other in Narcotics Anonymous.

*Not all addicts reach jails or institutions in order to hit
their bottom. In his story, originally published in the Little
White Book and later included in our Second Edition, this
"different" addict explains that his disease kept him confined
to a life of fear and loneliness. He found serenity in
a simple life in Narcotics Anonymous.*

I Was Different

My story may differ from the others you have heard, in that
I was never arrested or hospitalized. I did, however, reach the
point of utter despair which so many of us have experienced. It is
not my track record that shows my addiction but rather my feelings and my life. Addiction was my way of life—the only way of
life I knew for many years.

Thinking back, I must have taken one look at life and
decided I didn't want any part of it. I came from a "good old-
fashioned," upper-middle-class broken home. I can't remember
a time when I haven't been strung out. As a small child, I found
out I could ease the pain with food, and here my drug addiction
began.

I became part of the pill mania of the 1950's. Even at this time
I found it hard to take medication as directed. I figured that two
pills would do twice as much good as one. I remember hoard-
ing pills, stealing from my mother's prescriptions, having a hard
time making the pills last until the next refill.

I continued to use in this way throughout my early years.
When I was in high school and the drug craze hit, the transition
between drugstore dope and street dope was a natural. I had
already been using drugs on a daily basis for nearly ten years;
these drugs had virtually stopped working. I was plagued
with adolescent feelings of inadequacy and inferiority. The
only answer I had was that if I took something I either was,
felt or acted better.

The story of my street using is pretty normal. I used anything and everything available every day. It didn't matter what I took so long as I got high. Drugs seemed good to me in those years. I was a crusader; I was an observer; I was afraid; and I was alone. Sometimes I felt all-powerful and sometimes I prayed for the comfort of idiocy—if only I didn't have to think. I remember feeling different—not quite human—and I couldn't stand it. I stayed in my natural state... LOADED.

In 1966, I think, I got turned on to heroin. After that, like so many of us, nothing else would do the thing for me. At first I joy-popped occasionally, and then used only on weekends; but a year later I had a habit, and two years later I flunked out of college and started working where my connection worked. I used stuff and dealt, and ran for another year-and-a-half before I got "sick and tired of being sick and tired."

I found myself strung out and no longer able to function as a human being. During this last year of my using, I started looking for help. Nothing worked! Nothing helped!

Somewhere along the line I had gotten the telephone number of a man in NA. Against my better judgment and without hope, I made what may well be the most important phone call of my life.

No one came to save me; I wasn't instantly cured. The man simply said that if I had a drug problem, I might benefit from the meetings. He gave me the address of a meeting for that night. It was too far to drive, and besides I was kicking. He also gave me the address of another meeting a couple of days later and closer to home. I promised him I'd go and have a look. When the night came, I was deathly afraid of getting busted, and afraid of the dope fiends I would find there. I knew I wasn't like the addict you read about in books or newspapers. Despite these fears I made my first meeting. I was dressed in a three piece black suit, black tie, and eighty-four hours off a two-and-a-half year run. I didn't want you to know what and who I was. I don't think I fooled anybody, I was screaming for help, and everybody knew it. I really don't remember much of that first meeting, but I must have heard something that brought me back. The first feeling I do remember on this program was the gnawing fear that because I'd never been busted or hospitalized for drugs, I might not qualify and might not be accepted.

I used twice during my first two weeks around the program, and finally gave up. I no longer cared whether or not I qualified, I didn't care if I was accepted, I didn't even care what the people thought of me. I was too tired to care.

I don't remember exactly when, but shortly after I gave up, I began to get some hope that this program might work for me. I started to imitate some of the things the winners were doing. I got caught up in NA. I felt good, it was great to be clean for the first time in years.

After I'd been around for about six months, the novelty of being clean wore off, and I fell off that rosy cloud I'd been riding. It got hard. Somehow I survived that first dose of reality. I think the only things I had going for me then were the desire to stay clean, no matter what; faith that things would work out okay so long as I didn't use; and people who were willing to help when I asked for help. Since then, it's been an uphill fight; I've had to work to stay clean. I've found it necessary to go to many meetings, to work with newcomers, to participate in NA, to get involved. I've had to work the Twelve Steps the best I could, and I've had to learn to live.

Today, my life is much simpler. I have a job I like, I'm comfortable in my marriage, I have real friends, and I'm active in NA. This type of life seems to suit me fine. I used to spend my time looking for the magic—those people, places, and things, which would make my life ideal. I no longer have time for magic. I'm too busy learning how to live. It's a long slow process. Sometimes I think I'm going crazy. Sometimes I think "What's the use." Sometimes I back myself into that corner of self-obsession and think there's no way out. Sometimes I think I can't stand life's problems anymore, but then this program provides an answer and the bad times pass.

Most of the time life's pretty good. And sometimes life is great, greater than I can ever remember. I learned to like myself and found friendship. I came to know myself a little bit and found understanding. I found a little faith, and from it, freedom. And I found service and learned that this provides the fulfillment I need for happiness.

Coming Home

These members share about reaching the end of the road and surrendering. Their paths to find recovery differed, but they all found that in coming to NA, they have come home.

These snapshots of our members' experiences finding NA are meant to be similar to the sharing at a topic meeting.

Reflections

When I finally had a moment of honest reflection about the severity of my drug addiction, I'd already been through the loss of relationships, jobs, esteem, credibility, and personal morality. I was experiencing deep spiritual chaos.

I asked myself, "What ever happened to all that joy and happiness I used to feel?"

One night I ran into one of my old using friends. To my surprise, he was drug-free. We spoke awhile and he let me stay with him that night. He introduced me to recovery. There was an NA group four blocks away, and I started attending daily. Soon I was asked to serve as the GSR alternate, and I realized my life had taken another direction. I was no longer that same lost person.

I went to my first rehab at twelve years old, just after I started doing drugs. Even though I disliked the feeling of being high, I kept using. I used drugs that I said I would never use. I thought about suicide every day and stuck a shotgun in my mouth at fourteen but couldn't pull the trigger. I was a convicted felon at fifteen and hated my life.

I used for about two and a half years in all. I stopped while I was in rehab for the third time, and I still felt miserable. I needed an answer. I was introduced to NA again in that rehab. I'd grown tired of living in and creating more pain. I wanted relief.

We read from the Basic Text, and this time I believed it. I started feeling that I was on a path that could lead me out of my pain. The day I left treatment, I went directly to a meeting. They told me they loved me and that they wanted me to keep coming back. And I did.

Even here in prison, my life can be peaceful, orderly, and useful. And by the grace of God I am making progress. At the end of my using, I was arrested for robbery. Though I knew I was an addict, I wouldn't admit it. Getting high was the only relief I felt I could get, but it was becoming less effective and producing more problems. Here, I connected with a sponsor by mail. He encourages me and helps me work the steps. I've learned to just follow directions as best I can.

My addiction progressed to the point where I couldn't speak in complete sentences. My mind was fractured, and I wouldn't sleep for days at a time. I began to take to heart what I learned in treatment—go to NA meetings. I threw myself into recovery, and I got a sponsor who taught me to laugh and have fun again without using.

My mother picked me up at the treatment center that had just kicked me out. She did not speak a word until we were a block from home, where she pulled over and said she loved me and wanted me to give this recovery thing a try. She might have said those words every day of my life for all I knew. But it was the first time I actually heard her say it, and I believed it when she said, "I love you." I had a glimmer of hope.

I'd known that there were recovery programs available and had met some of the NA members at the youth center on Wednesdays. They were an odd group that reminded me of hippies from the sixties. They often hung around and talked with us kids after the meetings. But it was the readings that hooked me in, talking about the disease of addiction, not a specific drug. It wasn't long before I found my place in recovery in Narcotics Anonymous. Today I am able to look for similarities, instead of being distracted by differences. This group of people took me in, and it was like being adopted by fifty older brothers and sisters.

The last night I used, I blacked out. When I came to, my car was parked sideways in the driveway and there was a bag of money on the coffee table. I thought I had robbed someone, but I couldn't remember. I knew inside I was through. I saw the sun rise and thought to myself, "I'm done getting high. Now what do I do?"

I'd heard of NA from a friend who had six months clean, and I went to a meeting. I approached a guy in front of the meeting place. I asked him if this was Narcotics Anonymous, and he hugged me. I didn't know what to think of that, but it didn't feel bad. I heard a lot at that meeting and some of it made sense. Feelings surfaced that I'd stuffed for years, and tears welled in my eyes when I heard the reading *Just for Today*. Some of the people even seemed happy. I met a man who had a calmness I wanted, and he agreed to sponsor me. I feel so lucky to have found NA.

At the end of my using, I was in detox for six days. I felt very shaky for a few weeks longer from the physical withdrawal. In former times I'd have written a prescription for myself and easily started the addiction cycle over again. Something was preventing me from doing what I'd always done. I was going to meetings every day and loved hearing addicts share about having good lives. I got a sponsor in my first weeks and called her every day. She encouraged me to get involved with service and started me on the steps right away. My brains were a bit scrambled at first, but she felt step work was an excellent way to help unscramble them. She was right.

Despite the warm welcome I got at my first NA meeting, I felt very uncomfortable there. I always got panicky in the face of the unknown. Being an expert in justification, I told myself that I was too young. The worst thing is that I believed myself! My disease continued to progress for two more years. One day, after a twenty-four-hour run, feeling desperate, I returned home to find the pamphlet *Youth and Recovery* on my nightstand.[6] I was in tears when I opened it. I felt so worn out. I started going to meetings, and although they didn't calm my fears at first, I kept coming back. I grew fascinated by the new language: acceptance, humility, amends, open-mindedness, and Higher Power. Thanks to NA, I felt I was finally going to learn how to live, and I realized I had so much to learn.

---

[6] *By Young Addicts, For Young Addicts* replaced *Youth and Recovery*.

He checked himself into treatment to avoid prison, but while
he was there he found hope in the pages of a Basic Text.
There was no NA in his part of rural Illinois, so he started
a meeting and he's stayed clean through his own
growing pains and those of the fellowship.

Start a Meeting,
They Will Come

I was forty-five years old, two prison terms behind me, facing twelve to sixty years on this latest possession charge. I was still using, going to an outpatient treatment center to fool everyone so I wouldn't have to go back to prison. Well, it worked! The con fooled them again, and I ended up with probation. If I could just get around all the drug tests, my problems would be over. Just my luck: I caught a dirty drop. Why didn't God answer my prayers? I only asked that He would help me pass the drug test. This time I really had to work a big con, so I admitted myself into an inpatient treatment center. I didn't need treatment, of course, but I had to make the law think I really wanted help.

The best thing that happened to me in treatment was that my counselor gave me a Basic Text from Narcotics Anonymous. I could hardly put it down once I started reading it. It seemed like this book was written about me. For the first time, I felt hope. The Basic Text was like a map to help me find a way out and build a new life. Even though I had only been clean for about two weeks, I made two decisions: I was going to become a member of Narcotics Anonymous, and I was going to start a meeting in my hometown. With the hope given to me from reading the Basic Text, I truly believed that a Narcotics Anonymous meeting would get addicts clean.

I come from a small town in Illinois, and across the river is another small town. There were a number of meetings for the AA Fellowship, but no NA meetings at all. I told my counselor that

I was going to start an NA meeting back home when I got out of treatment. He told me that I wouldn't be able to get it done, and that I should go to a halfway house instead. But I'm stubborn, so I didn't listen.

I got clean in June, was released from treatment the first week of July, and on 3 August 2000 we had our first Narcotics Anonymous meeting! It was slow getting started. There were only a couple of us for the first few months, but we persevered. Word got out that there was a new meeting. Members came over from Iowa to help us through their outreach service. One of them brought us the steps and traditions posters and other readings. I was so grateful. This is when I first realized how much love that the NA Fellowship has to offer.

These meetings didn't just happen by sheer luck. We have had our share of growing pains. Picture a room with ten to fifteen addicts, all on the First Step, with no experienced sponsorship for direction. Talk about being powerless and unmanageable! And we all thought we knew everything. We made every mistake you can imagine. Relapses were common. Arguments occurred over members bringing bibles and other non-NA material to meetings. Then there were the dating games, which caused new resentments and even some relapses. The hardest thing for me was that many of the addicts who came shortly after I did kept looking to me for direction. Heck, I was on the First Step too!

Remember, we are in rural Illinois, not Chicago. The large metropolitan areas with established NA communities were at least sixty miles away, and might as well have been on the other side of the world. If you had an issue with other members, there weren't any other meetings to attend so you could avoid each other. You either worked through your resentment or went out and used. We had only one meeting.

I realized that if this was going to work and I was going to survive, then I had to take action. I started attending a group out of town, found a sponsor, and got some help. Thank God for sponsorship. When we reached out for help, recovering addicts came to share their experience, strength, and hope with us. As a result, we learned better ways to work the program and carry the NA message. After five years, we are still making mistakes, but we survived and are getting stronger. In the past year we have joined an area service committee. We travel every month to other NA communities and now receive more support from "out-of-towners." As our members got more stable in their recovery, we started doing the same type of outreach service that had helped our group in its early stages. As a result, there are now several active NA groups within a thirty-mile radius of our home group. This is another great experience because we are truly giving away what was so freely given to us.

Our area holds an annual convention and a few other big events. This is a good opportunity for our small NA fellowship to experience the benefits of being a part of greater NA, so we often have caravans of addicts cruising on a "recovery quest." The interaction with addicts I don't see as often helps me experience the importance of the phrase "principles before personalities": When I come back home, I try harder to look past the flaws in others. Hopefully they are learning to forgive my shortcomings as well.

The Twelve Steps of Narcotics Anonymous have helped me to change from the inside to become a better man. I feel the most spiritual when I let my Higher Power work through me to help another suffering addict. One of the greatest blessings that I receive as a Narcotics Anonymous member is seeing newcomers arrive all beat up and scared, not knowing what to do, doubting if this will work for them, and then seeing them start to change. They surrender, begin sharing honestly, and get the light of recovery in their eyes as they work through the steps.

NA is alive and well in rural Illinois, thanks, in part, to a counselor lending a Basic Text to a con. I have learned a new way of thinking and live a better, more productive life than I could ever have imagined. At this writing I have over five years clean, and our home group just celebrated its fifth birthday picnic. My home group has held over 3,600 meetings. Just for today, through NA, many addicts are living the promise of freedom from active addiction in our area. For this I will remain forever grateful. If you start a meeting, they will come!

This addict from the "wrong side" of Chicago's south side lost his best friend and his marriage to the disease of addiction. Recovery hasn't restored the things he's lost, but it has helped him make amends.

The Point

My sponsor says this is an example of "God showing off." I'll tell you the story and let you decide.

My best friend's mom never liked that we hung out together. She'd tell him not to bring "that curly-headed boy" to the house. I lived on the wrong side of Chicago's south side; he lived in a neighborhood favored by the folks who wanted a better and safer environment for their children. But he and I were tight, and we did most everything together. We were both adopted, and we looked and felt like the brothers we never had.

I joined the army at the tender underage of sixteen. My home life was insane. The family that adopted me, a half-black baby, from a German orphanage had become a pretty dysfunctional alcoholic scene. My second stepdad used to beat my mom in drunken stupors, and then she'd beat me. One day, following a particularly brutal display of codependent relationship dynamics, I came to the conclusion that if this was love, you could have my share. I knew that I could no longer live in that house.

I walked into an army recruiter's office on a Thursday, and Sunday night I was in Fort Polk, Louisiana. Five months later I was injecting heroin in Amsterdam, Holland. Four months after that I was honorably discharged—I had told them I was underage. It had become too hard to keep up a heroin habit and do the duties the army expected every day.

I came back to Chicago and started going to college. My friend and I became roommates. The winter of 1975 was cold. The notorious Chicago winds were blowing hard, and the temperature was below zero every day. On the day after Christmas we were

165

in our basement apartment with our coats on to fend off the cold, watching television and smoking weed. A tropical scene came on the screen showing sunny California with the beach, palm trees, and a beautiful woman driving a convertible Mercedes. I looked out our window, then looked at the TV and told my friend, "Enough of this weather; I'm going to California." He immediately agreed, and we left Chicago that weekend to pursue all the promise that sunny California offered. We arrived in San Francisco on a cold, wet, windy January afternoon. It was nothing like the TV show; it was almost as cold as Chicago. I wondered if I had made a mistake.

Nevertheless, we made the best of it and settled into our new life. He decided to go to college and work on a degree. I decided to immerse myself in the huge underground drug scene. My life became as our literature describes: I "lived to use and used to live." I was going in and out of jail, and my friend was continuing in his education. He had hooked up with a nice little square girlfriend. I had a girlfriend too, but she certainly wasn't a square. She was my using buddy, and together our addictions flourished.

In 1982 my son was born. He was the answer to my prayers: Having been adopted, I had never known anyone who was blood-related to me. I wanted to be a good dad, but my addiction would not allow anyone or anything to come before it. I had a primal need to use, every day, at any cost. I remember how guilty I felt when my son walked into a room and I had a belt wrapped around my arm, or when he fell asleep waiting for me to come out of the bathroom, where I was nodding off. He meant the world to me, and this was the best I could do.

One day that same friend called me to hook up and get high. He was a closet addict. He impersonated a square in the daytime and would occasionally come to my dark side of the world at night and use. There was some dope on the street at the time that was overdosing people, and I copped a few bags for us. We both shot up, and we both passed out. I woke up and looked over to see my friend still out. I tried to revive him, but he wouldn't come to. I staggered to the lobby and asked someone to call 911. The ambulance came and took him to the general hospital.

They took him out like they were taking out garbage. I guess they had seen so many addicts that they had lost any semblance of compassion. The cop looked disgusted as he asked me if I wanted to come along. I told him I would be there shortly. I went back to the room and did another shot. That is the insanity of my disease. I woke up about six hours later with a needle hanging out of my arm.

I remembered that I had to pick up my friend from the hospital. When I called from the lobby to find out which room he was in, I was informed that he had died. I couldn't believe it; I loved him, and he was gone. I felt so bad and guilty for my role in his death. I couldn't understand why God would let him die instead of me. Actually, I thought that God was reaching for me and picked him by mistake. I was devastated. I called his girlfriend, and I can still hear her screaming into the phone.

My addiction became suicidal. I overdosed all the time, always disappointed that I woke up. I remember crossing the street so people who knew me wouldn't see how low I had gotten. All I did was use, but I couldn't use enough to make the pain go away. And I didn't know there was another way. I didn't know that addicts like me got clean. No one came to the Tenderloin area of San Francisco to twelve-step any of us. I had no clue about Narcotics Anonymous.

One morning I was sitting on the dock of the San Francisco Bay in a "deuce and a quarter" that I never put more than $2.00 worth of gas in.[7] It was about 5:30 am. My three-year-old son was in the back seat, and his mom was in the front seat, begging me to get them something to eat. All night long I had been shooting speedballs of heroin and cocaine. I knew that once I shot up, we would need to go get more money to use. She didn't

---

[7] A "deuce and a quarter" is a Buick Electra 225.

know that we were broke, since we started the night with over $600. I wrapped the belt around my arm, and looked in the rear-view mirror. I told my son to turn over, because the rule was he couldn't watch me shoot up. He looked lovingly at me and smiled. And then I looked in the mirror at myself and had the proverbial "moment of clarity."

I saw what I had become. My teeth and eyes were yellow, my face was broken out, my hands were swollen with track marks all over them, there was blood on my jeans, and my neck was green from wearing a fake gold necklace. I was a mess. Then I looked again at my son. He was peeking at me, smiling. And I knew: I knew that if I kept using he didn't have a chance. I knew I would never teach him how to drive, or play baseball, or tie a tie, or get ready for the prom, or ride a bike. I didn't care about my own life, but I realized that it wasn't fair to deny him a life. I looked at his mom and realized that she had been following me everywhere, and I was leading her right to hell. Then I did something that I think nearly every recovering addict can remember, probably right to the moment. I cried out, "God help me." That was the first time I genuinely asked for my Higher Power's help to stop. I had wanted to stop for years, but didn't know how. That cry for help didn't have an immediate reaction that I could see. I finished off my drugs and convinced my sobbing girlfriend that we needed to go get some money to use again.

I know now that God's delay is not God's denial. I was arrested that day and sent to jail. In jail it was arranged for me to go into treatment. My brief stint in the military qualified me for a veterans' program. It was there that I was introduced to Narcotics Anonymous. I am so grateful for "H&I" meetings,[8] because that's how I was introduced to the program that would save this addict's life.

The first Narcotics Anonymous meeting I went to, I knew that I was home. I saw addicts like me recovering. I realized that it was possible to live free from our addiction. I was given hope

---

[8] Hospitals and Institutions

where I had been hopeless. I was given tools where I had been helpless. I was given a family where I had been alone. I was excited at the possibility of having another chance at life. I got a sponsor, and he told me that he loved me, no matter what. He has been my only sponsor for the last nineteen-plus years. And he has continued to love me no matter what. I got custody of my son when I was two years clean. I was able to teach him to ride a bike, to go to Cub Scout meetings, and eventually to drive and even to tie a tie. His mom decided to continue to use, and she still struggles.

Back when I had three years clean I was doing an inventory on my mother who had adopted me. She had died during my addiction, and I was so resentful that I didn't even go to her funeral. In the course of my inventory I realized that much of my resentment was really hurt. I find it easier to be angry than be hurt. I wrote an amends letter and went to Chicago to read it at her grave site.

Before going to the cemetery I stopped at a little beach on Lake Michigan that we called The Point. I sat there and worked on my letter and swam in the water. For the first time in my young recovery I began to feel serene. The critical voices in my head seemed to quiet down, and I felt an overwhelming sense of peace and calmness. I spent the whole day there basking in the sunlight and my newfound serenity. Being at The Point had never had this kind of impact on me before. As I left and was driving, I realized that I was near my old friend's house. Something told me to go by and see his mom. I hadn't seen her since his funeral, where she could hardly even stand to look at me. I wanted to tell her that I was clean and that I was sorry. I rang the doorbell, and no one answered. So I wrote a little note on one of my business cards. I had started a career as a substance-abuse counselor. The note said, "Dear Mrs. C. I just wanted to let you know that I'm a member of Narcotics Anonymous and I'm clean over three years, and I work helping other people get clean. I'm sorry for what happened to…and I miss him very much. Love,…" I dropped the note in the mail slot on the door and walked back to my car.

Before I could get to my car a gentleman opened the door and called me back. He was her new husband, and he didn't know me. He invited me in and seated me on the couch. A few moments later my friend's mom walked in the room and was visibly shocked to see me. He handed her the card, and she silently read it. Then she started weeping, she opened her arms to me, and we hugged and both began to sob. She asked me if her son knew how much she loved him, and I assured her he always did. She told me she had always blamed me for his addiction but realized that he had always had those addict traits and it wasn't my fault. She said she was happy that something good came about from his death. We then went into the basement, and she gave me pictures and we told stories about my friend, her son. We laughed and cried and hugged. It was an incredible healing experience. As we were saying our good-byes, she told me, "Before you go, be sure and visit The Point, because that's where we spread his ashes." I cried again because I realized that I had just had what was the first of many spiritual awakenings in the program of Narcotics Anonymous.

Today my life is a gift. I'm coming up on twenty years clean. I've been married for fifteen years and have another wonderful son. I met my German birth mother ten years ago and now have a family of blood relatives. My heart has been awakened, and I have learned how to love and be loved. I have been working in treatment for over eighteen years, and I've written two books for African Americans.

I just returned from the NA Thirty-first World Convention in Hawaii where I was reminded of how this program is changing the world one addict at a time.

Thanks, NA, from the bottom of my heart.

They used together and got clean together, but this addict got active in the program and his brother did not. This Saudi Arabian member found in the loss of his brother a powerful drive to carry the message.

Carrying the Message

Using in Saudi Arabia means shame for the addict and for the family. If anyone tells a family that their son or father is using, the denial is often greater than that of the addict himself. My family had to deal with not one son, but two. Eventually they could no longer be in denial about either of us. I found help in Narcotics Anonymous, but my brother did not.

My family was always unstable, and eventually my parents divorced. When my father and mother were in the middle of the divorce I found the time, the reason, and everything I needed to use. I started leaving school at midday to drink and smoke with my friends. I started with prescription drugs and sometimes alcohol. As the years passed it became hash. I didn't complete high school.

In Saudi Arabia you can buy drugs in the streets, but only in special areas. It is a Muslim country and alcohol is not allowed, but alcohol is made illegally in certain houses. Sometimes you can find whiskey or other things that come from outside in expensive places. In these places I found a sense of pride. I formed a circle of mates who would meet just to use drugs together. It very quickly went out of control as the need to belong to the group became the most important thing. We were all too weak to resist these peer pressures.

At first, my brother used heroin and I used hashish, and I was upset because he was using heroin. I went to visit friends after Ramadan, a very important holiday in our religion. We used to smoke hashish together, but this time I found they were using heroin. All I said was, "Oh, you have something new here?" As

171

my addiction progressed I found myself in the same marketplaces as my brother where they sell heroin. The dealer only said, "We finally see you here!"

I tried to control my addiction by using small quantities for short periods. Then it totally consumed my mind. All I could think about was how to take it today and how to find tomorrow's dose. I started neglecting my work and my family. I spent all my money in order to take my dose, which now became my bread. Using became my only way to practice my daily life, even though I started losing myself and my health. I was asked by my family to leave my house. I went to stay at my father's house and found a new place to take drugs.

My family demanded that I give up drugs and I promised I would, but to no avail. My sickness was stronger. My family encircled me to force me to cut my friends off. I told them I would and then would lie and find excuses to take off and see them. In order to acquire drugs I started stealing from my siblings' wallets and cheating my colleagues. I hurt my loved ones but was unable to stop. My life deteriorated. I felt abandoned and rejected, and this only made me hurt more and take more.

Eventually, I went to the hospital, mostly because of pressure from my family and my work. I was absent from work often, and they sent me to the hospital to find out what was wrong with me. That's when I first found out I could not stop using because my body was sick. Everyone had told me about the pain in the joints, the nausea. I realized what they meant once the drugs weren't available.

I went back to using as soon as I got out. Everyone gave up on me, and I gave up on myself. But my prayers to God—even under the influence of drugs—had an effect on me. I was finally hospitalized again, this time by choice, when I felt that the drugs stopped working. In the hospital I was forced to attend a meeting brought in by NA's committee for hospitals and associations (the equivalent of hospitals and institutions elsewhere).

I used to take drugs with one of the speakers. I rushed to him after the lecture to ask how he had managed to stay clean all that time. His answer was through the NA program. He told me that after I got out of the hospital he would take me to NA meetings. When it was time to leave the hospital, he took me first to my family, then to a meeting. I was astonished by the welcome I got at the meeting after I had been rejected by everybody else. I was amazed by the similarities of the sickness and suffering and by the varied lengths of clean time of the members. During the meeting I was asking myself if I could really be like them. The answer was yes. I had become like them, and I belonged to them for four months.

After the fourth month I had an appointment with the doctor to follow up on my condition. I consulted my sponsor beforehand, and he told me to explain that my health had settled. The doctor asked me if I suffered from insomnia. My sickness surfaced, and I complained about staying up for a long time before I could fall asleep. He prescribed medication. In only a few hours I started replacing that medicine with other drugs. In a few months I fell back to the same bottom—or worse—that I was in before. I asked my sponsor for help, and he asked me to accompany him to the hospital. I agreed, and then I finally rejoined the fellowship.

My brother ended up in the same hospital, and we began to stay clean together. I worked hard on myself, and my brother worked two jobs. Most of his time was spent with work. He didn't work in NA. I went to NA every day and was involved in service. I asked the man who had carried the message to me in the hospital to be my sponsor. My sponsor took me to work from the hospital every day during that time. My brother did not have such a person in his life. My sponsor had three years more than I did at the time. I stayed close to him from the moment I met him in the hospital. My brother stayed close to no one and became consumed with his life.

My brother didn't stay clean. I tried to help him. I tried to speak with him, but I couldn't find the open mind. I knew that when he promised to stay clean for me it wouldn't work. Our wives are sisters, and when they came to visit I saw that he was using. I sent some friends to talk to him because I thought I might not be the best one to help him. I would feel nervous talking with him, and maybe if it wasn't family he would be more relaxed. The last time he went to the hospital, when he went to Umrah (our smaller pilgrimage), he looked good. I never saw him alive again.

I was with my family, with everyone, when we found him dead from a relapse. I said, "I tried and tried to help you but I know the disease was stronger." I felt so sad I couldn't help him. This has made me more active in my recovery and has helped me with the members I sponsor and the members I try to carry the message to.

It has been two years since I lost my brother to the disease of addiction. The message that I carry is that my brother and I used drugs together. He stopped using for seven years with me, but he wasn't coming to meetings regularly because he was consumed with his personal life. He was facing its hard conditions without attending meetings or working the steps. Even when he gave up on himself, the NA fellows never gave up on him. He ended up relapsing, and in his last relapse he gave up his last chance at this life. It was his last dose, and he died like others did before him—it is the end of our sickness.

We know we can't force the addict to recover; we can only carry the message to every addict still suffering the sickness of addiction. I thank God that He showed us the way to the NA Fellowship. Today—thank God—with the help of my sponsor I have been clean for eleven years. I stayed clean through the death of my brother. I have been able to use that pain to help others. I have a job and family that make me proud. I no longer need to live in shame. Today I have found the connections with my family and friends in the NA program that I was looking for in the drugs. Today, the message that we carry in Saudi Arabia is that addiction is not something we need to be ashamed of or embarrassed by. The message that we carry is that any addict can stop taking drugs, lose the desire to take them, and find a new way to live. Today, there are addicts recovering in Saudi Arabia — thank you, NA.

She found NA when she was only fifteen. From her very first meeting, she knew NA was where she needed to be. Now, more than twenty years later, she's gone from a hostile, wasted teenager to a grateful member of the program.

Young Addict, Young NA Fellowship Grow Up Together

Any addict can find recovery in NA ... even a fifteen-year-old girl from an island in South Florida who learned to drink coffee and hang out with mostly thirty-year-olds, because she knew her recovery depended on them—even when they hit on her, teased her about getting clean so young, told her how lucky she was that she didn't have to go through real pain, as she suffered silently from her past: sexual abuse, drug overdoses, promiscuity, arrests, violence, loneliness, guilt, paranoia. The thing she wanted so badly to say was that although she was different (younger) in their eyes, her pain was just as devastating to her as the pain of a homeless junkie, or anyone else. She was ready to quit; she was asking for help. There were NA members who told her she was too young to be an addict. Others avoided or shunned her. Fortunately, there were those who told her that she earned a seat in Narcotics Anonymous, and to stay and fight for it.

I remember the first time I heard the message of recovery. Stumbling in wasted after the bell rang for my freshman high school English class wasn't unusual.[9] When I walked in that day, I realized that something was different. The class was quiet, and some woman was talking to the teacher.

I made my way to the back corner. Other students, trying to avoid my frequent hostility, moved out of my way. I was just wiping the sweat off my sunglasses when the teacher introduced us to the lady. She said the visitor was a former drug addict and

---

[9] "Freshman" year is the first year in high school.

was going to tell us about her drug problem. Everyone near me started cutting up after I asked her if she'd brought us any of the drugs she had left over.

As she started talking about her childhood, I wadded up paper in my mouth and shot it toward her with a straw. Someone threw a crumpled-up homework assignment at her as she talked of her arrests and drug overdoses. I laughed and encouraged everyone to be as disrespectful and obnoxious as possible.

The whole time we taunted her, her voice remained calm and steady. Despite my lack of apparent interest, I heard every word she said, every word.

I had already wanted to, tried to, and promised to stop using drugs, but I always failed. Incredibly, I come from a wonderful family with loving parents and two older brothers who I admire. My closeness to them was being destroyed, and I felt totally unable to do anything about it.

Later that day, two of my clean friends, who had tried many times to help me clean up by lying for me, carrying me into class or home, begging me to quit, stealing my drugs, and threatening to snitch, approached me. They asked me to skip my next class to meet someone. When we got there, it was her—the lady who both fascinated and terrified me.

Before I left, she told me she would like to take me to a Narcotics Anonymous meeting. She said words that would later give me comfort. She confidently said, "You never have to use again, just for today."

At the end of that first meeting, I found myself in the front of the room with a plain white poker chip in my hand. I later found out that the white poker chip was a symbol of my surrender and a reminder that I was gambling with my life if I threw it away. Strange as it seems, at that age, knowing nothing about NA, I felt that I had found something that would change my life forever! For some reason I knew that I was okay, that I had found help.

That is how my recovery journey began, leading me to places I never could have imagined. Over time, I would learn about the traditions and the NA service structure. There at the beginning, I had no idea that one day I would enjoy being of service by making phone calls, greeting newcomers, handing out literature, setting up tables and chairs, making coffee, taking out the trash, and cleaning the floor of the meeting facility.

Despite pressure from all the other teens "just doing time," I was blessed with the willingness to get a sponsor and build that relationship. I had no idea that I would be sponsoring many women over the years because I had something worth giving, and was willing to give it because someone else gave it so freely to me.

I was blessed with the gift of taking recovery seriously. I listened and stuck with the "winners," like I was told. I trusted my sponsor's suggestion to attend the world convention in Chicago and met and shared recovery with addicts from all over the world. Many of them are still clean today, and I consider them my brothers and sisters. I have also seen many addicts whom I love die.

I didn't know that one day the woman who shared her story in my class would relapse, overdose, and die after having three years clean. I didn't know that one day I would pick up a twenty-year medallion at the group she started, my home group to this day. I had no idea of my good fortune for grabbing onto NA not only at my young age, but also at an age when NA was young.

I believe in the NA message to my core, not just from all the gifts of recovery, but from the terrible pain I've faced in recovery as well. There were lonely, horrible times that I didn't want to live through, and the times when I couldn't hold on, but God, the Twelve Steps, and other recovering addicts pulled me out of them, clean!

The Narcotics Anonymous message that I struggle to live each and every day in my heart is still as relevant for me today as it was when I first heard from that woman who had the courage to share her story in my high school class: "That an addict, any addict, can stop using drugs, lose the desire to use, and find a new way to live."

Any addict, even you!

At the end of his using even the other street boys and the dealers didn't want him around, but NA felt like home from his very first meeting. Sometimes he is the only person in the room, but that only renews this Kenyan addict's commitment to recovery.

A Quiet Satisfaction

In the streets of Nairobi, Kenya, East Africa, my name kept changing as my addiction progressed. Toward the end of my using I was just "the junkie in sunglasses."

Born in the ghettos of Nairobi, I knew at a very early age about the reality of drugs, crime, prostitution, rape, and death. That's part of the package in the slums. My mum passed away when I was ten, and my sisters were sent to a children's home. I was lucky to be taken in by my Sunday school teacher, a missionary from Norway.

I attended the best high school in the region, with a reputation for great discipline. My schoolwork was good. I excelled in sports and was captain of the school football team. I played for the national team and was "Sportsman of the Year" at my university. I had everything to live for. The future was looking bright for this ghetto boy.

I started drinking and smoking cigarettes in college. Smoking contributed to the onset of severe asthma, and soon I was unable to play football. To escape, I took to excessive drinking. I cursed God for taking away my favorite sport. Eventually I would take any drug that was offered to me. I graduated with a lower second-class honors degree—and a habit.

Upon graduation I got a job with a pharmaceutical company, and my addiction skyrocketed. What a combination: an addict with the keys to a drugstore! I was using heroin for a few weeks, then detoxifying myself with drugs that I took from the company. Not surprisingly, my boss decided to let me go.

My personal relationships were also falling apart. My fiancée was devastated when I canceled our wedding three weeks before the ceremony. Luckily for her, she got a transfer out of town. We already had a beautiful son who was caught in the middle of all this. I was a junkie on the loose. Heroin had me in its grip.

The trips to doctors and psychiatrists started. My doctor said, "You will end up in the street and die of an overdose. Guys like you never make it," and with that I felt I had permission for full-blown drug use.

As predicted by my good doctor, I was in the street hustling within a year. I scammed my friends and former workmates. Periodically, I moved to remote towns to clean up. Eventually, when I returned to Nairobi, my feet would lead me like a zombie to the using joints and I would be back at square one. I saw crazy, crazy stuff during this time. I once held someone's hand to help him find a vein, and as he passed away from an overdose I picked his pocket. Then I rushed to buy the same stuff. Whatever he was using must be really good.

I lived among street boys and watched as they abused each other. I felt nothing. I had to beg, and when I became too much of a freeloader, even the "scum of the streets" avoided me. I was unwanted by the world, including my fellow users. Dealers began to hate guys who shot up. Nobody wanted a guy to die on their doorstep. It was bad for business.

Fortunately, I was not a good thief, which kept me out of jail. Having no money to buy drugs and not knowing how to steal contributed to my willingness to change. With my willpower, self-help books, faith in God, and geographic changes, I could pull myself together and stay clean for short periods, but eventually the pain of not using would supersede the benefits of my newfound freedom from active addiction. I visited witch doctors, and I have marks on my chest to show for their efforts. Nothing worked.

I had been off heroin for three months when I met a guy I had used with. He looked all cleaned up. I wanted what he had. He led me to my first Narcotics Anonymous meeting. My intuition told me I had finally found the help I needed. In the meeting I recognized some other guys I had used with. I made myself a cup of coffee and knew I was home. I needed to see someone I knew get clean in order to believe that recovery was possible for me.

Though I was in and out of the rooms several times after that first meeting, I now knew that I had a choice. In my heart I knew that the solution to my drug problem was in the rooms, that NA was my hope for recovery. I have never doubted this fact.

I am now three years clean. In these last three years I have watched others walk in just like I did, and I have seen the changes that take place as they keep coming back. Witnessing this has been one of the greatest gifts of my recovery.

Meetings in Kenya are small in numbers and in clean time. The average meeting has four to fifteen members; most of them have less than a year clean. There are language barriers for members who can't communicate in English. Recently, public awareness about NA has been increasing. Meetings are starting in Mombasa and Malindi, our coastal towns. There are some conflicts in the fellowship here, which I am told is part and parcel of growing groups. I admit that we could have done better. However, I mark the progress. I hear the laughter. I see the meetings growing—but sometimes it's still difficult to get more than one person in a meeting.

Personally, I enjoy the quiet when no one shows up to the NA meeting. It renews my commitment every time I find myself alone in a room—although most meetings, these days, have a minimum of four members (and sometimes even twenty).

There are great friendships in the fellowship here. We make cakes for birthdays and have a good rapport—you know we addicts are really down-to-earth people. There is a lot of laughter after meetings. My cell phone reads like an NA phone book. We go bowling together, to the movies, to dinner. Recently, one of my new friends in NA taught me how to scuba dive, jet ski, and parasail. I could never imagine doing things like that and having fun. My friends, my true friends, are now in NA.

Service has been the cornerstone of my recovery. My friends tell me that I underrate all I do, but I feel apprehensive sharing about service. I try to serve with humility—nothing compares to the joy of service, of sharing the NA way, setting up tables, attending meetings, connecting members with each other, passing on books and other NA literature, corresponding with those visiting Kenya, holding public information workshops, bringing together new groups outside Nairobi, and now, recently, sponsoring other members. Surrounding countries like Rwanda, Uganda, and Tanzania are starting to ask for literature. We are working on getting them what they need. What a quiet satisfaction there is in being useful. It makes me feel even better when I don't mention it. Please do not take this as being proud of what I do.

My recovery has been based on three fundamental truths that work for me: One, do not pick up no matter what—all feelings eventually pass; two, go to meetings; and three, pray. I tell my sponsees these same things. My experience is that everything else sorts itself out with this as a base. I have a lot more to learn about the NA way.

Recently, I've learned that I have hepatitis C and have been getting answers from members in the fellowship who live miles away about how to deal with it. With this new challenge, my friends in the fellowship (and even their families) have been asking me what they can do to help me. I tell them that they are doing enough just being willing to support me. I am also back to school in a postgraduate program. I've been talking to the son I almost lost during my addiction. He recently told me he loves me. He is twelve years old and has never said anything like that before. I can't express how much this means to me—especially after all the damage I caused.

Through my recovery I am reestablishing relationships and making new ones. I am also discovering myself and slowly finding out what I can do and be. It far exceeds what I ever imagined before finding NA.

Our fellowship here is still young. Visiting NA members have given us so much. I have found people I identify with, tools to live by, and a purpose that has filled the void that existed throughout my life. You are welcome to visit us here in Nairobi, Kenya, any time. God bless Narcotics Anonymous.

When he got to NA he was also in a drug-replacement program.
He wanted what he saw in the rooms of Narcotics Anonymous,
but was afraid of returning to his old life if he quit methadone.
For ten months he went to meetings every day—
and finally he got clean.

The Only Requirement

Our Third Tradition states that "the only requirement for membership is a desire to stop using." I don't know if I had a desire to stop using when I came to my first NA meeting, but I sure had a desire to stop hurting. I was very, very tired. Tired enough to be curious about NA. Tired enough to listen.

At my first NA meeting, something very powerful happened to me: I met addicts who were recovering. I knew lots of addicts, of course. I had been on the streets for years at that point, and every person in my life was an addict. But all of my addict friends were still using. I had never met a clean addict before. This was something very new and attractive to me. These people shared their stories, and I identified instantly. Clearly they were people like me. The only difference was that there was something else going on their lives besides the daily struggle to score and stay out of jail. They shared about living in recovery. There was a light on behind their eyes, and their lives seemed to be full of hope and possibility.

At that first meeting, I was the last person in the circle to share. I identified as an addict but stated truthfully that I had a lot of reservations about never using again. I told the group that I was taking a break from the street and had stopped shooting dope, but that I was on methadone maintenance and also still using other substances. To my surprise, no one judged me. They welcomed me to the fellowship of NA and told me to keep coming back. "You are right where you belong," they said. They gave me telephone numbers, a meeting list, and something even more powerful: their acceptance.

I don't know why I decided to be honest at that first meeting. Years on the street had made lying and deception my natural response to every new situation. But for some reason, I realized that there was no point lying to these people. The only person I would be hurting was me. I thank my higher power that I was guided to speak simply and honestly about where I actually was, rather than to put on a front. That decision probably saved my life. Because I told the truth, people in NA were able to tell me the things I needed to hear. What really impressed me was that no one told me what to do. Instead, they shared their own experiences. It was up to me to decide how to use this new information in my own life. Over time, I began to accept that the tools that were working for others could work for me too.

One of the biggest challenges I faced as a new member in recovery was the fact that I came into the fellowship on methadone maintenance. I had a lot of reservations about getting clean and was particularly scared about getting off methadone. Being in a drug-replacement program had helped me get some structure into my life after years of living on the street. I now had a roof over my head and was working again. I was afraid that if I gave up methadone I would return to the insanity of homelessness and life as a criminal. As always, the wisdom and experience of other NA members helped guide me through this dilemma. Nobody told me what to do. Instead, by quiet example, they showed me the possibilities of a life free from active addiction. Over time I came to believe that being employed and off the street was not enough. Until I stopped using, whether the drugs were legal or illegal, I was not going to experience the full benefits of recovery.

I made the decision to begin the process of detoxing from methadone maintenance. Getting clean was very hard for me, both physically and emotionally. I came to NA meetings on a daily basis for ten months before I experienced my first day clean. There were no role models for me: I was the only person at my methadone clinic who was voluntarily detoxing. Every day I would have to run a gauntlet of drug dealers peddling pills as I walked to and from the clinic. Another challenge that I had to face was within the rooms of NA. I had learned from my very first meeting that it was important that I share openly and honestly. When I shared, I told the truth: I was not yet clean, but I was working really hard to get there. To my surprise, some people were really upset when I shared in NA meetings. One person came up to me after a meeting and told me that I had no right to share until I was clean. I was really confused and hurt the first time this happened. It was the first time I had not felt welcome in NA. Fortunately, an older member overheard the exchange and took me aside. She told me that the only requirement for NA membership was the desire to stop using. She reassured me, "You just keep coming back, honey; you're right where you belong." I thank my higher power that I listened to her message of love and acceptance. I did keep coming back. Every time I talked about my struggle and my doubts, members would share something from their own experiences that was helpful to me.

The wisdom and experience of other NA members was critical to the process of my getting clean. They even helped me get health insurance and get into the hospital so that I could complete the final stage of my detox under medical supervision. Thanks to NA, when I walked out of that hospital—clean for the first time in my adult life—I had a sponsor, a home group, and a service position waiting for me. Most importantly, I had admitted that I was powerless over addiction and had come to believe that only a power greater than myself could restore me to sanity. I didn't realize it at the time, but by choosing to keep coming back, by listening, by learning, and by following the example of other NA members, I had made a decision to turn my will and my life over to a power greater than myself. By the grace of that power, I am still clean today, twenty-one years later.

*She walked into NA—literally—and was treated with more love
and respect than she ever had been. For this Mexican woman,
a chance encounter on the beach opened
the door to hope and freedom.*

Restored to Dignity

Obsession and compulsion were present in my life way before
I started using drugs. From the time I was very young I had
a problem with the way I used things: how I ate, watched TV,
slept, bit my fingernails, and demanded attention from others.

My family's history is marked by war, armed conflicts, and
migrations. My grandparents left Poland and went to Chile,
running away from World War II. I was born in Chile the same
year there was a coup, and my mother sought political asylum
in Mexico, where I was raised. I always felt different; I was never
able to determine exactly where I was from or where I belonged,
and I had difficulty relating to other people. I didn't have any
concept of God, because I come from a leftist family that is
deeply atheist. I lived in isolation.

I was desperate to belong, to be accepted, and to have friends.
When I was ten years old I went to a party where there were
drugs and I got high for the first time. I passed out and a couple
of men put me in a sleeping bag and almost kicked me to death.
They were also using and thought it was fun to hurt another
person. I accepted that I was going to suffer whatever was necessary in order to hang out with people who used drugs. I felt that
I had found the key to enter other people's worlds. Sometimes I
wonder how I ever thought I could control my using. From the
first time, it was a disaster.

I cannot say at which moment drugs became the most important thing in my life. But the degradation progressed rapidly. I
didn't obey any rules. I constantly ran away from home, and I
learned to exchange sex for drugs, shelter, food, and protection.

Honestly, I didn't feel anything for anybody. But drugs...made me feel something. Nothing else mattered. I was still shy and afraid, but as long as I could get loaded, I could lock myself up in my own world where nothing could touch me. I didn't know that there was a God, but I knew that hell existed, and I was living it. I harmed a lot of people, especially those who loved me the most.

I graduated from school only through the blessings of my Higher Power.

After graduation I went to work and found that having money meant having drugs, and that meant having power. I believed I had my life under control. If I had drugs, I could buy other people and make them do what I wanted. But there weren't enough drugs or money to fill the huge gap that I had inside of me.

I couldn't relate to anybody who was not using. I had boyfriends who didn't use drugs. They were good, loving men who wanted to be with me. But I saw them as inferior, dumb, and boring because they didn't use. All those relationships ended quickly.

Pretty soon I returned to the same place: selling my body, cheating, and stealing to continue using. I was arrested. I had street fights and physical confrontations with my family. I would wake up in the street with barely any clothes on because I had pawned or lost them. It didn't matter who I used with; anyone who had drugs could go to bed with me. After every moment of crisis I would convince myself that it wasn't so bad and I could try it once more.

When I didn't have drugs, I destroyed everything around me. I cut myself or I hit my head against the walls and doors. I also hit other people. I ended up alone because nobody could stand to be around me. There were holes in the doors of my apartment from all the times that I hit my head in desperation.

My life was horrible. I had lost any kind of hope that I could change. I didn't have any idea that Narcotics Anonymous existed. I believed that I had to keep using. I didn't imagine that there were alternatives; neither my family nor I could afford to pay for a treatment program.

I was introduced to Narcotics Anonymous in a very strange manner, which kept me from being able to close my eyes to my own life. I found NA on a beach on New Year's Eve. There was a group of addicts celebrating their recovery around a bonfire while I was going crazy looking for drugs. I literally bumped into them! I was so high that I couldn't talk. I had no idea who these people were, but they seemed so happy that I thought they probably had some good drugs. I was excited when they invited me to sit with them. I thought they were going to give me something really powerful and that I was going to get higher.

Instead of giving me drugs, they treated me better than anyone had before. They didn't ask anything from me; they just stayed with me, and that made a difference. They waited a few hours until I was able to speak, and then they told me: If you want to, you can stay clean, just for today.

I can't explain what happened in that moment, but I spent my first day clean with NA members on that beach. I thought they were funny, and there were a couple of good-looking boys, but deep inside I didn't believe them. I couldn't believe that I would be able to stay clean. However, that day passed and I didn't use. When I went back to the city I had five days of clean time—five days that I spent with members of Narcotics Anonymous I had never met before. As soon as I got to my house I knew that I would not be able to stay clean alone. I ran to a meeting.

When I got to my first meeting, I was dirty, alone, and afraid. But I felt the care and concern of the members I had met, and I wanted more. Those days I had spent at the beach were sensational: No one had hit me or humiliated me. I had not done anything wrong. I was tired of my life and myself, and I didn't have anything to lose, so I opened the door.

I began to attend meetings every day, and I stayed clean. I didn't know exactly why I was in the rooms of NA or why I continued to come back. But I wanted what those people had, the sparkle in their eyes, the smiles, that indescribable light that recovering addicts have, which has helped me to recover.

What happened to me is truly a miracle. I am still clean, ever since that first encounter with NA at the beach. Years have gone by, and now I live with dignity. My first months clean were beautiful, because I was being taken care of. I hope that all addicts who are seeking recovery have the opportunity to receive as much love and attention as I did when I first came to meetings, because I got just what I needed and much more.

I followed suggestions when I got to NA. I attended ninety meetings in ninety days. I found a sponsor, and I began to work the program. It wasn't as difficult as I first thought. After a while I felt so good that I thought I didn't need as much help and that I could attend meetings less frequently. It's not a new story; other NA members have shared similar experiences. My recovery process has been more painful because many times I have lost the willingness to change and my defects of character have ruled my life. I hold onto resentments, especially when I feel I have a right to be angry. But resentments harm me more than anybody else and they don't allow me to move forward, so I continue trying to forgive. I also need to learn how to receive guidance, because I still don't always react appropriately when someone offers me a suggestion. I have never liked to be told what to do.

But the feeling I get when I'm with members of NA, when I go to meetings, or when I attend a convention, is such that I eventually do the right thing. Today staying clean is the most important thing I can do. To accomplish that, I need the Twelve Steps, a sponsor, a Higher Power, and service. I have lived through many bad experiences being clean, because I am stubborn. I tend to prioritize other things like my work, my mate, and fun. When I do this my life becomes a disaster. I am not a quick learner, but

I am beginning to understand that as long as I take care of my recovery, everything else will get better.

Today, Narcotics Anonymous makes more sense to me than anything else. Giving to others fills me up more than drugs, sex, food, or money ever did. I have a Higher Power now and that makes me feel more tranquil. I trust that no matter what happens I won't be alone. Today all things are better balanced.

I am very dramatic. When I don't get what I want, I suffer too much. I must learn to allow things to happen, always doing the best I can. But the emptiness I feel today is not as deep as it was in the past. I am not very stable emotionally, and I have occasional obsessive thoughts. I still have a lot of work ahead of me. But nothing compares to the nightmare of using. I know that I don't have to make a storm in a glass of water.[10]

There's a lot to be done for the fellowship in my country. There are more meetings now than when I met the program, but many people still don't know that Narcotics Anonymous exists here. I didn't know. Today it is my commitment to let everyone know that we exist, because I don't want addicts like me to believe that it is not possible to recover.

Life on life's terms has ups and downs. People I loved have passed away. I went through a divorce, and I lost a job. But I no longer hurt myself the way I did when I was using. I don't cut myself, and I don't bang my head. You have taught me that today there is no reason to use again.

I want to be here and be part of all this. To feel that I belong to this fellowship has been fundamental to staying clean. I once thought that if I survived to my thirtieth birthday I would kill myself. All my idols were musicians and artists who died young from overdoses. Today I am thirty-two years old and I love to be alive. The best experience of my life has been to see how the eyes of an addict who begins to recover don't have that look of death anymore. Seeing that awakening is worth more than anything else. Forever and ever, thanks for opening the door of life to me.

---

[10] A Spanish idiom: *Hacer una tempestad en un vaso de agua.*

A host of bad choices ultimately led to relapse for this addict with thirteen years clean. It was a hard road back to recovery, but NA loved her until she could love herself.

Second Chance

As I sat on the edge of the couch with my head in my hands, I felt completely bewildered. I was crying, but I didn't feel any tears, I was screaming, but there wasn't any sound, and I was watching my husband of twelve years pace the house like a caged animal. I was too nervous to talk to him, and afraid not to. Our NA friends from around the country were ringing the phone off the hook. They all had suggestions and ideas. There was a lot of whispering going on; plans were being made. My whole life was in complete and utter insanity. This all seemed so surreal; a few weeks earlier at my NA home group I had picked up my thirteen-year medallion, and less than a month later, there I was, sitting on my couch...a newcomer. Today I know that my relapse started long before that.

Over the years I have heard many addicts say, "One bad thought and one bad action could lead to relapse." For me, at the time, it wasn't about the thought because I didn't think; I hadn't any thought at all. For me, it was entirely about my bad actions. I was in my office, sitting at my business partner's desk, and inside a slightly opened drawer I saw a pile of crystal meth. I reached in, took it out and played with it a little bit, and snorted it. Period. I certainly wish I had thought something, anything; but I didn't. I had stopped thinking well before I was faced with the opportunity to do that "one bad action."

Today, I know so many factors played into my relapse. I hardly went to meetings, almost none at all. I hadn't been keeping in contact with fellow addicts, and I had held onto a self-centered resentment with my sponsor that separated us for a whole year.

The list could go on and on: dishonesty, complacency, greed, arrogance, judgment.

For a long time I had felt immune to relapse and had an attitude of "better than." When I got clean the first time, I considered myself a "high bottom" addict. Sure, I used a lot of different drugs, just about anything I could get my hands on, but cocaine and pot were my drugs of choice. I was a middle-class girl who turned up her nose at "dirty" drugs like meth or crank. The progression of my disease, for all those years clean, is hard to believe. When I relapsed, I used like there wasn't any tomorrow, like there wasn't any price to be paid. I recklessly tore through the lives of those who loved me. The greater the pain, the more I used, without any thought of living or dying. Overnight, my addiction once again held me prisoner. I started gouging at the skin on my face and pulling chunks of flesh from my body from that very first day! I continued to believe that I was infested with bugs for a very long time. I was hooked, and even though I kept using, the drugs weren't getting me high any longer. I just kept getting more and more detached mentally, physically, emotionally, and spiritually. I knew that I had unleashed a huge monster. I remember feeling so trapped—by the thoughts in my head full of Narcotics Anonymous and by my body full of drugs.

When I heard my sponsor's voice on the telephone, the resentment that had separated us for so long disappeared. I was really comforted by the sound of her voice. Her words took me to a safe and vulnerable place that I hadn't been to in quite some time. But they also confirmed for me that I had gotten myself into a real nightmare, a nightmare that neither she nor anyone else could fix for me. Surrender was a long way away.

The very last place that I wanted to go to was treatment because of all my judgment about treatment in the past, but I knew once my sponsor and other NA friends started suggesting it, that was exactly where I was headed. In a moment of clarity I admitted that I didn't want to become a statistic of "jails, institutions, or death." I knew that I was in serious trouble. Instead of feeling grateful that I was being given the chance to get clean again, I felt angry, hurt, scared, and crazy with paranoia. I had lived the miracle of the program for thirteen years, and now I felt like an alien. It felt like I didn't fit anywhere, not in NA and certainly not on the streets. I didn't stay clean. I was mentally unstable and a danger to myself as well as to others. I kept fighting the process like a soldier at war. I left the inpatient treatment facility against the advice of my counselor. I was so raw and completely full of rage. Unfortunately for me, it took three trips to treatment to finally "get it."

Getting off drugs was not easy, but it was the easier part. My pain, shame, guilt, and complete confusion were all too much to take. Instead of calling my sponsor or support system, I ran… from everyone and everything. I went from town to town. I landed back in my hometown and checked into yet another treatment center. I finally realized I was the problem. I went to their outpatient program for only three days, but I did continue to see their addiction specialist for over a year. He drug-tested me on a regular basis and was very NA-oriented. I needed that kind of accountability. I was so unpredictable. I didn't trust anything, most of all myself.

A lot of my relapse is a blur to me. I haven't any memory of the very last time I used before entering treatment, but I will never, ever forget walking back through the doors of NA. I was terrified. I sat through that first meeting wanting to get loaded and run. I was sweating. I was shaking, and my stomach felt like I was going to be sick. I didn't think that I had what it took to do this whole recovery thing again. I truly believed that I was just a "has-been." My sponsor suggested that I share at the next meeting that I attended. The only thing that I said was my name, and that I had relapsed with thirteen years clean. I have never experienced anything like that night. I expected judgment and criticism, but what I actually received was nothing but love. I was embraced by the addicts in that room. I arrived at the meeting feeling hopeless and left feeling like I too had a fighting chance.

I had to do everything differently. For a long time I felt as if I would never be "normal" again, and regardless of stubbing my toes along the way, I just kept trying. As much as I would love to say that I was grateful at that moment for being clean and that nothing else mattered, I can't. I was stuck in the place of "how I used to be, or how I used to look" for a long time. The majority of my "clean life" before relapsing was a beautiful thing. I had some good friends, great family, and a dedicated marriage. Once I picked up, everything, every aspect of my life, changed. My friends and family were scared to death that I would end up dead, and my marriage hit the skids, to say the least. I was so overwhelmed by feelings; I thought I would just die.

Numbing those feelings felt like an option for a long, long time. It wasn't until I began writing on my steps again, getting honest with my sponsor, and sharing in meetings that my thinking began to change. The more meetings I attended, the better I felt. I had to realize that what I had put myself through was a trauma to my body and mind. I had to quit fighting the grieving process that was necessary for me to begin to heal, trust, and change. It was necessary for me to grieve the woman I once was, the life I once had, and the marriage that my husband and I had worked so hard to build in order to accept the woman I was becoming, and make a new life for myself. I learned to be gentle with myself, as I would with any newcomer.

The knowledge that I had accumulated the first thirteen years had to be put aside so I could become teachable. I had to learn the gift of humility and vulnerability. I learned to be honest with myself as well as with others, no matter the shame I felt. I learned how to ask for help and accept it when it was offered. The days of thinking that meetings were a social affair or fashion show were over. For me, meetings were essential to staying clean; this was the real deal. I was here this time to save my life.

Today, looking back, it feels as if that period of my life was forever ago. I can remember being on my knees, praying to my Higher Power for the obsession to use be lifted, and begging for a quiet heart and peace of mind. The desperation I felt during that time just makes me shudder. Other than being clean, I just wanted to feel comfortable in my own skin, and not be overtaken with nightmarish thoughts and using dreams. Today I am worlds away from that woman who entered treatment over seven years ago. I am comfortable in my own skin, and best of all, I do have a quiet heart and peace of mind. I am extremely grateful to my Higher Power, my sponsor, and all the people who helped guide me back to the quality of life that I am once again living. I have a deep compassion for the still-suffering addict, be it the addict who is sitting in the rooms of Narcotics Anonymous, the addict who has yet to find the rooms, or especially the addict who left and has yet to find the way back again.

I can only pray that I will never let fade the memory of the pain it took for me to return to the program, and always remember I was loved back, not judged back. I want to always remember so that I can extend that same respect to another addict. I have so much today, but honestly, none of it was possible without a lot of hard footwork. I had to begin by forgiving myself for disrespecting the very program that saved my life the first time twenty-one years ago, for disrespecting my marriage which began in recovery, and last but not least, for disrespecting myself for returning to a life of drugs and disease.

I don't live in shame today about what happened, but I have learned from my mistakes. I share honestly and openly with other addicts. I would give anything and everything under the sun to have taken a different route, but because I can't I need to accept the responsibility for my own actions and grow from it. I believe today that if I had never relapsed I would have twenty-one years abstinent and that is all; but thankfully, I have seven and a half years clean with tons of heart and soul, dedication, and a love that I can hardly put into words. With the help of others, the Twelve Steps, and the principles of this program, my marriage was saved. I have gained trust within my family and friends again. I am no longer an outsider looking in; I am a part of. It has been a long road back, but I believe I am one of the lucky ones.

NA helped this Israeli addict rediscover his love of life. He had always felt like an outsider before he got clean. Now he has a home group and understands fellowshipping to be a spiritual principle.

Sowing the Seed

In Israel, we sing at meetings. If it's your turn to get a keytag, we sing a song that has became an NA anthem in Israel. It's a song about a simple guy who doesn't want much. And this guy has made a mistake here and there, but he can see the future and it looks good as long as we all stick together. We sing at every meeting. We go to the European conventions and everyone knows that the Israelis are the noisiest fellowship. We never stop singing.

We also have a "count-up" at every meeting. We start by asking if there's anyone attending the meeting for the first time — then it goes to two weeks, then to one month, then up to three months and then six months ... it can go on and on up to twenty years. We hug all the newcomers who are courageous enough to say, "I have three days today." We hug you if you have two days clean or two years clean.

We recruit newcomers to do small group tasks. A group may have twelve officers: One newcomer makes the coffee, one brings the cups, the other opens the room, and the other closes it. In my first three months clean, I was the key-holder. I didn't actually open the meeting, but I held the key until the trusted servant who opened the meeting came.

This was so important to me because it showed that I belonged. From my early childhood, I had felt like an outsider. In elementary school I was never invited to parties and had no friends. I became a real troublemaker. If I couldn't get love at least I could get attention. At home, I felt as if I was standing in my parents' way. My parents were busy with their careers and did the best they could. I grew up with caregivers who took care of me during the day, and I joined my parents when they returned from work.

In high school I became a DJ and played music in the school-yard. But that attention wasn't enough. I still wasn't content, and after a year of high school I dropped out. I spent all of my free time at the beach using. I was fifteen years old. I had two years until mandatory military service. My parents gave up hope, and I spent more time in the streets than at home.

On my first day in the army I found what I was looking for, drug partners. I had thought that military service would moderate my drug use, but it turned out I used more and different drugs. It didn't take long to realize I wanted out of the military. I went to an army shrink and told him I was having nightmares. I was so high, I could only mumble, and I was sent to a psychiatric hospital for observation. It was an open hospital, so I received no medications. I was there during the day, and in the afternoons I left to hang out with my friends to get high. Two months later they discharged me. I was free.

I took the first flight to Amsterdam. A friend picked me up from the airport, and on the way to his house, he offered me heroin. I told him I don't do heroin, I only do cocaine. Ironically, a year later, heroin was my favorite drug. I was homeless, no job, no food, but as soon as I put my hands on money, I spent it all on drugs. At night I went to the marketplace and took leftover food from the garbage. I slept in empty apartments with no heat or water, but I was sure that I was on the top of the world. Six months later I was back in Tel Aviv selling drugs. I thought that I was an important man. I justified my actions by telling myself that I needed to sell drugs to keep my habit. In recovery, I realized that one of the reasons I sold drugs was to keep people around me.

Eventually, I was beaten, lonely, and alienated. I felt like a failure, and worst of all, I wasn't ready to stop using. One day a using friend suggested we go to an NA meeting. He told me that NA was a group of addicts who meet together and help each other. At that time there were only seven NA meetings a week in Israel and they were all in Tel Aviv. The only reason I went to that first NA meeting with my friend was because I knew that we were going to go out afterwards and buy more drugs. There were forty or fifty people at the meeting, some of whom I knew. This was the first time in my life I saw junkies who had stopped using. I didn't believe that this was possible. I went to another meeting a few days later and I saw people laughing and enjoying themselves, but I was not ready to give up. Today I know that a seed was planted inside me at those first meetings. I started to believe that there was another way.

People used to tell me, "You've got so much potential." I didn't want to hear about going to school, having a steady job, or building a family. I never completed anything. I love NA because it is spiritual, abstract, and endless. We don't measure recovery by our accomplishments. We do the best we can each day.

It took me another ten years of pain and suffering before I was ready to surrender. I lost all my friends and stopped communicating with my family. I isolated myself to the point of not even answering the phone. I stopped functioning as a dealer. I stopped eating and let my personal hygiene go. I slipped into a long period of deep depression. The only thing I did was stay home alone and use drugs. There I was, a guy who loved life, loved to party, loved company, suddenly thinking about ending it all. I felt like there was no hope, and that was the biggest shock for me.

I went to an NA meeting. It was summer, the room was hot, but I was shivering and wearing a heavy leather coat. There were only two other people there, and they were arguing about how to set up the meeting. It almost came to blows. I knew from my previous experience that NA was much more than this incident. Deep inside me I knew that NA could save my life. Soon people came, and even though I didn't know anybody, I felt like I was among friends. Someone reached out to me, and I joined him in another meeting that night. Those first meetings were very significant. I kept coming back and stayed clean. At some point I understood that if I wanted to stay clean this time I had to make a decision to keep an open mind and get involved. I really wanted to be part of the fellowship. Today I know that fellowshipping is a spiritual principle.

During my first years in recovery, I used to go to a meeting in an Arab neighborhood not far from my house. At this meeting, Arab and Israeli members spoke Hebrew and shared about recovery from addiction. When it comes to NA, there are no politics involved. We sit in meetings together; we serve together; we celebrate our recovery together.

I chose a home group and committed myself to that group. I took a service commitment. I opened the meeting space, cleaned the floors there, and got it ready for the meeting. Today, I am still a part of that same home group. It is a place where people can find me, and I know that I can find my friends there too. I have a sponsor, and I work the steps. But most importantly, I keep coming back no matter what.

Until I got clean, the only job I had was dealing drugs. I worked a few hours a couple of days a week and made a lot of money. In recovery, the first job I had was delivering newspapers on my scooter. I was making less in one month than I made in one day dealing drugs. But I delivered the papers and used the time for meditation in motion. Today I work with homeless addicts, and I went back to school to learn how to be better at my job. It is a miracle that this addict has a job helping others.

Service taught me to care about other people and respect others. I learned to respect my family, and they see the changes I have made through the program. Six years ago, I lost my father. He was ill for a long time, and before he slipped into a coma, I was able to make my amends with him. He told me that I looked

good and asked if I was still going to "those meetings." He for-
gave me. I wanted him to get well, but prayed for acceptance of
God's will. When he died, the pain was so strong I could not stop
crying, and seeing my mother hurting as well was devastating.
I did not know how I was going to get through this. I called a
few NA friends, and within half an hour I was surrounded with
love and support. This was my first experience of handling such
severe emotions clean. I was sure I was going to break down,
but through prayer and the support I got from my NA friends,
the opposite happened. I found the strength and courage to go
through the mourning process without using. Not only that,
but I found that I was able to be there for my mother while she
grieved. This was a humbling experience.

When I first got clean, I thought that I was giving up so much:
my friends, my status, my good times. I even gave up listening
to music at first. Now I know that I've received much more in
return. I have lots of new friends who are recovering addicts,
and I am a respected member of society. I am well appreciated at
work, and music is still my passion. Once, when I got fired from
a job, I was devastated. I was confused about my higher power's
intentions for me. I confronted my sponsor with my lack of faith,
and he told me to pray and check God's will for me. The pain and
the blow to my ego were too big; the fear of how I would pay
the rent was overwhelming. My sponsor told me that God has a
better plan for me. Later, after some time had passed, I realized
how right he was. When I am in pain, I remember that pain is
my best teacher. When I have attacks of self-pity, I visualize my
higher power looking at me and asking his secretary, "Get me his
file." He looks at the file, smiles, and says to his secretary, "This
guy doesn't realize all the good things that he is going to get." I
am full of hope. I am grateful for everything I have been given.
I love you, NA.

A simple act of kindness showed this Dutch addict that he belonged in Narcotics Anonymous. He worked through his fears that a relationship with God would be barred to him because he is gay and learned to trust the power of love.

Sandwich

I remember the upstairs hallway where I was sitting. I looked at the woodwork of the stairs and thought it would hold a rope.

I also knew that I would not do anything to die, even though I did not want to go on.

I looked in the phone book for a helpline. I called in and talked to a man. He said I could meet him for coffee and that I did not have to say anything, but if I wanted to I could.

I went to see him and tried to keep my sadness inside. I drank a cup of coffee and was glad I wasn't at home where the walls were closing in on me. The man told me about the meetings he went to, and asked if I wanted to join him. I wanted to; I did not want to be alone.

Before the meeting we went to his house. He understood, or maybe I told him, that I had not eaten in a few days. He made me a sandwich. That impressed me. I had done things against my conscience. I had lied, I had manipulated, and worse, I had used violence. I wasn't worth it, and still that man was there for me.

He took me to my first meeting. I don't remember what was said, even though several people spoke to me. I know I cried. I remember the warmth I felt when I was with those people. I felt I shared something with them. I felt I belonged, that I belonged to them. I had never felt anything like that.

I had always felt different with everybody, even my family. We lived in a village, but we weren't born there and the people spoke a strange dialect. I went to a different school than the kids from my block. I did not have real friends, and my older brother died when I was in elementary school. My parents were always fighting, and I was ashamed. I often fled the house with my mother. After a few hours, my father would find us and bring us back. When I was young, I learned that for adults, yelling, fighting, using, and running away were normal ways to deal with problems. I was a smart and sensitive boy with an unsafe start in life.

That feeling of belonging I had at that first meeting was therefore so important—it made certain that I kept coming back.

It was hard to stay clean those first weeks. Each day seemed to go on endlessly until the next meeting. When I stopped using, it was as if I had been in a deep, dark cave for years and suddenly I stood in full sunlight. My eyes had to adjust to light that sometimes hurt terribly. Everything, good and bad, became more intense. Living without anesthesia, I did not understand the feelings that would suddenly surface. Sometimes I thought I was going crazy. I could be immensely sad without reason, sometimes for days. Other addicts who remembered their own struggle assured me that everything would be fine. I did not have to understand everything immediately. There would always be someone to fall back on. I was safe. I kept coming back, and it got easier. The obsession disappeared.

When I was first going to meetings, I thought my problem was a recent development. I had been having a toxic relationship with a man I thought I loved. I completely effaced myself, and thought that was love. The fights, when we used, could spin out of control so badly that we would go at each other with full wine bottles.

But as I opened my eyes to my own reality, I started to see that my problem dated much further back. I remembered when the alcohol came out of my pores the week of my mother's funeral, even though I was only twenty. I remembered that I had had fights in bars before; that relationships had ended before; that I had wanted to die before and had made pathetic attempts to do so. I had been in situations before where people wanted to kill me. This wasn't the first time I had been through any of this. But I had always tried to find my salvation in drugs, obsessive sex, relationships, smoking, etc. I had been fleeing into addictive behavior for a long, long time. NA provided me with a safe environment in which I could say anything and share everything. This security enabled me to look beyond the last couple of years to see patterns that had been there for decades.

When things got out of hand, I had always thought that it was the result of some outside force. I was intelligent; I still had my house and job; it could not be that bad. If only people would see me for what I was worth. If only I lived or worked somewhere else. If only the weather were nicer. If only there had been no military service. If only my brother had lived, or my mother. If…if… if only I was not addicted. I had my reasons. I was a victim.

I learned to recognize feelings. The safe environment of NA gave me the chance to face my own fear. My fear was deep, and deeply hidden—fear that I wouldn't amount to anything, fear of being deserted, fear of emptiness…. I couldn't fight this fear by myself. I couldn't even name it. Old feelings of emptiness and loneliness can still take hold of me. But NA's Twelve Steps and the people in the program, who I love so much, have shown me another way. The security and solidarity that I get from the program gave me room to breathe. It gave me freedom of choice. I don't have to respond to situations the way I did before.

At first, I did not like the word God. It made me think of people and institutions that judge others, like churches that would ban me because I am gay. It frightened me. I was afraid I would not fit into a twelve-step program. I shared this at meetings. I talked to other addicts and learned that spirituality is something personal. What matters is my understanding of God, not anyone else's.

With their help, I learned to trust a power of love that is much bigger than me.

When I told my father I was an addict, he told me that his father had died from addiction. My grandfather was apparently not the bohemian from the family stories. He was an addict. As a young boy my father had to go to the pub to beg him for money for the household. That man died from alcohol after he left his wife and kids in poverty. Out of shame, my father had never told that to anyone. Learning his secret gave me more compassion for my father—and more compassion for myself. I have a disease that has occurred in my family several times. I did not choose to be addicted. I am unable to take the disease away. And other people, whether or not they are addicts, have their stories. Beginning to see how powerless I am and getting more understanding for the powerlessness of others allowed me to breathe again, and has given me the space to find more good in myself and others.

When my father died, I was able to be there for his widow and others, as a mature man who could be a support. I don't have to approve of what I have done, or what others did. But I get more and more freedom to untangle myself from a negative past, negative behavior, and negative thoughts. This has made my life extremely more beautiful.

I don't have to be overwhelmed by feelings anymore. It's easier for me to let go. I am able to make more room between my feelings, my thoughts, and my behavior, room that is necessary to choose. I don't always succeed in making the right choices. I still have my dramas and my panic. I am a human being and not perfect. But I can see a lot of progress, and I am very grateful.

I'm blessed. I am in a happy relationship in which I learn healthy ways to deal with confrontation. I have friends. I am able to give love and to receive love. I am an addict. That is no longer a handicap, but a drive to shape my life in a positive way. So much has changed since the day when I wanted to die and that man showed me I was worth caring about. I didn't even feel worthy of the sandwich he made, but I did feel like I belonged in NA, and I do. It is important for me to remain watchful; the disease is here and will remain, so my recovery should continue as well. I learn more and more to trust the endless love and power that lie in the spirituality of the program.

I am no longer a victim of others, or of myself. I don't have to use anymore, no matter what happens. I am responsible for my recovery. If I fall back into an old feeling of self-pity, then I have the means to deal with it. I am not alone; I have people to support me when I ask for it. When I have a moment of despair, there will always be someone to talk to. It's not always going well, but it is always getting better.

This addict from Iran was "the most important person in the room" for two years before he got clean. Now he devotes himself to NA—sponsorship, the steps, and service.

The Spirit of Service

I am an addict from Iran. I was introduced to NA in 1996 at a detention house. This introduction led to a new way of life, not out of willingness but out of powerlessness and desperation. I had arrived at the center nearly unconscious and slept for two complete days. I had smuggled in some drugs, but when I went to use them, they were gone. It seemed to me that all my room-mates were high, even though they all denied it. I was very agitated and disappointed. I endured the pain without complaining, but the desire to use was with me the whole time I was there.

Now that I have been clean for a number of years, I am able to see there was evidence of the disease of addiction long before I started using. I didn't like my own belongings or even my parents' names; I always wanted to be someone else. I wanted to be powerful, capable, and prestigious. I wanted to be a grown-up.

At age eleven, I smoked my first cigarette. It burned my throat badly, yet I felt like a man. It helped my self-esteem for a moment, but soon those feelings went away. At thirteen, I was introduced to drugs. I immediately felt that I had found a way to create feelings of power and control in me. The more I used or the more powerful a substance I used, the better I felt. By the time I was sixteen, I was using the most powerful drugs around. For the first three years I enjoyed it. Gradually, one hit at a time, drugs became my higher power. Day by day I was getting older and weaker, while the drugs seemed younger and stronger.

I started thinking about controlling my drug use. On every attempt, the drugs defeated me. I would use to sleep; instead I stayed awake. I would use to stay awake; instead I'd fall sleep. I would use to find friends; instead I'd find enemies. I used to fight; instead I made up. Everything was controlled by the drugs. I felt shame and guilt and would regularly judge and punish myself. Denial, justification, and dishonesty created distance between me, my family, and the rest of society. My feelings of anger, resentment, and hatred fueled my justification for using more and more.

I have experienced much hardship due to my addiction: many different jails, mental hospitals, suicide attempts, theft, and selling of my family's belongings. One of the most painful experiences happened during the 1984 war. At that time, many everyday products were rationed and we had to use government-issued coupons for our purchases. On a number of occasions, I sold the rations of my baby's powdered milk on the black market and used the money for drugs. After getting high, I would cry and beat myself up. Sometimes I would feed my baby only sugar water. My heavy using lasted twenty years; for the last seventeen, I was looking for a cure that I couldn't find, until finally in that detention house I was introduced to NA.

Upon my arrival at my first NA meeting, the greeter welcomed me with a warm and loving hug. I was lost and confused. It had been a long time since anyone hugged me—even my mother. I thought, "These people are lunatics. They don't know who they are dealing with." I was looking for differences and finding fault with the meeting. Eventually there was a part of the meeting where people announced their clean time. "This is not possible; they are all lying; they are all high," my head was screaming. Even in prison I would use anything I could find to get high.

That was and will remain one of the most sacred days of my life. They told me the newcomer is the most important person in an NA meeting. For the next two years I was the most important person in every meeting, since it took two years for me to get clean. I thought that I was different. I thought maybe there was another way for me to use if I could change the type or the amount or the timing of my drug use. I continued struggling until the miracle happened for me as well.

One day, on the way to my connection, something amazing happened: Somehow I turned around and went to visit one of my NA friends instead. We talked only for a few minutes about ordinary stuff. But when I left I felt different. My obsession had disappeared. To this day I don't know what happened in those few minutes; what I do know is that was the beginning of my recovery. All that I had done was continue going to meetings, wholeheartedly asking God to help me stay clean, and I kept in touch with other NA members. Against my every belief that this program would not work for me, it did. I started feeling intense hope instead of my usual obsession to use. It seemed like I had become a different person with a new set of feelings who was about to begin a new life. I felt excited and happy and the world seemed beautiful to me.

That same night I got a sponsor and told him that I wanted to work the First Step right away. He told me to read the First Step a few times so we could talk about it later. I stayed up until morning and read all of the Basic Text. Starting the next day, I carried the book around with me and continued reading it. Every time I reviewed the First Step, something new would become clear. I couldn't believe that I could stop using, but the truth was that I no longer had an obsession to use. I spent most of my time with people in the fellowship and became more and more hopeful. I could truly laugh and feel joy. I looked at the sky, and it seemed that I hadn't really noticed it in years.

Every day I shaved, put on clean clothes, and was the first one at the meeting. I shared at meetings and afterwards would spend time with other addicts. I no longer denied my problems, because I felt that everything would be okay. I would call my sponsor over ten times a day. He was patient and treated me like a good friend. It was a curious thing; for the first time I was willing to listen to someone unconditionally. I had become teachable. And I kept feeling and getting better. After a couple of months clean I ran into one of my old using buddies. We would talk for hours when we were using. But this time we had nothing to say to each other. It was as if we were strangers.

From the beginning my sponsor made me aware that this was only the beginning and that I needed to get into action. He told me that to stay clean I need to work the steps, go to meetings, and be of service. At first I couldn't understand what he was telling me. I was clean after many years of trying; I felt happy. However, after a short time I realized that if I didn't make some major changes in my life soon, I would go back to where I was before. Today I believe that a person who is clean and has not worked the steps can possibly be more dangerous than someone using.

When I started service work, I realized how sick I was. Attention seeking, self-centeredness, selfishness, resentment, the desire for revenge, and many of my other character defects got in the way and caused problems for other members. One day at a time, our fellowship continued its growth, and I grew up and got wiser as well. A little at a time I got in touch with humility, God-centeredness, acceptance, forgiveness, and other spiritual principles.

At that time in Tehran there were only two groups, and each met three times a week. I helped out by making tea, setting up chairs, and cleaning up afterwards. I started feeling that this was my home, and every time a newcomer arrived, I would go talk to him and share my experience. I noticed the positive effect of my words, and that made me feel good. I felt useful. People started asking me to sponsor them, but my sponsor suggested that I work some more steps before doing so. He said that meanwhile I should continue to share my experience in recovery with others. Gradually, by working the steps, sharing, and working with newcomers, the spirit of service grew in me. I became thirsty for service in NA. Today I recognize that service is my responsibility and my way of appreciating the fellowship.

My relationship with God improved. In the beginning I simply prayed and thanked God for being clean, and that was enough to give me a sense of serenity. Through working the steps I realized that as I kept changing and getting better, the world around me also kept changing for the better, and that God was with me on this path of transformation. I started to know myself and became familiar with my strengths and weaknesses. My relationships with people and my community kept improving. I found the ability to resolve my problems one by one. I experienced a new sense of peace and freedom by practicing the spiritual principles contained in the steps, and that helped me be more successful in my work. My faith helped me to recognize that my pain or defeats were possible lessons for future success.

Prayer and meditation became part of my life. The first time I worked the Eleventh Step my sponsor asked me if I'd ever thought about what God's will was for me. After a few days of considering this, the answer came to me that God's will for me was to serve others. When I shared this with my sponsor, he smiled and told me that now I was ready for the Twelfth Step. I believe that I truly became a member of NA once I worked the Twelfth Step. My sponsor suggested that to work the Twelfth Step better, I should increase my knowledge of how the program works. He encouraged me to attend meetings focused on the traditions and concepts of service. I read service material. I gained a better understanding of spiritual principles and a better understanding of my defects, which were obstacles in the way of my sincere service. Practicing spiritual principles has helped my life outside of the fellowship as well—to the point that today I am an economically and socially successful person.

The NA program offers us only one promise: freedom from active addiction. Every day I thank God I have received this and so much more. Today I do not need to use drugs and do not need to die. I feel a loving God with me at every moment. I feel good about others and myself. I no longer need to seek approval or recognition. Serving NA is my way of repaying the fellowship that saved me from certain death, and doing service is a part of my amends to society for the damage that I caused during my using. Service is gratitude in action, and it gives me a feeling of usefulness that is extremely meaningful to me. Every day I ask God to give me the power to carry out his will.

As an entertainer she traveled the world, but found herself
in the isolation of addiction wherever she went. This dancer
found grace out of the spotlight, in the rooms of NA.

A Brazilian Full of It!

Narcotics Anonymous rescued me from the depths of despair and gave me back my life. I was born in Rio de Janeiro and grew up in the north of Brazil in a big family. My father was angry and full of morals, but my mother was gentle and really good to us. Life was difficult, but I felt loved. We were taught to love others and be responsible. I thought of myself as special.

I was seventeen when I got drunk for the first time. I hated the taste but loved the way it made me feel. It was like the doors of the universe were opened to me. In 1974 I started dancing with a folklore company and was introduced to marijuana by another dancer. I absolutely loved the way I felt: Something was glowing inside me, making me feel strong. After that first one, I wanted another and another. When we went to smoke he took me behind the theater and told me not to tell. The secrecy was very exciting. The progression to other drugs came soon.

We traveled in Europe, and even without speaking other languages, we found drugs. I became more and more dependent on using. I was invited to stay in London and join a Brazilian theater company. Most of the actors used, and I felt at home. In the play all the actors were nude onstage. The first night I got really loaded to be able to take all my clothes off.

When the company went back to Brazil I stayed in London. I spent all my money on drugs and wound up living in a squat with other addicts, stealing from shops to eat, dancing topless for money. I experimented with acid with another addict—I tell you, we got more than we asked for. I got pregnant, and the decision to have an abortion was like deciding what to eat: There were no feelings (today when I think about it, I feel a lot). Two days after the abortion I was introduced to cocaine—that love affair lasted more than ten years.

The dance company was rehearsing another show, so I went back. I took LSD with me to sell. It was crazy, but I was so arrogant I never thought about consequences. In Brazil I started dealing. I knew it was dangerous, but I felt invincible.

I was approached by a buyer, and we arranged to meet. I was set up, and I am alive today only because I mentioned a friend one of them recognized. When they left I was shaking, my heart beating so fast I thought it would explode. One of them got arrested, and someone told me that the police were looking for a woman with red hair—that was me. I shaved my head.

I got pregnant again and had another abortion. In Brazil that was very difficult. I went to a backstreet doctor and contracted an infection. I was in pain, and I had to tell my mother so she could take me to a private doctor. I knew my mother was suffering, and my sisters were all angry. My family didn't know how to deal with me. They didn't know what was going on, but they knew it was serious. I was stealing from them to get drugs. I was so unhappy, a figure of despair, in denial, lying, pretending things were okay. Everything that I did, I did like there was no tomorrow. I was powerless.

At the end of the next tour I stayed in London again and met the man who would become my love, my husband, and my hostage. I moved in with him. I was so happy that for a while I didn't use much. My boyfriend was supporting me. I looked after the flat, studied English, and sewed to make money. We were happy.

We went to a crazy party—they had everything. That night, my boyfriend couldn't find me to go home. I returned two days later with an excuse. I started using cocaine again, smoking grass every day, and becoming unreliable. My boyfriend was taking such good care of me, and I was behaving so badly. I didn't see what was happening, but I started using more and more and hiding it from him.

I got a contract to work as an entertainer in Cannes, Monaco, and Nice. The show was in the evenings. All we did during the day was go to the beach and use. I was high all the time. I discovered my addiction to gambling. I could not stop until I lost all the money I had taken with me and all the drugs were gone.

I had an affair. I felt guilty, but I was an addict wanting more of whatever was available. I was using cocaine all the time. One night I used so much before the show that I couldn't sing; my voice didn't come out, and my nose started bleeding. I had to leave the stage. That had consequences for the whole group, but I didn't care. When the manager came to talk to me, I flirted with him until it was forgotten.

In 1980 I went to work in the Caribbean. One night after the show I went out on a yacht with a man. We used a lot. He passed out. I was half-conscious, and I knew something was wrong. I could feel my heart beating inside my mouth, and my left side was paralyzed. I thought, quite calmly, "I am going to die." Then I thought, "I don't want to die," and I realized to my horror that we were in the middle of the sea. I was losing my senses. I felt really frightened. I prayed to God not to let me die. I promised that I wouldn't use again. Somehow I was able to turn on the shower, and the cool water helped the circulation return. When I got back to where I was staying, one of the musicians was using. He offered and I took. I was powerless, and my life was unmanageable.

When my boyfriend met me at the airport he didn't recognize me. He was horrified; he said I looked like death. I had lost a lot of weight. For the next two years I did weekend shows in different cities, taking my drugs with me. Sometimes I was aware of the madness: It was like my body was twisted, my hands gripping the glass so tight that it would break. I was unmanageable, confused, and unhappy.

My boyfriend asked me to marry him, and we went to Brazil. Even on my wedding day I was high. I was just able to stand through it all, not embarrassing him or my family too much. My last year of using was a nightmare. I stopped performing or even taking care of myself. I didn't care what anyone thought. I would go to dealers and come home days later.

I was called to do a gig in Paris and thought I could do with a change of scene. After the performance I went out, and to this day that evening is a total blackout. On my way back to London I stood out like a sore thumb, in a tight leopard-skin dress, attracting attention. I was arrested in the airport in London. I was really angry. I didn't know why they were arresting me. I had this policeman saying to me how bad using drugs was, and in my head I was saying, yeah, yeah.... That was the beginning of the end of my using. It was August 1986.

My recovery journey began when a friend took me to an NA meeting. We had used together, and he was nine months clean. I was very sick, very thin, and didn't know if I was coming or going. My husband sent me to a treatment center. I didn't feel human. In place of me there was a huge pool of arrogance, denial, delusions, fear, pain, despair. It was more than I could bear. After being in treatment for three months, I left, waving my middle finger at everyone.

Having been abstinent for three months and having gone to NA meetings, even reluctantly, it was clear to me that I was done using. But I had to make sure. Everything I had heard in meetings was true: My short, devastating relapse left me with feelings I couldn't understand, and I went back to treatment. It was hard to go back, but I am grateful for having found courage and determination to stay and really look at the disease that wanted me dead. The emotional pain was intense, and there were moments when I thought I was going to die, but the love and care of other addicts helped me to carry on and to take it a day at time. Sometimes I could only take it a minute at a time, and that was okay too.

Surrender allowed me to slowly return to humanity. I recognized that I was dead inside. I was physically, spiritually, and mentally sick. I decided to stop fighting and let people in, and bit by bit I was restored to sanity. I went into a halfway house for women. My first thought was, "But I hate women!" I told that thought to go away, and it worked (I do that a lot). I began to look at my anger, self-pity, and denial about what I did when I was using. Trusting the process, using the program, being helped and helping others, I found that I had compassion and that I cared.

When I did Steps One, Two, and Three for the first time it was like switching on the light. I started waking up every morning with this new feeling inside me—hope. Writing Step Four was definitely a turning point. I was able to face all the rubbish and start to recognize the good in me. I realized that I could nourish it and become a better person. There was a lot of work to do, but I wasn't afraid to let go, grow up, and go forward!

Going through Step Five, sharing with another human being the true nature of my wrongs, is one of the most humbling things I've done. The day I did Step Five it was raining; the sky was covered in dark clouds. Afterwards I went for a walk on the beach. It was really cold, and I was crying. When I looked up there was a patch of blue in the sky and the sun shone for a minute; for me that was my Higher Power saying to me that I was going to be okay. I felt happy, a spiritual awakening....

Narcotics Anonymous is in my life. It has allowed me to see, to feel, to be the real me, and to achieve great things over the years. I could not be where I am today if I didn't practice prayer and meditation. My Higher Power is loving, kind, and truly my friend. I learned to accept my life as it is, not as I would like it to be. Working the steps is still a primary purpose in my life. I love going to meetings and growing. I like talking to other addicts and always have time for the newcomer.

Recovery gave me the opportunity to become a mother, one of the most wonderful things that has happened to me. Life is not perfect. When my daughter was three years old, she was diagnosed as autistic. Through the years she has been a real challenge.

She is lovely and we can have fun together, but at times she is impossible to live with. I am lucky to have such a supportive husband. We've been married for twenty years, and when I can't cope, he takes over. My daughter is sixteen now, and we have a son who is thirteen. The program helps me with my life and its challenges. Today I believe that everything is going to be all right. I have some very difficult days, but I have tools to help me see the way through.

When I came to recovery I was emotionally and spiritually dead. It was like I was in a deep, dark hole. I could not see anything, no hope, only despair. Going to meetings, sharing, things started to make sense. I learned from other people's experiences. Being willing to shut up and listen, doing service, having the courage to leave my safe environment, I changed. Before I knew it I was out of that hole for good, with huge prospects for my life. I practice the Twelve Steps daily, and am grateful that today I can admit when I am wrong. I can learn from my mistakes. I am not so hard on myself anymore.

I am eighteen years clean. My recovery journey is full of wonderful happenings. I love my life, my sponsor, and my sponsees. I have my own business. If someone had told me when I came into recovery that I would be able to manage my own business, I would have thought that they were joking. NA also helped me go back to singing. I was invited to share at a convention, and when I finished everyone asked me to sing. I didn't know what to do, but they kept shouting, sing, sing, and to my surprise, I started singing and I loved it! Thanks, NA. With the help of the steps, a Power greater than myself, sponsorship, and service, I've been able to see my potential. I've found me.

When he reached the point where he couldn't live
with or without drugs, this Australian addict
attempted suicide. He survived through grace,
and now he's been clean more than sixteen years.

Another Chance to Live

In the life of every addict there are crossroads: times when we could stop using and take responsibility for our lives, if we make the choice. I went through the crossroads one day in the bus station toilets, and chose the wrong path. I think I was supposed to die, but by the grace of God, I was given another chance.

I have been clean for sixteen years. I got clean when I was twenty-two, so I have lived most of my adult life as an NA member here in Australia. I have a full, rich life, thanks to the program of Narcotics Anonymous.

As an adolescent, I was governed by the compulsion to take drugs. The results were trouble, violence, prison, and poor health. My using was punctuated by legally required visits to counselors, probation officers, psychologists, etc. Rarely could I hear what these people were saying — or hear anything above the rumbling din of self and the desire for drugs. I was so focused on getting what I thought I needed that I ignored most of the moral boundaries most people take for granted. I stole, lied, cheated, scammed, robbed; in the end, I was exactly what the Basic Text says: "reduced to the animal level." I hunted the streets like a wolf, looking for money and drugs. Deep inside I still had a conscience, but I couldn't access it; I couldn't afford to. It was buried under a pile of emotional rubble. The task of cleaning up all that rubbish was too great. There were too many things to deal with to live a normal life. My life became a misery of unresolved responsibilities.

I believe every human's real job is looking after themselves, and I couldn't seem to do that. Eating, sleeping, drinking water, exercising, staying warm or clean seemed irrelevant and virtually impossible. The result was a vicious cycle of hunger, poor hygiene, and bad health. Between the layers of self, these inabilities hid a particular emotional pain that I carried. I couldn't feel it or articulate it properly until I got clean. I don't know whether I brought this pain from childhood or whether it came into the world with me, but I still carry it. It's not always present, but it arises from time to time as I move through these layers. If I get rejected, left out, treated as second best, or am not wanted in some way, the pain can become acute. I used to medicate this pain with drugs. For a long time they made me feel better, but in the end the drugs became their own particular pain. They drove me to the edge of sanity, to the brink of death, and now I no longer see myself as having that option. For me, using drugs is suicide.

When I was twenty years old, I spent time in a maximum-security prison for burglary. In there I saw some of the most brutal human behaviors that I have ever witnessed. After two excruciating years, I was released, with an absolute commitment to stop using. I lasted for one hour before I was stoned on about four different drugs and went into a blackout. My life spiraled out of control for the next few months. My powerlessness was evident, unmanageability undeniable. I woke up from a blackout with blood on me that wasn't mine; I had a pocket full of money and no recollection. I was frightened about what I was becoming.

One night I was trying to sleep through withdrawals. I had taken some heavy tranquilizers, but they hadn't worked properly. I was in a stupor of frustration and futility. The pain of my whole wretched life was caving in on me. I worked myself into a weeping, cursing, violent rage, smashing the room, scratching and punching at my own face. My housemate was terrified and called my parole officer.

The following day, an intervention was done by my parole officer, a counselor, and my mother. They told me they were going to send me back to prison unless I went to NA and did ninety meetings in ninety days. I said I would do whatever they wanted. They told me that wasn't good enough: I had to make choices for myself, because recovery couldn't occur until I really wanted to change. I was caught in a limbo of conflicting desires. Of course I wanted to change, but I couldn't; I wanted to use, but I couldn't. I felt there was nothing left to do, so I decided to kill myself. I left the intervention that day filled with a sense of absolute doom and desolation. I did a robbery, bought as many drugs as I could, and overdosed in the bus station toilets. I wanted to die because there didn't seem to be an alternative to the misery that my life had become. I went through the crossroads that day and chose the wrong path—but by the grace of God, I was given a second chance.

I woke up a couple of hours later, crumpled on the floor of the toilet, completely defeated, my life a shambles. I walked, trudged, not knowing what to do or where to go. In that state of blind desperation, the winds of chance blew me into a detox center across the highway. They took pity on me and admitted me, even though I wasn't the required forty-eight hours clean. I lay naked, curled up on the bed, sobbing that night, feeling a particular sense of freedom, because deep inside I think I knew it was over. I had surrendered. I just didn't really know what that meant yet.

At that detox they took people to meetings daily. I struggled through those painful first few days, but on a Wednesday night, at a meeting in a homeless center, I heard and felt the NA message for the first time. I didn't have to use drugs anymore; there was a way out. I was inspired by the other people who were clearly junkies but didn't seem to be using. They made me believe there was a chance for me to really stop and have a go at life. I feel sad now, writing this; I am much more emotionally in touch with my old mad life now than I ever was back then.

I couldn't imagine how life would play out. I just saw a black hole of the unknown, but I had decided, just for the novelty, to give it a go for a couple of days and see how long I could last.

I lasted forty-nine days. Then I relapsed, and the compulsion to take drugs was back on me like a ferocious animal. My life spiraled immediately out of control again, and I realized that the previous forty-nine days had been the most trouble-free in the last ten years. The relapse lasted for about two months before another detox and the death of another friend through overdose. I have been clean now since the 25th of January 1989, and my clean time is my treasure. I protect it with my life, because it is my life.

I have gone on to do many of the things that it seems to me a person should do. I own a house and a business. I went back to school and got an education. All the normal social and material assets have returned. But more than any of that, I have loved—at times deeply. I feel things—I feel everything! I guess I had always been scared of that, but it is amazing to feel, brilliant and frightening, sad and awesome all at once. I am excited to be alive. I am excited about what is to come. I still suffer with existential angst from time to time, and wonder what we are all doing here on this planet, but I have decided on a purpose, and that makes it easier for me: I care about people getting clean. I have dedicated myself to NA and to serving others. I attend meetings regularly. I participate in the local area and the region. I sponsor people, and I have an NA sponsor. I live the steps to the best of my ability, and I am trying to become the best person I can be. I believe that by living like this we give others permission to do the same. NA gave me the key to another life and this is it: "We keep what we have by giving it away."

She thought she was a traveler, but it was really a need to escape herself. This addict from Norway found her way home on a Mediterranean island.

At the End of the Road

I came to my first NA meeting because of a twelve-step call. It wasn't that I hadn't tried to stop using; I had done nothing else for the last few years. But I tried by myself—my way. I was traveling around the world, changing cities, countries, and continents. I would have changed planets if I could have. I tried everything to get away from drugs. I stopped on various occasions. I substituted one drug for another. I tried changing boyfriends. I had a baby, thinking for sure that would stop me from using. But if I couldn't stop using for me, how could I stop using for someone else? Nothing or no one could stop me.

As far back as I can remember I have had a need to escape from myself and my feelings. As a child I lived in the world of books and fantasy in an effort to escape from emotions like fear, shame, inadequacy, insecurity, inferiority, and oversensitivity. I became someone else. I went away from my family as often as I could to experience something different. I had to have excitement, something new all the time. I left home at sixteen years old. By that time I had already started to use drugs. I joined the hippies in the early seventies, and I left Norway and went to Denmark. I continued using, and I started to smuggle drugs because I was not able to keep a job. I went on to India—on the hippie trail—and I ended up at the "end station," which was Goa, in India. Here, I was hanging out with freaks from all over the world. I could get my hands on all kinds of drugs. I thought I had arrived in paradise. It looked like it from the outside, but there is no such place as paradise for an active addict. The drugs turned against me. I was imprisoned by my addiction, and I tried to get away time and time again. I continued my criminal behavior and became an international drug smuggler. I ended up in jail, but I continued using while incarcerated. I became an extravagant consumer of drugs. I had developed a lifestyle of drugs, parties, and travel. But the emotions I tried getting away from caught up with me: The shame, fear, inferiority, despair, and loneliness only got bigger and bigger. I could not go on anymore. At one point I was sure that I would die a using addict. I was close to death. I had developed chronic bronchitis, and the attacks became more and more frequent. One doctor told me I would die from this.

This was the condition in which two members of Narcotics Anonymous found me and brought me the message of recovery. They saved my life. They told me I had a disease, and that recovery was possible. I went to a treatment center and there started to attend NA meetings. I moved back to my native country after having been away for nineteen years. While spending a few months in the south of Europe, I had the opportunity to attend my first local NA convention and my first regional European convention. I went back to Norway, started an NA meeting in my hometown, and became active in trying to spread the message about NA to the public. I mostly sat by myself at this NA meeting, but when I stopped listening for footsteps and instead focused on the fact that I was there for my own sake, things went much better. I was a member of NA, even if I was there alone.

After one year I moved down south, still clean, and got involved in an already-established NA community with a couple of groups going. We formed a service structure, and slowly but surely, NA started to grow in Norway. I started to work the steps, and I also, slowly but surely, started to grow.

I have the disease of addiction just as much today as I had a few years ago. I am powerless, but I have a power greater than myself in my life today who has helped me be restored to sanity. Just for today, I no longer need to escape from myself and my feelings. I hand my will and my life over to God as I understand God, which has relieved me of trying to control people, places, and things in order to get things to be the way I want them to be. It is up to God now—the results, I mean; the footwork is up to me. I attend meetings regularly, where I try to focus on bringing a message of recovery and giving back what other members so generously gave to me. I have had the opportunity to work a few Fourth Steps that have revealed my old, unhealthy behavior patterns. I got rid of the shame and guilt that had become such a burden. I had the opportunity to focus on my assets—parts of me that I did not know I possessed. I never in my wildest dreams imagined that I could share so honestly all of myself with another human being, my sponsor, in the Fifth Step. By sharing about myself, I found love and acceptance in the eyes of another woman. And by daring to be myself, I could start to like myself. I am just another human being with defects of character and shortcomings. What a revelation.

Further, in the Eighth Step I made a list of people whom I had harmed, and I put myself first on the list. I hurt a lot of people, but none as much as I hurt myself. I had nothing but contempt for myself, so there was no limit to the pain I inflicted on myself. Others whom I hurt were usually people close to me. They were people I loved while I was charging through life with my self-centered need for instant gratification. I made direct amends to those people when to do so would not hurt them more. Instead of inflicting more hurt, I practice love, compassion, and forgiveness. My experience is that it is much easier to make direct amends than indirect ones, because the latter takes much more time.

I keep on making amends to myself on a daily basis. I take care of myself today. I thank my Higher Power on a daily basis for my life and for my recovery. These are two gifts that it is up to me to take good care of. I do that by working NA's program of recovery and also practicing a healthy lifestyle. I have stopped filling myself up with chemicals. I eat healthy food, I rest, I do exercises, and I set boundaries where needed. I treat myself with respect and love today because I deserve it.

In the Tenth Step I do a daily inventory, and I look at my behavior throughout the day. Today I'm more able to say, "I'm sorry, my mistake," when I do not act according to my values. I pray and meditate on a daily basis, and I try to act according to God's will. I can often tell God's will today by the way things feel. If an answer hits me like a bolt of lightning, it is usually my will. If an answer develops over time, it is usually God's will. I am no longer controlled by self-seeking behavior.

This is what a spiritual awakening is like for me. I have gone through a radical personality change as a result of working the Twelve Steps. I am still actively involved in doing service. I continually work my Twelfth Step. I have a message to pass on today, a message of recovery from the disease of addiction. I can only keep what I have by giving it away, and there are many ways I can carry the message.

I was not clean during that first twelve-step call many years ago on a Mediterranean island. As I put my small daughter to bed that night, I took the last of my drugs. I sat on the kitchen floor for hours, crying in despair. Those NA members told me that my recovery was up to me. It was up to me to ask for help. By the time I went to bed that night, I had made up my mind. I wanted to be free of drugs. The process of surrender began that evening, and when I awoke the next morning I had hope, for the first time in years.

I still like traveling and I still like hanging out with addicts. I have had the opportunity to experience NA as a worldwide fellowship. Before, I met using addicts from all around the world. Now, I meet recovering addicts from all around the world. What a difference and what a privilege.

Regardless of...

The disease of addiction does not discriminate, and neither does Narcotics Anonymous. Our literature explains that NA is open to anyone "regardless of age, race, sexual identity, creed, religion, or lack of religion." No matter where we come from, how we were brought up, or what we do for a living, NA's doors are open to us. These members write about finding love and acceptance in the program, and within themselves, even when they least expected it.

These members share briefly about finding recovery in NA "regardless of age, race, sexual identity, creed, religion, or lack of religion."

Reflections

When I came to my first NA meeting at the age of fifty-two, I heard a woman say, "If there is anybody here for their first time, please come to the front of the room and get a white keytag." All sixty people turned around and looked at me. I went to the front of the room, not knowing I was about to have the first physical contact with another human being in over four years. The wonderful woman who gave me the tag held me in her arms as if she were holding one of her own children and whispered in my ear, "You never have to use again." She gave me something I hadn't had for many years—hope.

Now I'm a senior citizen at sixty-five years old with thirteen years clean, and a grandfather of two kids who teach me the spiritual principle of unconditional love. To be able to do something for someone other than myself has been the most rewarding experience of my life.

I am an Eskimo, born and raised in the dark, frozen north. When I wore my hand-sewn parka my mom made, the kids would tease me. I hated my parka, my mom, my ethnicity, and myself. Drugs took the edge off and helped me forget. Eventually, I left with a scholarship my tribe offered. My disease progressed, and I spent most of my money on drugs. A friend I considered to be worse off than me said he was going to an NA meeting. I asked if he wanted me to go for support, and I went. Little did I know I would relate to all the readings and things others shared. I felt so good when I left that first meeting.

So much has happened since then. For a long time, I could not share in front of others. With my sponsor's help and by working on myself, I've been able to share over a dozen times. That is amazing. Working the steps and going to meetings have helped me get better with myself, my culture, and my ethnicity. Today I am proud of who I am.

The first time I shared in a meeting about being gay was very hard. I had five years clean and regularly attended the same meeting. I never spoke about being gay. I referred to my boyfriends as "she" or "her" whenever I talked about my relationships. I was asked to share my story at a large meeting and knew that my newfound honesty demanded I share the truth about me.

The night I was scheduled to speak, my sponsor unexpectedly brought his wife, who is not a member, to the open meeting. She had invited me to her home many times for dinner and is a devout Christian woman. I didn't want her to know that I was gay. I was afraid she would reject me. I prayed to keep my commitment to share openly that night. Despite my fear, I told my story honestly for the first time. When I finished, she looked directly at me and gave me a big, beautiful smile that said everything was fine. People came up to hug me, and no one teased or ridiculed me for being gay. From that time on, I knew I could recover as a gay man in Narcotics Anonymous.

As a Native American, I was taught that I was born with a spirit and I was blessed with seven guardian spirits. In my active addiction, they scattered and could not help me until I was willing to help myself. What I came to believe is that addiction is a living, breathing disease that will take what one loves the most. It will tear one's life apart until all is gone. I recall telling my husband, in despair, that my spirit had left me.

I was eventually banished from my land and my tribe. I was facing over two years in prison. I was tired, and I wanted change with all my heart. My deceased sister came to me in spirit and said, "You can stay clean now." I believed her. With NA, I have been able to humble my life. I have made amends to all the people and my ancestors in public. In an open vote, the tribe chose in my favor, and I now have my people back. My spirit has survived, thanks to my recovery.

I was raised in a sincere, devotional religious family. The church was the center of my social life, and I attended religious schools. However, I didn't fit in well, even when I wanted to. I got pregnant out of wedlock, and this devastated my family. I saw my dad cry for the first time. I chose to go forward with the pregnancy, partly due to my religion and also because I cared for the father. I gave birth to a beautiful boy and relinquished him to another family. The painful truth is that I succumbed to pressure from family, church, and society.

After college I discovered drugs, and my run didn't end until I was mentally and spiritually destroyed. I landed in treatment and found a woman who would be my sponsor for the next nineteen years. At around eight years clean, I felt a lack of spiritual growth. I came into contact with a spiritual leader of a tradition from India. I began to study that path and experienced the sensation of being in love with God. I was afraid that the NA Fellowship would reject me because of my dedication to this path, but my community was surprisingly supportive. More recently, I have been developing in a spiritual tradition not from India but from Mexico. I have a teacher who has been showing us a way that honors the spirit and the earth. I have assets that are beginning to reawaken, and I am rediscovering a long-sleeping part of myself.

Several years ago I found the son I had given up for adoption. It is very strange and wonderful. I am not the mother I might have been had things been different. It is best described as "intimate strangers," and it is an ongoing story.

It took two months of being clean and actively involved with NA and the steps before the obsession to get high was lost. And it's never come back. As an atheist, I looked to other addicts in the program as "the power of example." I understood power to be the ability to effect change. I saw power in those around me who were clean and enjoying the world they lived in and seeking solutions to their everyday problems. And to me, seeing is believing.

Everything I've learned in recovery has been from other addicts, those with similar problems who worked to overcome them. I do the same things as other members, except I don't believe in prayer. I believe that if prayer worked, there would be no unhappy people in the world. Yet NA does work, as long as I involve myself in the steps and traditions as a way of life.

After a lifetime of feeling different, this lesbian addict found the key to connection in a common needs workshop.

Finally Connected

I spent many years struggling against the overwhelming tide of active drug addiction. As a lesbian, I felt hated and thought that life could never offer me the things that seemed to come so easily to others. Convinced that my sexual orientation was the ultimate problem with my life, I grew angrier and more defiant toward people and institutions every day. Alienation, legal problems, shame, guilt, loneliness, degradation, and despair reached such a frenzied cycle that eventually suicide seemed like the only option. From a hospital emergency room, I was referred to a treatment facility.

I was introduced to the program through members who facilitated Narcotics Anonymous meetings in the treatment center. My only contribution to these meetings was the resentment, anger, pain, and hopelessness that surfaced nearly every time I shared. The meeting facilitators were always telling me things would get better. Although I fought it every step of the way, the caring and concern they showed stayed with me.

Eventually, I began to listen to what other people shared during the meetings. The group readings interested me in spite of my feeling that I was different from everyone else. I started to look forward to these meetings for temporary relief from my pain, confusion, and fear. One day I realized that I was staying clean; I welcomed this change like a drowning person discovering a float. This was my "signing on" to the program. I understood that the only way to avoid returning to the cycle of destruction I left on the streets was to replace it with recovery, and I uttered the words "I am an addict" with new understanding.

As I stayed clean, more privileges were granted to me in the center. I attended outside meetings, spent time with addicts who were willing to come get me, and went to activities hosted by various NA groups. For the first time ever, I was living and having fun without having to use drugs. Life had improved dramatically in such a short time, but I still lacked a real sense of belonging. Other addicts shared with me about being gay, but I thought that they avoided sharing this in the meetings because they were ashamed. I wanted to attend a gay and lesbian Narcotics Anonymous meeting to finally have my unique lifestyle and feelings of alienation truly validated. Finally, the center allowed me to attend a common needs meeting. I couldn't wait to explain to the group how ironic this title was for such a meeting. My needs were not common. I was a lesbian trying to work a program designed by straight people.

I left that first common needs meeting disappointed; no one brought up the obvious fact that being gay was different from the norm. The meeting did not run any differently than any other meeting I had attended up to then, and I had expected it would. I returned every week, thinking it would be different, but the addicts there talked about the same things I heard in other meetings. It took some time for me to see that I was expected to get a sponsor, work the steps, and go to meetings just like everybody else. When I finally found the courage to explain my indignation and disappointment to another gay recovering addict, I got laughter in response. I was told that staying clean came first; the solutions to my problems would follow. I was amazed this person didn't recognize the injustice and hatred that gay people faced in our everyday lives. Getting clean was wonderful but could never resolve the real problems we confronted as gay, lesbian, bisexual, and transgendered individuals. I kept these feelings to myself, hoping that one day I could help another gay person to understand that it is possible to get clean despite the alienation and hatred we faced.

Shortly after this resolution, the addicts who came to the treatment center excitedly announced there was going to be a

Narcotics Anonymous convention in the state. Their enthusiasm and willingness to support us at this convention won over the center director. I found myself on my first out-of-town adventure with one of the supporting staff. During our car ride I learned that she was also a member of Narcotics Anonymous and believed that, with the help of the fellowship, any addict could successfully work the program and learn to stay clean. She was part of the group responsible for this convention, and most certainly for my attendance. We talked about staying clean all the way there, and something inside me broke just a little bit. I told her I was scared. Staying clean in the center was easier now, but I was scared to think I would have to leave soon and stay clean alone. That is when I heard the most profound thing ever told to me by any recovering addict: In the Fellowship of Narcotics Anonymous, you are never alone. I never wanted to believe someone so badly.

I was overwhelmed by the number of people at the convention. I wasn't sure what I was feeling. The next day it was suggested that I volunteer to greet and hug people at the convention. This was difficult for me, but the other addicts didn't seem to notice my awkwardness. Because I had no better ideas and nowhere to hide, I did a four-hour shift.

I attended the gay and lesbian workshop that afternoon. I was thoroughly drained from hugging and greeting, and unable to voice my frustration and discontent. My thoughts were cloudy, and I had to work hard to fight back tears. I listened to every drop shared at that workshop.

Although the message had been shared at the other common needs meetings I'd attended, this was the very first time I heard gay and lesbian addicts talk about the internal struggle of learning to identify. I realized it wasn't hatred from society that kept me from feeling connected; it was my own hatred I would have to combat. No one had done as much harm to me regarding my sexuality as I had done to myself by feeling unique, victimized, and closed-minded. Finding my place of peace would have to come through working the Twelve Steps with someone who had knowledge and experience. Maybe I was just too tired to block out the message that afternoon. All I know is that I could no longer find the energy to intellectually battle with people who wanted to help me. This is when I truly began to feel my way into the program of Narcotics Anonymous.

The experience at that first convention changed my attitude about my own life, and I craved that powerful feeling of unity and group spirit. My willingness skyrocketed. I was ready to find a sponsor, share my thoughts, do step work, and listen to others.

After leaving the center I found myself volunteering for all types of service work: coffee-making, greeting, stacking chairs, talking with newcomers. I shared at meetings about my struggle to understand the steps, instead of about the things I found unacceptable in the world. No one in NA has ever turned me down for a service position because of my sexual orientation. Women in Narcotics Anonymous have provided me the opportunity to sponsor them even though I'm a lesbian, and when I am looking for a sponsor, being gay has never been a condition. The belief that my sexual orientation would always be a wedge between me and others has melted away. My home group sent me to area service meetings, and I enjoy the opportunity to be involved at that level. After some time in service at the area, I joined the planning committee for the very convention that sparked the change in my attitude.

The opportunities to work with others and become a part of this fellowship have soothed the aching need I had to belong somewhere. Through working the steps and practicing the program of Narcotics Anonymous, I have discovered so much about myself. One of the gifts I have received is the deep desire to work with others. This is the medicine I apply to the old scars left by anger, fear, resentment, and alienation. My gratitude for this way of life cannot be expressed through words on a page; it is expressed whenever I have the opportunity to help other people on their journey of recovery. I thank the members of Narcotics Anonymous for creating spaces like common needs meetings where I can explore some of the feelings I dragged into the program with me. I had no idea the solution would begin with acceptance of myself. From this position I naturally developed the capacity to accept and care about others. It is truly a "we" program, and I have never been happier or more content than to learn that I have always been just like everyone else.

*Addiction took him away from his Orthodox Jewish roots,
but recovery helped him forge a new relationship with
a God of his understanding.*

One Third Step for Me,
One Giant Leap for My Recovery

I was born in 1954 and adopted at birth by an Orthodox Jewish family in New York City. My parents were honorable people. My father was a righteous, humble man, dedicated to his religion. I couldn't have had better parents. They always told me the truth about being adopted. Even though they loved me very much, I felt abandoned by my natural parents. I believed that I was unusually lucky to have a family who loved me, but that I really didn't deserve one. I felt different, alone, and less than. And I knew there was something that I could do to make myself feel better, only I didn't know what it was.

I was raised in the traditional Orthodox way. We went to temple weekly, prayed three times daily, ate only kosher food, and observed the Sabbath and the holidays. I learned to read Hebrew at the same time that I learned to read English. I brought my parents great joy as a youngster. When I was twelve years old, I ran into a burning house and helped an old blind lady to safety. I made the front page of the paper. My parents were very proud of me. But all I wanted was to be the same as everyone else. We dressed differently from other people, we acted differently, we spoke a different language, and we ate different food. I really wanted to be cool.

Addiction was not learned behavior. I was an addict for as long as I can remember. I first used fantasy to get out of myself. I would dress up as Superman and run around with my arms in front of me, as if I could fly. I badly wanted to be a superhero. I was taught about the power of prayer: If I prayed at the right time, in the right place, and with the right intention, my prayers would be answered. I prayed often that God would allow me to fly and have superpowers. I wasn't going to use my powers to rob banks. I wanted to help people in need. Yet God did not let me fly. When I outgrew superhero costumes I "substituted one for another," and started playing air guitar. Every day after school I would go to my room, put on a record, stand in front of the mirror, and play along with the band. I wasn't a Jewish kid from the Bronx. I was the fifth Beatle. I was the sixth Rolling Stone. Then my mom would call that it was suppertime, and I had to go back to being me.

Then one night my folks came home after an evening out to find me passed out on the living room floor with an empty bottle of my father's wine. I never played air guitar again. I had found a new way to get out of myself.

About that time, I read an article in a magazine about people who took a particular drug, thought they could fly, and jumped off a building to their deaths. Anyone else reading this article would say, "I'm going to stay away from that," but not me. I said, "Now I know how I am going to fly, after all." My thinking was that they didn't die because they were using, they died because they were stupid. "I'm gonna take that drug, and if I think I can fly I'll start flapping my arms while standing on the ground, then fly up to the top of the building." That was my logic.

Before long, I strayed from my religious observances. Every time I had to choose between my heritage and using, I painfully and reluctantly chose using. I was drawn further and further away, into a lifestyle I knew nothing about and didn't really like. My father tried everything he could to help me stop using. He would have done anything. As much as I respected and loved my parents, the disease of addiction caused me to bring them nothing but shame and sorrow.

I used every day, switching from one drug to another, drifting from one city to another. As I pushed people away, they began to give up on me, and I began to give up on myself. Everything I did ended in disaster. A failed marriage, a failed career, a failure in every respect. I cleaned up for one day to attend my son's bar mitzvah, and in the middle of the reception I had to get back to the crack house. I had nothing left to live for. I was a stain on my family name. I was ashamed of who I had become.

In December 1993, I finally checked into a detox. I weighed in at 112 pounds.[11] My thighs and arms were the same thickness. I looked liked a concentration camp survivor. I was angry, arrogant, closed-minded, hateful, stubborn, and completely in denial. Boy, did they have their hands full with me. They tried to convince me that I had a drug problem, but using was my solution for every problem I had.

When I quit school because I was using every day, I didn't have a drug problem, I had an education problem. When I left my parents' house because I was using, I didn't have a drug problem, I had a family problem. When my wife left me because I was using in front of the kids, I didn't have a drug problem, I had a marital problem. When I sold the family car for a couple of "eightballs," I didn't have a drug problem, I had a transportation problem. This was the condition of my denial when I was introduced to Narcotics Anonymous.

I made it through detox and treatment, and ended up in a halfway house in upstate New York. I attended my first NA meeting the night I arrived. I raised my hand and said that I was new, and they sent a meeting list around the room to gather phone numbers from other members for me to call. I still have that list. It rode in my wallet for the first ten years of my recovery. Now it is laminated and I keep it in my living room. Every now and then I look at the names, and most of the people are still clean.

I started doing service work very early in my recovery, and have benefited greatly from finding humility through service. I began working steps with my sponsor. For a long time I struggled with the Third Step. I couldn't understand the difference between spirituality and religion, and I had to establish a new relationship with a Higher Power. This struggle has been the greatest

[11] Fifty-one kilograms

challenge in my recovery. It has also been the most rewarding experience of my life. My sponsor thought that I would work through the Third Step in a few months and would start writing my Fourth Step by the end of my first year. Instead, I spent almost twenty months searching for a loving, caring Higher Power who would "guide me in my recovery, and show me how to live."

The problem was that my idea of a Higher Power was an old man with a long beard who had a scorecard of my life in one hand and a lightning bolt in the other. He was definitely going to send me to hell. How could I possibly make a decision to turn my will and my life over to him? Yet it was clear to me that those people who had worked the Third and Eleventh Steps had a serenity about them which I did not have. I wanted that so much. I had to find a new definition of a Higher Power. I searched the library, the Internet. I went on spiritual retreats. I went to services in a temple and spoke to the rabbi. I spoke to a lot of people in the fellowship about their Higher Power. Some of these were good experiences, and some were not. I kept searching.

Slowly, things began to change. I started talking regularly to my Higher Power. I started seeing my Higher Power working in other people's lives, and started thanking him for that. I started seeing evidence that my Higher Power was working in my life. I started to pray for other people, and I started seeing some of my prayers being answered. Then I put a special time aside on a regular basis to ask my Higher Power's help in my endeavor to find him. And then one day, while I was meditating, I noticed that my Higher Power was no longer carrying that lightning bolt around with him.

I slowly noticed myself changing. I started to see the good side of everyone around me. I started to understand other people's problems, and I prayed for them to find a solution. And after building a relationship with my Higher Power and the NA Fellowship, I couldn't see that scorecard in his hand, either. I came to the revelation that I was a good person, and that I was not going to end up in hell. It's hard for me to imagine now that a person can do hospitals and institutions service work and still think that he is going to hell.

I am still on this journey. I am still growing. My love for my Higher Power is getting stronger every day. Something still calls me to return to my religion. I tried attending services again when a fellow addict invited me to go to temple with her on the holidays. It wasn't as bad as the last time. I am gradually getting more comfortable with my relationship with my Higher Power. I know that today I cannot return to the Orthodox religious practices of my youth. But I am coming closer and closer. My relationship with my Higher Power reminds me of a story my father used to tell about a father whose son had strayed away. One day, after many years, the father sent a messenger to find his son and tell him to return home. The son replied, "I can't." So the father sent the messenger back to say, "Then come as far as you can, and I will come to meet you the rest of the way." My Higher Power has come the rest of the way to meet me.

I know today that my Higher Power is completely okay with where I am, but he continually places opportunities in my path for me to grow spiritually. These opportunities are often cleverly disguised as catastrophes. Either they can be experiences, or they can be learning experiences. It's up to me. I have a choice.

I really am grateful for the program of Narcotics Anonymous. My life now has purpose. I love myself and everyone around me. I am grateful to my predecessors who saw to it that there was a seat for me, with a reading on it, in NA. I owe them a debt of gratitude. The only way I know to repay that debt is to get involved, and make sure that there is a meeting with a seat available for the newcomer today. I am so grateful that I have been able to stay clean. I reach out to newcomers, and I look for people who are struggling with their concept of a Higher Power, and share my experiences with them. Today, I am truly grateful that God did not let me fly. This program works.

NA's message got through to this Maori addict. She got clean out of spite, but she stayed clean because of hope.

Kia Ora Koutou

Ko … taku ingoa.	*My name is….*
Ko Hikurangi te Maunga,	*My mountain is Hikurangi,*
Ko Waipaoa te awa,	*my river is Waipaoa,*
Ko Rongopai taku marae,	*my Sacred Place is Rongopai,*
Ko Ai-tanga-Mahaki toku iwi,	*my tribe is Aitanga Mahaki,*
No Aotearoa ahau	*I am from New Zealand*
and I am an addict.	*and I am an addict.*

Where do I begin a story that I shouldn't be here to tell? I am a Maori woman who came into this program kicking and screaming. I was twenty-eight and had been court-ordered to attend a treatment program in Auckland, New Zealand. I believed treatment was a "get out of jail card" for me, and I would use when I left.

I knew I was an addict when I first used alcohol at the age of thirteen. After that first drink, I remember thinking, "Hey, I really like this feeling," and then I proceeded to black out. I binged for a while, drinking on Friday nights, but went from using alcohol to smoking dope, to hitting the doctors up for prescription drugs, to injecting hard drugs—wow, the progression was fast. I was shocked at how quickly it happened. By the time I was eighteen I was a single mum with a two-year-old daughter living on welfare in public housing, using on the government methadone scheme. From the beginning, my goal was to be an addict. I loved the feeling of being out of it. I was heavily involved in the criminal underworld, and the chaotic lifestyle was exciting.

My family loved me dearly, but I continually ripped them off. All the promises I made to them were empty. "I promise I'll stop, mum; just need some money to organize myself." "I promise I'll turn up. I promise I will get help. I promise I'll be there for my little girl's birthday...." Yeah, right. My family knew my addiction was killing me, but I couldn't see it. They decided to care for my children to keep them safe from me. What a blessing that was.

I tried to change. I moved, thinking new city, new start. I would get a couple of months, but once I started again I couldn't stop. I tried relationships to get clean, but I always chose addicts. I tried mental institutions, but they gave me more drugs. I tried finding god on my own, but that didn't work. I couldn't understand why I continued to use when my life was crumbling around me. Physically I was shot: I lost all my teeth and I weighed about six and a half stone.[12] I was devoid of any concept of a higher power and my *wairua* was broken.[13] I really only thought of one thing: how I could use and get more drugs. I could not see any cure. I was an addict, and addicts use drugs, full stop. If that meant killing myself in the process, then so be it.

By the end of my using, it wasn't pretty: I was wanted by my so-called friends for ripping them off, my *whanau* didn't want to see me because all I brought was cops and trouble,[14] and the cops just thought I was a nuisance addict who created a lot of paperwork; they wanted to put me away, out of their hair. I hated myself and everyone around me. I couldn't even kill myself properly; I would wake up in the emergency ward and think, "What the hell are you keeping me alive for?"

I was sitting on the wrong side of a window at Auckland Police Station, where my partner was trying to get me bail. He had brought our children with him and they were crying, wanting to know when mummy was coming home. My partner pleaded with me to stop using and to look at the pain I was causing our *whanau*. For that brief moment I told myself, this has to stop. Deep inside, I had had enough. The next day I appeared before the judge and was told to either go to treatment or go to jail. I thought I took the easy way out and chose treatment, but it would have been far easier to go to jail for three months than

---

[12] Ninety-one pounds or forty-one kilograms.
[13] *Wairua* is spirit.
[14] *Whanau* is family.

go to all those groups! Who wants to find out how you really feel inside? Who wants to find out that all the relationships you had were based on nothing but your addiction? Who wants to find out that you have an incurable disease, but that it can be arrested? Not me!

On my first day of treatment, I took the bus with all my suitcases to my dealer for a last taste. I arrived at the treatment facility an hour late. When I got there, the manager told me I was too late—that 8:00 am was the time to come in. I was told to come back a week later. I was furious that she could refuse me, an addict crying for help (stoned, actually), and I told her that this was bull and I would show her! Out of pure stubbornness I set out to prove that I could do this. That was the decision that saved my life. I have been clean over nineteen years since that first day.

The miracle that happens when one addict helps another is without parallel. I started treatment not knowing what to expect. Every morning I would wake up with my body screaming to use. I would talk to myself and say, "For the next ten minutes I won't use," and it would pass. Those ten-minute slots turned into days, then weeks, and then months.

Through NA I started to hear the message of hope. Slowly my clean eyes saw people in the rooms who I had used with. These people were no-hopers in my mind, and they had stopped using. They looked happy. This gave me hope that maybe I could do it, too. My muddled head started to get clearer as the drugs came out of my system. I was learning to practice the steps in treatment and soaking up all the healing that happens with addicts helping each other, yet I still had reservations about staying clean. I didn't think I could do it. I had no belief in myself. I graduated from treatment, but out in the real world I was full of fear. I hung in there at all costs because I was too scared to go back.

I found that freedom from active addiction comes with a price. I did everything that I was told to do. I left the love of my life because he was still using, and I knew that I wouldn't stay clean if I went back. I never hooked up with any of my using mates for fear of picking up. I gave up my house and all my possessions to move across town. I wanted to start a fresh life for myself and my children.

I was told when I left treatment to get a sponsor, go to meetings, and don't use at all costs. To tell the truth, that's all I did. I went to meetings, worked the steps, and didn't pick up—even though every day for the first two years, my first waking thought was that I wanted to use drugs. After I had earned the respect of my *whanau* I was able to have my kids come live with me. I was still a single mum with small children living on welfare in a state house, but I was clean. I had NA meetings and our Twelve Steps to help me. I learned a valuable lesson: Thinking about using drugs does not mean actually doing it.

I started to accept my powerlessness over addiction. The first two years of recovery were a grieving process for me. I grieved for my old lifestyle, I grieved to use drugs like wanting an old familiar lover, I grieved for my old friends, and I grieved for the rituals of using. Slowly, as I moved away from this grief by staying clean a day at a time, I was letting my addict go. I felt empty inside.

That's when I started to get a handle on the Second Step: "We came to believe that a Power greater than ourselves could restore us to sanity." I so love this step! It allowed me to see that I needed to fill myself up with something else. NA meetings, my sponsor, the group, and working the steps would all help to restore me to sanity. Each day in those first two years was hard, but it was "a program of firsts"—the first time getting through feeding myself and my *whanau* clean, the first time meeting with teachers and getting the kids to school clean, the first time paying bills on time clean, the first time opening a bank account clean, sharing in meetings clean, having coffee with other recovering addicts clean, the first time I had sex clean (that's a biggie). Slowly, I started to change. I remember the first day I woke up without having the desire to use drugs. It took two years, but the desire was removed for that moment. Wow, that was a huge milestone. For a moment, my sanity had been restored. I started to feel good about who I was and where I belonged in this world.

I started to understand the message of hope for this addict. After that miracle, I decided to get off the dole by going back to school, and got a degree in social work.[15] I had left school at fifteen, had no formal education, and thought I was a dummy—but it was possible because I found the rooms of NA. My family was pretty stoked as well, as I'm the only one in my family who went to university. I have been a productive member of society for a while now, holding down a straight "Mary tea-towel" job for the last fifteen years of recovery. Sometimes it blows my mind: I'm in these professional meetings thinking, "Is this really me?" I pinch myself sometimes at the miracles in my life. I have the biggest gift: my children's company, respect, and *aroha*.[16] That has been truly a miracle. I bought my first house in recovery. I have a wicked job that I love and get paid for. I got my driver's license at thirty and have a car. I have money in my bank that I worked hard for. I don't have to rob and steal to make ends meet. I am no longer standing on street corners waiting for the man to turn up. I don't have cops busting my door, and I have this unshakable faith that all will be well, no matter what happens, as long as I don't pick up, I go to meetings, and I trust my higher power.

If you are reading this and are new to this program, please give yourself a break. Go on, take it a day at a time, minute by minute if need be, ring someone in NA, and get to a meeting because I promise you there is hope for us addicts, and miracles happen way beyond your wildest dreams.

Arohanui: God's will for us all.[17]

---

[15] "The dole" is government assistance.
[16] *Aroha* is love and compassion.
[17] *Arohanui* is big love.

When she got clean at sixteen in Chicago, she had no way
of knowing that more than twenty years later she would wind up
in Italy, feeling how service connects us all.

Growing Up in NA

I made it to NA for all the usual reasons, and thanks to the fellowship and Twelve Steps, I've literally grown up in NA as NA has grown up around me.

I got clean in Chicago in 1983, when I was barely sixteen and all the meetings in the metropolitan area could fit on just one sheet of paper. Much of our literature hadn't been written yet, we had poker chips instead of key chains, and my first Basic Text was a photocopy of the literature approval version. There were few women and no one else quite as young as I was in the meetings I went to. At six months clean I was taking my shift answering the NA helpline from a pay phone in the halfway house for juvenile delinquents where I was living.

Looking back on it now, it seems like NA and I were both adolescents who grew up together. It was a period of rapid expansion in the fellowship—every weekend we traveled to meetings or workshops, or planned social events, learning how to stay clean together.

How you identified yourself in a meeting became of the utmost importance—we were forging our own identity as a fellowship, saying yes, we can recover in NA, just NA. There was no avoiding service in those days, and being the addict that I am, I was rather obsessively involved for the first nine or ten years of my recovery. I was blessed to be a part of a lot of new beginnings: opening an area service office, creating two regional service structures, planning local and world conventions, developing NA literature.

What have I learned after spending more than half my life in NA? Simply that the fundamentals are just that, fundamental.

There is no substitute for being of service, having a good sponsor, working the steps, and going to meetings. I was fortunate in that I got clean so young that I have literally grown up with twelve incredible tools for living—the steps. I have had to confront many difficulties during my recovery. But with the tools of recovery I've been able to overcome and, even more importantly, learn from and grow through all of it.

When I had about ten years clean I moved to a very remote Native American reservation where there were no NA meetings. I was able to stay clean and continue to work the steps by maintaining strong relationships with other addicts and my sponsor (who I was with for fifteen years).

Today I know I can do anything I choose to in life, as long as I am willing to do the footwork. Working the program has helped me become the responsible, productive member of society that our literature talks about. I went from being a high school dropout to having a master's degree and working with Native tribes nationwide in Washington, DC. I was still feeling jittery the first time I had to get screened for White House clearance to meet the president, until I remembered that I was a juvenile when I got clean so my record would be clear! I have traveled all over the world and gotten to do work that I believe in and that would benefit others.

I was back in Chicago for several months around my twentieth anniversary. So many of my old crowd were no longer around, for all the usual reasons: One was in prison, several dead, lots using again, and a number still clean but not going to meetings anymore. As I seem to do every year around my clean date, I was examining my recovery and looking for reasons to keep going to meetings myself. It seemed like I always had the most clean time wherever I went, and I felt a real need to be around other "oldtimers" and hear what made them keep coming back. Thank goodness I did what I had been told to do all these years: I went to meetings and I shared. I talked about my lethargy and doubts (including the classic "I got clean so young; maybe I wasn't really an addict."). I actively sought out people with time and questioned them on where they found their motivation to continue in the program. I reconnected with a woman I had known since she got clean fifteen years earlier, and we began working the steps together again. I did another Fourth Step inventory. In short, I followed the program's suggestions. What I got in return was another spiritual awakening and a new lease on my life in recovery.

And now I am writing this from Italy. I have started a new career, something I love and that is just for me, and I am back to doing service in NA. I am an active member of my home group and Narcotici Anonimi in Italia. I have a sponsor, and I sponsor two amazing women. The program here seems very much like the NA I walked into many years ago, and I am excited and honored to get to be a part of another growth cycle in NA, this time halfway around the world.

Three years ago I attended my first Italian NA convention. Each meeting at the convention was based on an entry from the *Just for Today* daily meditation book. At my very first meeting I heard a man from Italy with fourteen years clean say that he read from it every day and it had helped save his life and keep him clean. I spontaneously burst into tears. When I was eighteen years old I was a regional literature chairperson and for two years coordinated what we then called the "daily book project." Every weekend we had editing workshops in my mom's basement where I would input the corrected versions in one of the very first personal computers.

During this time I had never stopped to think about the impact we might have on someone else. I wouldn't realize it until years later when I was half a world away at a convention. There I heard another addict speak in Italian about his life changing as a result of the literature we were working on in my mom's basement. Today I understand how what we do in our own lives and recovery can be felt around the world. Through NA and the service we do for the fellowship, every single one of us is connected in some way. Coming from a Native American tradition, I had always been taught that we are all related and interconnected, but I never thought much about this early in my recovery because I was so young and busy trying to stay clean and grow up. I now understand why I need to keep coming back, no matter how long I've been clean. I finally understand what my family had been trying to tell me all those years. *Mitakuye oyasin.*[18]

---

[18] We are all related.

At nine years clean, he was diagnosed with depression and schizophrenia, diseases he continues to treat with medication and therapy. This addict learned that while mental illness is an outside issue in NA, dealing with it in his personal recovery is very much an inside issue for him.

A Serene Heart

I am a grateful recovering addict who recently celebrated twenty-five years clean through NA and the grace of God...and I live with the mental illnesses of severe depression and schizophrenia. And yes, I've been blessed with a very fulfilling life. I have noticed that many people who readily admit they are addicts can't admit that they struggle with their mental health. There are different levels of stigma attached to addiction and mental illness. I understand the fear of admitting something unpleasant. After all, as an NA member, I had to squarely face my fears when I first owned up to being powerless over my addiction in Step One. Later in my recovery, I learned that mental illness is not something that can be hidden away or minimized. I have to be honest and admit it, in and out of the rooms. Fortunately, the paths of NA recovery are many. For those who live with permanent, debilitating diseases in recovery, I hope my story will help courage blossom within you.

My earliest memories are of continual abuse and yelling, with frequent visits to the hospital. I behaved differently from what was "normal," and was diagnosed as mentally retarded and hyperactive. Consequently, I was accorded the kind of upbringing prescribed for "special" children: social isolation, close supervision, and limited stimulation. In grade school, I spent half days in special education programs. But when I was seven, I read an entire encyclopedia in three weeks, plus numerous books intended for adults. Suddenly they decided I wasn't mentally retarded, just very hyperactive. But I still wasn't allowed friends and was kept from activities because of my acting out. Being isolated, I developed a fantasy life.

I first used drugs around this time, and using took away the sense of alienation. Drugs allowed me to feel like I belonged to something, even if it was just another fantasy. I smoked weed and abused my prescriptions to cope with an alcoholic family and a troubled social life. Not having friends at school, I felt like it was always "them" and "me," the abnormal kid. I ran away from home at twelve, beginning a cycle of living on the streets and in communes. The first time I overdosed, I was fourteen. Later, I robbed a convenience store at gunpoint for a book of matches. I knew I was crazy, and the drugs made it okay.

The fun times were over by the time I was fifteen. Sleeping in dumpsters, freezing in garages, constant starvation, and self-abuse accompanied my drug addiction. I drifted from one group to another. I was constantly haunted by the feeling that I was different from other people, that I was an alien walking among the earthlings.

I looked for companionship in psych units and rehabs, but no girl would have anything to do with me. I certainly wasn't the high school dating type. I wanted to be loved, but I tried to believe that using drugs made love unnecessary. I finally hooked up with a girl I met at a rock concert. Using my homelessness as an excuse to move in with her family, I ripped off her parents and we took off for the streets. By that time, I was overdosing every few weeks. One of those times I was hospitalized, and she left. Feeling doomed, I tried to kill myself in a variety of ways. Finally, I overdosed into a coma. At the hospital, they didn't know who I was. I had no ID; I was found dying in an alley somewhere. The doctors told me afterwards that the coma was the kind people usually don't wake up from. No one had visited me. No one cared. Full force, I felt the total emptiness in the heart that comes from addiction. I had nothing for a life. I couldn't even remember my name.

At this point, when I was most hopeless, I was graced with the awareness that I wouldn't have to feel this way again if I did everything in my power to stay clean. I went to AA, and there, I ran into the only NA member in my community. When he explained NA recovery to me, something clicked. Nothing else had worked for me, whether I was sincere or not. Could it be that I just wasn't around the kind of people who could really understand me? Together we started a meeting. By example, he taught me the value of being dedicated to my personal recovery and to NA. We'd drive hundreds of miles to support fellow addicts in other communities. I wrote out the steps, and practically lived and breathed recovery. I had absolute faith in Narcotics Anonymous. I strongly believed I would be transformed into a better human being if I followed the path of recovery. By the time I had ninety days clean, I had started several meetings and was sponsoring newer members.

Miracles happened. The spiritual awakening described in Step Twelve manifested in my life. I *knew* what it meant to be spiritually awake, and I could *live* it. Not only did I stay clean, I lost the desire to use drugs, or even to behave like an addict. Addict behaviors were as distasteful and spiritually empty as using drugs. Never having worked before, I was able to hold down a job at a treatment center. Starting off as a counselor, I quickly became an administrator. I served on service boards in and out of NA. God blessed me with leadership abilities, and I was filled with willingness to be of loving service. I went to ninety meetings in ninety days, *every* ninety days. Learning consistency this way, I was able to discover and cultivate my talents on behalf of the fellowship and in my professional life. Daily prayer and meditation brought balance in my life. I could have intense conviction, but convey myself to others with gentleness. I experienced love for the first time, the deep love for other human beings that comes from a soul that is serene.

By the time I had eight years clean, I had a life that I could only have dreamed about. Not that I did it alone, of course; I had all the assets that come with NA recovery: a Higher Power, the experience of my fellow addicts, and the strength of their recovery. Years of prayer and meditation were rewarded with a genuine conscious contact with God and the awareness that I was participating in my Higher Power's plan. I had earned the respect of my fellow NA members and the community. I even had a soul mate, a wonderful lady who was clean in NA. I was *living* life, rather than just surviving.

But life changed. Over the next couple of years, I endured many dark days. My wife dropped out of NA, started sleeping around, and eventually relapsed. I quit my job. In the midst of this instability, I was still asked to serve on NA service projects. My first thought many mornings was "I can't handle it; I want to kill myself." But I kept showing up, assuming this was normal for someone who had lost so much. In meetings, I heard other NA members share about facing extreme emotional pain and surviving. I decided I would just ride it out. But it started getting weird.

The depression didn't go away. Instead, it got much worse. I heard voices and saw people who weren't there. I *knew* I wasn't using drugs, but I was hallucinating. In less than a year, I went from living in a six-bedroom house to being homeless. I couldn't even hold down a menial job. I had to sell blood to get food. I would spend days sitting in a chair, doing nothing, feeling nothing. At meetings, I struggled to find words to share what was going on with me. I was sleeping on NA members' couches and floors.

Several loving NA members confronted me with the fact that I "wasn't myself," and insisted that I see a psychiatrist. Recalling my childhood experiences, I recoiled at the idea. When I wouldn't go, they took me to the hospital. The medical team said I was severely depressed and schizophrenic, and prescribed medication. But I refused to take the meds, because I didn't want a mood-altering drug in me. And besides, hadn't I been "well" for nine years of recovery? But my heart kept becoming more distant. That dreaded total emptiness that I had felt when I was beaten down by addiction … it came back. Once again, I felt alienated, hopeless, useless, and worthless. And I wasn't using drugs.

Doctor after doctor told me I was mentally ill, the illness was disabling, and that it was something I'd have to live with for the rest of my life. I felt a deeper sense of defeat than when I first admitted I was an addict. What had I done to deserve this? Why did God allow this to happen to me? Hadn't I lived the principles? Hadn't I done everything one is supposed to do in NA? Aren't good people supposed to have good lives? Even more frightening was the uncertainty about the future. With drug addiction, NA is a proven way up and out of the hell of using. But with a mental illness, what kind of "recovery" would there be? How could I live the rest of my days … clean … with the many losses that result from mental illness? There was no hiding my problems, and there were no solutions in sight. I felt that my life was utterly ruined. How could I face the fellowship?

The confusion I felt inside was mirrored by how others responded to me. Some told me that I wasn't clean because I was taking meds. The same people who intervened to get me psychiatric help later accused me of getting disability benefits dishonestly. Others blamed my mental problems on "too much service work" or "never having worked an honest Fourth Step." Many men I sponsored decided not to work steps with me anymore. Other NA members said I was faking my illness. Fortunately, my sponsor was a very loving presence through all of this. Other NA members kept encouraging me, reminding me that NA isn't just about people, it's about principles. At times, I could feel the Higher Power in my life reminding me that I was loved, mental illness or not. Despite all the pain, the fellowship buoyed me with enough wisdom and caring to help me through this very difficult period.

Some of the most precious wisdom in my recovery is born out of my ignorance. Through the initial year or two of living clean with a mental illness, I learned a valuable lesson: *Mental illness is an outside issue in NA, but how I deal with it in my personal recovery is very much an inside issue.* Tenth and Eleventh Step journaling was critical in helping me get a grasp on where my recovery ended and my mental illness began. I had to make the distinction in order to stay clean. I learned that struggles with recovery never put me in the hospital, and that addicts aren't psychologists or psychiatrists unless they have a PhD after their name. When I first got clean, I had to learn how to explain addiction to people who had no experience using drugs, while also learning how to make sense of my addiction internally. The only way I could do this was to work the steps and learn what addiction and recovery really were. Now, I had to explain mental illness to NA members who had strong misconceptions about it. I had to rely on the steps to learn about my mental illness and how to live with it, clean.

Accepting the losses brought about by mental illness has been an ongoing challenge. At one point I was in a locked psychiatric unit, and some NA members were bringing an H&I meeting—but I wasn't allowed to go, because I wasn't considered stable enough. The only thing separating me from an NA meeting and a sixteen-year chip was a locked door. In a very real sense, this is what it's like to live with a severe illness in recovery: Ongoing illnesses shut the door on possibilities. But I need to deal with it with spiritual maturity, so I can enjoy emotional stability.

I can't compare myself with other NA members. During the sixteen years I've lived with mental illness, I've never dated, rarely worked, and sometimes lived in abject poverty. I have been hospitalized numerous times and have spent days, weeks, and months emotionally paralyzed and homebound. There have been long periods of time when the only thing I could do was go to a meeting, and times when I couldn't go at all. When I'm in a heavy episode, I can't even pray or meditate. I can work the steps until I'm blue in the face, and the mental illness won't go away. When I feel that I'm beyond hope, it's difficult to reach out to others. But I'm continually reminded that I don't have to walk this walk alone.

Understanding why some days are better than others is like knowing why I caught a cold last week instead of this week. In recovery from addiction, there are no guarantees, except that I'll stay clean when I live clean. When I work the steps, I don't follow a plan: I've learned that the plan will fall into place when I keep moving forward in recovery. That's why it's important to me to keep working the steps—so more can be revealed. The same is true with mental illness. Medication isn't a guarantee that I'll feel better. Therapy is a good tool, but understanding my illness doesn't make it go away. I've learned to apply those tools to the mental illness, and NA principles to my addiction.

In NA's traditions, I'm told that principles come before personalities. But what comes before principles? What gives an addict the strength and courage to live by the principles when recovery doesn't make sense? Why stay clean when it's impossible at times to feel the joy of recovery? I believe that the loving God described in Tradition Two that manifests in our group conscience, as well as in our service work, our fellowshipping, our work, and our play, is the same God that strengthens my personal recovery so I can live within the principles. Given the reality that I will face severe illness each day, and still being able to stay clean, that's an incredible miracle! Spiritually, I'm in a state of grace. I don't always feel it, but it's always there. I should have died many times over when I was using. Now I live with another disease, equally painful, equally life-threatening. I know many people in and out of NA who have killed themselves because of mental illness. I'm not going to be one of them. It's not an easy path, but I know that I'm alive because NA has blessed me with a clean life. Recovery makes it possible for me to treasure the moments when I have a serene heart, and to be grateful for the miracles, large and small, happening all around me.

As an African American gang member, he didn't think
he had a future. But NA kept its promise, and now he has
eight years clean and the life he always wanted.

From Gang Leader to Meeting Leader

I grew up in South Central Los Angeles. As a child, I had such severe asthma that I needed shots every other week to keep it under control. I felt different from the other kids, since I couldn't run or play without suffering an asthma attack. Fist-fighting became my way of dealing with the feelings I had about being different.

In junior high, my condition got better, but my violent behavior got worse. The home I was raised in was on the border between rival street gangs. I was afraid of those guys, but I wanted them to like me. One day I found a joint on the playground. I was too afraid to smoke it, so I gave it to an older guy who was a member of one of the gangs. After that I was allowed to hang out with them. I learned their walk, their talk, and their behavior. After I hit my first joint, I really felt a part of the group. Soon smoking weed was a daily event. One night I hit what I thought was weed, but it was PCP. I started experimenting with different drugs.

Once I was introduced to freebasing cocaine, that was all that mattered. I am the father of two boys and two girls, but using cocaine was all that I focused on. I started selling all the things I had acquired, including my prized custom lowrider.[19] My homies and my family tried to stop me, with no success.

From the age of thirteen I attended at least one funeral a year, sometimes two or three. With so much death around me, I always thought that I would be next, so my behavior was that of some-one who really didn't think he had a future. As the years passed,

---

[19] A "lowrider" is a car or truck that has been customized to ride very close to the ground.

my drug use and violent activity with the gang increased. I lived a life of crime, lowriders, drugs, and violence without really knowing that it was a problem.

In 1990 I was kidnapped by a rival gang, because a deal for some guns had gone wrong. The first guy put a gun to my chest and squeezed the trigger...it misfired. The driver told them to do it outside the car. I was taken out of the car, and started wrestling with the second guy for the gun. He put the gun to the side of my head and I heard a pop, felt the heat, and saw a bright flash. I saw another flash and felt the heat from a second shot, which went into my neck. They left me for dead, but I stumbled out of that alley into a grocery store, where someone called for help. En route to the hospital I heard the paramedics say that they were losing me. This was the first time I actually believed in a Higher Power.

While in the hospital I was told that I had been shot three times, twice in the neck and once in the head. The doctors removed one of the bullets from the back of my head; they left one in the back of my neck, and one is still lodged under my tongue. I was released from the hospital a month later and went to stay with my mother in Atlanta, Georgia.

I stayed clean on my own for a while, but eventually I started using again. I was introduced to the program of Narcotics Anonymous, and I shared clean and lived dirty until I couldn't anymore. At eleven months clean I relapsed, and suffered months of using. I went back into treatment, and I was able to accumulate eighteen months clean. I used again, and again lost everything that I had obtained—most of all my self-respect. They told me: If the drugs don't kill you, the lifestyle will. I had to become willing to change my thought process and, more importantly, my behavior.

I joined and became involved with a very loving and powerful home group in Atlanta, where I met my current sponsor, who told me that I would need to surrender to win. Surrender up to that point had been a negative word for me. My thought was if you surrender, you automatically lose. How can you surrender and still win? Then it was explained to me that by surrendering to the program, I would not have to fight anymore. This was what I was continuously doing: fighting a losing battle. I came to realize that I could only stay clean if I surrendered to the program. The members of my home group—in fact, my entire area—took me under their wing and showed me unconditional love. I am a firm believer that my Higher Power works through people, and the people are NA. They have been entrusted to help me—to not only stay clean but become a better person overall.

I am currently enjoying eight years of recovery with my wife and children. I am a successful professional, a student about to receive a bachelor's degree, and a proud, devoted father, grandfather, and husband. With my Higher Power and the program of NA, I am living the life I always wanted. I have learned that this is a program of progress, not perfection, and I still have major changes ahead of me. The only way I will be able to obtain the freedom that so many before me have achieved is first of all not to use no matter what, to implement the Twelve Steps, and to help others by carrying the message of hope. Narcotics Anonymous made me a promise years ago, and that promise was freedom from active addiction. Thank you, Narcotics Anonymous, for keeping your promise.

Because she is HIV-positive, this transsexual addict
was nearly denied surgery. Waiting helped her build
a stronger relationship with a Higher Power.

Terminally Unique

My name is ..., and I'm just another addict. Sometimes I need to remind myself of that: I'm just another addict. As a postoperative transsexual woman, I am not unjustified in feeling unique; there are fewer than 50,000 of us in the United States. We're a minority ridiculed and discriminated against by many and often rejected by our friends and families. It can be a painful existence, and my disease loves to exploit resentment, fear, self-pity, and self-loathing.

Nobody knows why some people are transsexual. In the end what matters is that I accept myself. Many addicts describe themselves as feeling like they never fit in, and as a child I felt this and more. As a teenager I discovered that marijuana cured my intense shyness and made me feel like I belonged.

I enlisted in the United States Air Force, and in the military I partied even harder, a "wild and crazy" guy. I fit in with my party-down buddies except for one thing: I started cross-dressing—wearing women's clothing—in secret.

I didn't know where this compulsion came from, and I tried resisting the urge. I could sometimes deny it for months, but the feeling always came back. I felt a deep shame about my secret, so I used even more to diminish the guilt.

In 1983 I fell in love with a woman who accepted my past as long as I was done with it, and I truly believed I was. I proposed marriage, we moved in together, and I started college.

School forced me to cut my drug use way back, and my "fetish" returned more strongly than before. I fought it for over a year, and finally my research at the college library strongly suggested I might be a transsexual woman—a woman trapped in a man's body—which led to a divorce only fifteen months after our wedding.

When I took the first steps to transition to full-time woman-hood, everybody freaked out. All of my "friends" cut me loose, my family backed way off, and I received abuse from total strangers. Even the housecleaning company I worked for would not permit me to work as a woman. I began to curse God for making me this way, if there was a God at all.

Motivated by rebellion as much as poverty, I turned to pros-titution—at least the people who paid me for sex were nice to me. Isolated in the sleazy Tenderloin district of San Francisco, with few real friends and feeling increasingly hopeless, I found relief in IV drugs. Three months earlier I'd sworn I would never use a needle. But that was common for my disease; I was always crossing lines I said I never would.

I admitted that my life was unmanageable, but I believed it was the transsexualism making it that way, so I tried going back to being a man. Shortly thereafter, I found out that I was HIV-positive. The next two years brought a downward spiral into increasing addiction, three months in jail, two psychiatric holds, three rehabs, and a half dozen overdoses, several of which nearly killed me. In short: jails, institutions, and (almost) death.

All three rehabs required me to go to NA meetings, where I heard a message of hope. In 1988, I finally admitted to myself that I was an addict. Four weeks later I was still clean; not even jail or basic training had accomplished that.

When my head was clear I began to feel my feelings again. I knew I had a problem. At six weeks clean, my most overwhelm-ing feeling was that I was a woman inside my male body. By ten weeks I knew for certain that if I did not deal with my transsexu-ality I would either go back to using or commit suicide.

I left that rehab homeless, jobless, and penniless, but I had a clean date, a sponsor, and a home group, and that was enough. I threw myself into NA, somehow believing everything would be okay. Miracles started happening within two weeks of leaving the rehab. Six months later I was living in a drug-free hotel and starting a corporate computer programming job. I gritted my teeth and presented myself as a guy to get hired, but I believed that someday soon I would be able to be myself, a woman, full-time. For six months I was a model recovering addict and an exemplary employee. I went to meetings daily long past ninety days, worked the steps with my sponsor, read all the NA literature, and had multiple service commitments. I had an experienced gender therapist, but I needed my NA program to deal sanely with being who I was.

Just because I was clean and no longer doing sex work didn't mean people stopped yelling "freak" and "faggot" at me on the street. Nor did my parents suddenly accept me. Some people stared at me in meetings. On some days I said the Serenity Prayer a dozen times. The closest I came to using that year was when I approached my manager with a letter from my therapist and explained that I was ready to start living full-time as a woman, including at work. Some of the weight lifted when she said that I was a good employee and she had no problem with it, but the final decision would be up to the divisional vice president.

My sponsor and my recovering friends said I'd done all I could, that I should turn it over to my Higher Power—easier said than done. Sure, when I shared in meetings I talked the HP talk with the best of them, but I had issues with God. I still hadn't forgiven Him or Whomever for making me a transsexual woman, so I had little faith. But instead of using, I doubled up on meetings and prayed like I actually believed. To my surprise, one month later I officially became the newest girl in the office. Just imagine if I'd given in to my disease and used!

After two and a half years of living and working as a woman, I grew complacent. I had money, credit, and friends. I'd forgotten the pathetic junkie that I'd been. I was deeply in love with a woman and living with her. I didn't have much time for meetings. I was sick of people staring at me, anyway. I even distanced myself from my sponsor, so I was completely set up for a fall. All of this time I'd been saving my money for the surgery that would make me anatomically female. My therapist agreed I was ready, but I was devastated to learn that none of the reputable sex change surgeons would consider me because of my HIV infection.

All of my fear, resentment, and self-pity came bubbling to the surface, but instead of going to my sponsor and meetings, I took solace in my girlfriend.

When that relationship became dysfunctional, I went straight into addict mode, using just six days after I took my four-year cake. I briefly came back to NA but relapsed again. I spent three and a half years forgetting that alcohol is a drug. I finally returned to the program, driven by liver disease that turned out to be hepatitis C. I started the steps again, but dug in my heels at Step Three. God was the one who put me in this male body where I would be forever trapped because of a deadly virus. Perhaps the new HIV medications could keep me alive, but so what? I'd be a freak for the rest of my life. I didn't want anything to do with God.

For two years all I did was go to meetings, but eventually I got away from even doing that. At three and a half years clean I found myself diving into deep depressions. Sudden rage was always close to the surface; I treated myself badly. I didn't want to use, though. I wanted to kill myself. Instead, I got a new sponsor, went back to Step One, and attended ninety meetings in ninety days. This time I worked the steps like I never had before. I studied the literature as if I were preparing for final exams. I wrote an essay on each step. I spent weeks on an exhaustive Fourth Step, and took an entire afternoon doing Five with my sponsor. I didn't hesitate when it came to Eight and Nine, either. I even made amends to people who'd screwed me over big time, because this was my spiritual housecleaning, not theirs. Within a year I'd completed all the steps as thoroughly as I could.

Over that year I noticed subtle changes. I wasn't so quick to anger, and I was much kinder to myself. Most of all, I no longer lived in perpetual fear or self-pity. My spiritual awakening came not in a flash of light, but slowly, over time. The first big test came at my fourth NA birthday, when the company I'd worked at for twelve years had massive layoffs. For some reason I didn't panic like I used to. Instead, I took a deep breath and looked for a new position in the corporation. Out of the blue I was offered a better position. The miracle of that ordeal was not the last-minute job offer but the calm response so unusual for me. It was the first sign of my growing faith.

The reason I now have an unshakable faith may seem strange, but it was my most powerful moment of spiritual awakening. In 2001 I learned of a gifted surgeon who could make me physically complete as a woman, despite my HIV. The catch was that my immune system had to hold steady. My T-cell count, the primary indicator of my health, has always fluctuated, and I tearfully confessed my worries to my sponsor. She told me I had to turn it over to my Higher Power, reminding me, "If you're supposed to have this surgery, then you'll have it." As my eyes filled with helpless tears, she gently asked me, "Who's in charge?"

It was what I wanted least and needed most to hear. By the time I hit my knees for my nightly prayer, I had turned it over. I slept like a baby that night. A few days before my surgery I had a stunning realization: My Higher Power had always known what was best for me. When I didn't get my way about whatever it was that I wanted, I'd never before stopped to consider that perhaps things happened for a reason.

I finally understand that I was denied this surgery in 1992 because I wasn't ready for it. I skimped on my recovery and mouthed platitudes about God, but I was nearly as fearful and self-centered as when I had a needle in my arm. I didn't really trust my Higher Power, and I could not have handled this roller-coaster ride. I thought I was ready, but God knew otherwise. It was actually a blessing that I was forced to wait. I just hope this profound lesson carries to the next time I don't get what I want when I want it.

I write this coming up on my ninth NA birthday, grateful my hepatitis is in remission, and I am nearly three years off nicotine. Aside from being clean, the greatest gift is true faith in my Higher Power, whom I choose to call Goddess. Faith helped me get past the disease that used to rule me. Whenever I catch myself drifting back into my defects, I just remember that Goddess is in charge. All I need to do is live the principles of the program to the best of my ability, and She will take care of the rest.

This Iroquois descendant ended up in an institution for "hard cases." When NA members brought a meeting in and shared, it was like seeing himself in the mirror for the first time.

A Textbook Case

I am an addict. In Narcotics Anonymous, I have learned what that means: who we are, what we share in common, where our nature leads us, and how together we recover.

My family descends from Canyenkehaka, the Iroquois people Europeans call Mohawks. I was taught that within all creatures dwells a soul which desires only peace and comfort, by the warming fire of the heart. The soul is the keeper of the spirit, which yearns to fly beyond the body and mind. We may be one with the Great Spirit only when our souls let go, setting our spirits free. This concept of spirituality makes sense to me. However, my soul is dark. Anything I let go of is covered with claw marks. Spiritual recovery began for me when I discovered Narcotics Anonymous and started working the Twelve Steps and living the NA way.

Early on I lost the simple faith I was born with. Oversensitive and exposed without it, I turned in on myself. My belief is that my soul took my spirit hostage out of fear and locked it away. I became a remote child living in a world of dreams. Perhaps I was always an addict. I attributed magical qualities to people, places, and things, as if a cure for my emptiness lay with them. Other troubled kids, secret hideouts, and toys at first—and lovers, hangouts, and drugs later—all became objects of obsession for me.

When I was seven years old I broke my leg pretty badly. I learned about unbearable pain and the horror and terror that attend it, and the ability of a chemical to relieve me of pain and fear. It was miraculous. Just like that, my problems disappeared. My bones were still broken. What mattered was that I didn't feel it.

Three things characterized my drug use from the start. First, I knew it was wrong, which made it more attractive. Second, I used to remove distress, whether physical, emotional, or psychic—generally rendering myself unconscious in the effort. And third, no consequences could dissuade me from using.

I took bizarre risks. By the time I was fourteen I had broken both arms, both legs, and a front tooth, and was rewarded with painkillers every time. I got into trouble with the authorities, and when I was old enough, got arrested. I was angry and self-righteous. My drug use steadily advanced. I was addicted to all kinds of things: to chemicals, sex, relationships, gambling, theft, and escapism in whatever form; to risk-taking, rule-breaking, overeating, overspending, overindulging, even to the chaos of my daily life. I was enslaved to impulsive thinking and compulsive behavior. I tried for a dozen years to quit, but nothing ever worked.

I ended up in an institution for hard cases, from criminals to psychotics. We all ate together in a big dining hall. My first day there I got stabbed with a fork when I sat in a chair occupied by a woman's imaginary friend. I remember looking around at all the other lost souls—hallucinating schizoids, catatonics, wet-brained lifers sulking in silent remorse, wrist-slashing teens who snorted saccharine off the tables—and I realized I belonged. The sum of all my resources and experience had landed me here. This was my family now. I realized the true extent of my illness, but I had no inkling of what ailed me.

One day several people from outside the facility came to speak. They introduced themselves as addicts, members of Narcotics Anonymous. They read from a little white book, and what I could grasp made sense to me. One of them told her story. She spoke of feelings that I had always had but never heard put into words. Then other people talked. I identified with their struggles and recognized the despair they'd felt. Yet they were full of hope and humor, which I found suspect. I decided that they were preaching some cult of temperance. Still, what I heard struck a chord. I showed up to hear more when they came back around.

When I was released I asked for Narcotics Anonymous meetings in my area. I listened as people shared their experience. Some had been through much tougher times than me. Others spoke of extended "clean time" or "coming back" from a relapse, both of which gave me hope. What fascinated me was the ability of NA members to express their feelings, good and bad. At one meeting this guy ran his hand down the center of his chest, saying, "This is the Grand Canyon." Another time a woman pointed at her head and called it "a thousand clowns on a carousel." Another spoke tearfully about a recent relapse and said, "I know I have a disease of shame, but this feels like shame times ten." That struck me like a sledgehammer. Clearly, this was where I needed to be.

While making meetings and learning about the nature of addiction, I was still hanging out with old friends in old places. After six weeks, I picked up. But now no amount of drugs could suppress the revulsion I felt about what I was doing. I fell back to old thinking and behavior, which divested me of any sense of humanity. Those were the worst ten months of my life.

During that run, I internalized what I had heard at NA meetings. It was true about the progressive nature of my illness. Staying clean for a time hadn't cured me. It was true about the involuntary nature of my destructiveness, my complete inability to control myself through willpower. I could see things that had brought about my relapse. Instead of sticking with people in the fellowship, I had run back to my using buddies. I had never worked the steps or taken a sponsor. The first time I read the Twelve Steps, I realized they were the most radical principles I had ever come across. But I couldn't be bothered with all that "spiritual nonsense."

The day came when I couldn't go on. I was sick of myself and felt nothing but anger, disgust, and shame. When I went to an

NA meeting, sat down in the front, and cried, I came in out of the cold for the last time.

I'd come to believe that the group was a power greater than myself which could restore me to sanity. With that hope, I started taking suggestions. I reached out for a sponsor to lead me through the steps. I made a decision to turn my life over to a loving Spirit which I could pray to. I asked in humble sincerity for relief from my self-destructiveness. My urge to use was lifted. It has never returned.

What a caring and wonderful family. We love, respect, support, and protect one another. Together, we reach out to newcomers. We sponsor our individual and collective spiritual growth. We carry the NA message of hope and freedom to suffering addicts. And we love and care for one another until we learn to love and care for ourselves.

Today, when I am challenged, angry, frightened, or confused, I work steps. Our steps work miracles in my life every time I practice them. In Narcotics Anonymous, I've learned who I am and what that requires of me. I learned that I am a "textbook case"—which is good, since we have a textbook solution in our Basic Text. I have learned to live on life's terms, to be grateful for Nature's blessings. And I pray daily to the Higher Power I was reunited with in NA: "Great Spirit, let my soul be at peace, my spirit free, and my mind untroubled and clean."

The process of recovery and the spiritual principles of NA
are a power greater than himself for this atheist addict.

Atheists Recover Too

I grew up without a teaching of god. My father, though raised in a very devout family, renounced all faith in the religion he had been taught. I too couldn't believe that there was something out there that had some magical power to do the impossible—to defy the laws of physics. There were many things beyond my understanding, but to attribute them to a deity was, in my mind, just another way of avoiding the fear of the unknown. Too many people used god, or the devil, as it were, to deflect credit due or to avoid taking responsibility for their mistakes. I viewed the institution of religion as a means of controlling the masses, and I didn't want to be controlled.

I made it my mission to refute this god in which other people believed and put their faith, but they resisted. In fact, in spite of all my efforts, I convinced not one person that they were wrong and that I was right. I just isolated myself all the more.

So, when I got clean I was apprehensive, to say the least. However, I was ready for a new way of life, so I just focused on today, and just for today I was on Step One. And there was no god in Step One. I got a sponsor who taught me about showing up and being dependable. He taught me about how to be available and not to be judgmental. He shared his experience and allowed me mine. The foundation of my recovery was laid in our relationship. I wanted what he had and was beginning to get it.

We moved on to Step Two, and it was time to cross the god bridge. I went on a quest to find a power greater than myself. I stepped out of my comfort zone and sought out people of both conventional and unconventional religious faiths. I opened my mind to what worked for others. I questioned, I listened, and I practiced. My search brought me to a number of different spiritual and religious groups, but I didn't find my place among any of them. What I was looking for was something quantifiable, something tangible to put on display — "See this? This is what I believe. This is the god of my understanding." Maybe if I could find that god, recovery would be easier. But that's not what I found.

With no breakthroughs, feeling lost and dejected, I decided to approach Step Two another way. Perhaps the steps, the fellowship, service, and my sponsor would be enough to help me find recovery, without a god.

Steps Three, Seven, and Eleven posed the greatest challenge because of their references to god and prayer. Steps Two and Six required some creative thinking as well. In practicing the Second Step, NA and the group became a power greater than me. By participating and being of service I was able to put the needs of the group and the suffering addict before my wants. My self-centeredness began to ease, and a restoration to sanity began to take place. I was right where I was supposed to be. I could see that my struggles weren't in vain, even when times were hard. I was experiencing life and growing as a result.

In the Third Step, I began turning my will and my life over to the process of recovery and to the spiritual principles that could be found in the steps. I was told to be honest about my belief, even if it was devoid of a god; otherwise the remaining steps would be of no value. I started to have faith in what recovery could offer me. With the strength and courage I found, I continued with the rest of the steps.

In Step Six, my defects of character were in the forefront of my mind. As I became more aware of their effects on my life, I tried to control my defects by suppressing them. The result was that they seemed to become worse, causing more harm, both to those close to me and to myself. I reached the place where I was entirely ready to be rid of my defects, and I moved on to Step Seven.

Believing that humility was an important aspect of the Seventh Step, I went to others for their experience. By earnestly seeking the experience of others, including those with whom I had little in common, I was performing acts of humility. I endeavored to live life by spiritual principles in order to relieve my shortcomings. Instead of merely trying to be rid of my shortcomings, I sought to replace them with something positive.

Step Eleven was a bit of a conundrum. "I'm an atheist who believes in the power of prayer," I became known for saying. The statement, meant to shock people, became a conviction. Prayer wasn't getting on my knees and petitioning a deity. Rather, it was how I lived. As a prayer, all my decisions became important and relevant, regardless of how insignificant they might seem on the surface. I saw meditation as a tool or exercise to help expand my awareness. It helped to put me in the moment and to maintain my presence of mind throughout the day.

The result was a spiritual awakening, a realization that I could stay clean, work the steps, be an upstanding member of Narcotics Anonymous, have a life worth living, and carry a message of recovery. All this was possible without a god. My initial fear of not being able to stay clean because I could not "come to believe" in a god had passed. I now had proof that it was possible, and the proof was in how I lived.

I have sponsored many people, some who struggle with believing in god and others who have a firm religious faith. Those who struggle find that they are not alone and are accepted as they are. Those with strong faith find that they too can share openly with me, and their beliefs are welcomed and accepted. Either way, my sponsees and I have the opportunity to grow together. I trust that what they come to believe has the power to help them, and they have the same trust in what I have come to believe. Sometimes we disagree on the particulars, but the particulars aren't what keep us clean. What keeps us clean is the choice that each of us makes not to pick up and to live this way of life to the best of our ability.

This is a spiritual program, not a religious one. I try different approaches to working the steps. I still read and try to expand my knowledge on spiritual topics, and I constantly review my experience and contemplate its meaning in my life. This isn't to say that I don't question what I believe from time to time, or that I don't struggle, because I do. Life isn't always easy. Sometimes I feel alone during hard times. Believing in a god is alluring, because I know others find comfort there, but I do not. Today I do have a spiritual solution, however. The steps provide me with a framework for applying spiritual principles. Service acts as a conduit to relieve my self-centered thinking. The fellowship reminds me that I'm not alone, and my sponsor is a guide through the process. I continue to be a seeker. Anyone with a desire to stay clean can stay clean.

*She got clean with her husband of twenty years,
and eight years later nursed him through terminal cancer
while both of her parents were terminally ill. Now,
at sixty-one, she shares that the program can help
any of us, regardless of age or circumstance.*

Never Alone

I am sixty-one years old and have been clean for fifteen years. My husband and I got clean at the same time. He was fifty-two at the time and I was forty-six. We had children older than most of the people in our meetings. NA seemed to us to be a bunch of young kids. I didn't think we could relate.

Even though we were the oldest people we saw at meetings, we stayed and heard the message of recovery in NA: that any addict can live clean and lose the desire to use. We went to a meeting every evening. Sitting in the rooms day after day with the same bunch of kids, we heard them telling our own stories. We heard people talking about the feeling of despair their addiction had led them to and the pain of trying to quit and not being able to. Hearing these stories, we knew that regardless of age, the pain of addiction was the same for everyone, and this was where we belonged. Eventually, we even met a few other folks our age.

I had been using since I was a small child when I'd raid my mother's medicine cabinet. In high school my best friend's father was an anesthesiologist. We would use the *Physicians' Desk Reference* like a catalog to decide what to take. Around this time, another friend turned me on to pot. She said, "Smoke this." I wanted to be as cool as she was, so I did. For the next thirty-three years I chased drugs from coast to coast and made them the center of my existence.

In the late 1960s and early 1970s it seemed that all of America had discovered drugs. I felt like I was in the vanguard of culture.

But when the rest of the country seemed to stop using, I didn't. When I finally wanted to, I couldn't.

Finally, at some point in the late 1980s, my husband became depressed. Imagine that! You fill your body with depressants and wonder why you're depressed. He went to treatment for his addiction and was introduced to NA there. He moved into a boarding house and went to meetings and tried to stay clean even though he was still buying drugs for me. He lasted three months that way, and then relapsed and went on a three-year run.

Meanwhile, I was using more than ever. I was strung out on something I didn't even like. Eventually the day came when I realized I couldn't give up the drugs, so I gave up on life. I knew there were people who didn't use drugs, and clearly their lives were better than the lives of anyone I knew who did use, certainly better than my life. But it never occurred to me that I could change, that I could be a different person, one who didn't use. I didn't want to do this anymore, and I couldn't see any way to stop. So I bought a huge piece and did it all. And God stepped into my life.

Even though it was the middle of the day in the middle of the week, my son stopped over at my house. To this day he doesn't know why he dropped by. He found me passed out but still alive and called an ambulance. This had not been a cry for help like I'd done in times past. This time I was seriously trying to die. I woke up in the hospital in five-point restraints.

I was given a choice between a ten-day voluntary commitment and an indefinite involuntary commitment. I chose to go voluntarily. The big surprise was the sense of relief I felt. I didn't have to pretend that I was okay. I didn't have to struggle to keep it together anymore. I needed help, and I was going to get it.

My husband had been to NA before, so he knew what to do. He would come to the hospital, pick me up on a pass, and take me to a meeting. Then he'd drop me off back at the hospital, go home, and get loaded. When the ten days were up and I was ready to come home, he realized that he would have to stay clean if I were to stay clean. So we both went to a meeting. It was his first day, and I had ten days more.

For the first year, we went to a meeting every day—sometimes two or three. We got sponsors, worked the steps, and did all of our socializing in NA. We had service positions. We got a home group. We made friends. We realized that the age difference was irrelevant because our feelings were the same as everyone else's.

It was hard at first doing the step work. Steps One, Two, and Three weren't too hard because the powerlessness and unmanageability were self-evident. I knew that I was alive because of a Higher Power. But Step Four was a different matter. How was I supposed to write about forty-six years of resentments and bad behavior? I had no idea whom I had hurt, ripped off, or damaged. I figured it was pretty much everyone I'd ever been near. I was guided by a more experienced member who told me my Higher Power would reveal what I needed to see at that time. I'd get to do the steps again, and more things would come up then. That made it possible for me to move on.

When I was in the middle of my Eighth Step I was invited to visit my family for a week. They lived 3,000 miles away from my home. I quickly went over my Ninth Step work with my sponsor so that I would be able to make amends to my mother, stepfather, brother, and sister-in-law all in one week. They all said the only amends I could make for them was to stay clean.

Life got good. I went to school and got a bachelor's and then a graduate degree. I started my own psychotherapy practice. My father even said he was proud of me, something he'd never said before in my life.

When I had six years clean, a friend with more experience in NA died of cancer. The fellowship gathered around him and supported him through his illness. In addition to the home health care provider, two addicts were with him at all times. One of his sponsees moved in and slept there. He talked about his experience as he was dying; he said he was growing from a thorn into a rose. He died clean, with great dignity and strength. He had taught us how to live clean, and he taught us how to die clean.

Two years later my husband was diagnosed with cancer. My father was dying of cancer, and my mother was ill with heart disease. Getting clean gives us the opportunity to deal with the conditions of our lives, whether we like them or not, in a way that we can feel good about. It doesn't matter what happens; it matters how I react when it happens. Losing my husband or my son was the only reservation in my First Step.

I went to meetings and talked about my reservations. I was afraid I wouldn't be able to stay clean without my husband. I wasn't sure I wanted to stay alive without him. We had been together for twenty-eight years, raised children together, traveled together, cared for one another through the worst years of our addiction, and gotten clean together. Since we had gotten clean, our relationship had deepened and flowered into one of deep mutual respect and unconditional love. He was my heart. I couldn't imagine life without him.

My husband was ill for six months. During that time we traveled to Mexico and to Hawaii. We went to the world convention in San Jose. It was there that I first learned how to reach out and ask for help. The people in the program were wonderful during his illness. His sponsees, my sponsor and sponsees, and friends from the fellowship all called often and came frequently to visit. One of my sponsees is a nurse. She wasn't working at the time, so she would come on a moment's notice to relieve me if I needed to go out. Loving, caring people surrounded us all of the time. Our hospice social worker, who had nursed another NA friend, told us that NA was the best support system he had ever seen.

I wasn't able to see my father before he died, because he died only eleven days before my husband. My mother died eighteen months after that. I was terrified that now I would be alone. I thought the pain of all that loss would turn my heart to ice. I thought I would suffocate because I couldn't breathe. The only thing I could think to do was to go to a meeting. I talked about my pain. I continued to talk about it until I thought people were running away when they saw me coming. I reached out to my Higher Power. I stayed on an Eleventh Step for the next several years. I came to know and to trust my Higher Power, whose only wish for me is that I use the opportunities life provides me with to heal and grow.

It was, and remains, very difficult. But I have not had to use. I've stayed connected to my program. I go to three to six meetings every week, even now. I have a sponsor. I work the steps. I sponsor many women. I do service, and I read the literature. I have a spiritual community and my faith, trust, and relationship with God have deepened and grown strong. I have good days and bad days. I still have so much to learn about how to live clean. When it gets tough, I go to a meeting or call a friend or work with a sponsee or help someone else or pray and pray and pray. I work Step Twelve by trying to practice the spiritual principles I have learned in NA in all of my affairs, both within and outside the rooms.

My life is full. I am so grateful to NA for taking a wounded, sick little girl of forty-six and teaching her how to live—clean.

*The youngest person in the room, this addict still felt
a connection right away and over time came to realize
that recovery from addiction is a bond that transcends age.*

Regardless of Age

The first NA member I ever spoke to was the same age as my mother. I have been clean since the summer after my freshman year of high school.[20] I'd been using drugs for just a few months. Those were the worst months of my life. In that short amount of time I had been placed in police custody, expelled from high school, and forced by my parents to check into a rehab. I knew I had a problem and I knew I needed help. The first time I had heard of Narcotics Anonymous was when I saw it listed on a brochure from my rehab. I didn't have a whole lot of options, so I decided to give it a shot. The first thing I noticed about NA was that everyone was much older than me. It was rare to see anyone within ten years of my age. These people were getting high before I was even born. When I was in kindergarten playing with blocks, they were dealing drugs, getting arrested, and living in the depths of active addiction. What could I possibly have in common with these old guys?

This question was answered before the meeting even started when an NA member who could easily have been my mother asked me if I was an addict. It was the first time anyone had asked me that and I didn't know what to say. I didn't need to say anything. I felt something. There was a connection between the two of us that transcended age. I could feel it in her voice, in her eyes, and in her spirit. There was something there that I hadn't felt before and I wanted to feel again.

I sat in the very back of the room. I don't remember anything that was shared at that meeting, but I remember hearing in the readings that "anyone may join us regardless of age." That was

---

[20] "Freshman" year is the first year of high school.

all I needed to hear. I was so desperate to fit in somewhere and belong to something that I just clung to those words and kept coming back. The more I listened to people sharing, the less I thought of their age. When I socialized with members after a meeting and went out for dinner, they ceased to be "older people" and became my friends. When I would tell them how I felt, they responded with a recognition that I could never get from nonaddicts my own age.

I am now in my third year of college and am living quite a peculiar life for a college student. On Friday nights when most of my classmates are out partying with drugs, I go to my home group of NA. I share about how I'm feeling, what I need to work on, and how I think I can get better. I go out after the meeting with other addicts who are over twice my age. I am still most often the youngest person at many meetings. It is a rare and precious gift to have the opportunity to get clean early in life. Recovery is a lifelong process, and I am grateful to have my whole life ahead of me. I need all the time I can get. When I see young people walk into a meeting, I try to carry the message that recovery is possible at any age. It can be tempting to think that I'm not sick enough for recovery. I didn't use hard enough drugs. My bottom wasn't low enough. As my sponsor told me, your bottom is wherever you choose to stop digging. Membership doesn't depend on extensive previous experience.

I try to give back to the younger members of NA. When I carry the NA message into juvenile treatment centers, I feel deeply grateful that I have been given a message that I now have the opportunity to give back. When I reach out and talk to young newcomers, I am reminded of where I started out and how far I've grown in recovery. A few years ago I got the opportunity to speak at a workshop called "Youth in Recovery" at my regional convention. I took this service commitment in a genuine spirit of humility. As I looked out at the crowd full of teenagers and young adults, I felt the presence of my higher power. I had never seen so many young addicts before. The room looked like a college lecture hall. Here were all these addicts just like me. I realized that I'm not so different after all. After the meeting, a teenager told me that I had shared his story. I can't begin to count how many times I've sat at meetings and thought the speaker was sharing my story, whether they were around my age or much older. I know that there will always be people with whom I can relate, on the level of specific experiences and on the spiritual level.

It's an odd thing when older members tell me that I'm so lucky to get clean so young. Yes, I am very lucky, and so is every other member of Narcotics Anonymous. I prefer to think of myself as a part of a fellowship full of fortunate souls, rather than some kind of exceptionally lucky individual. I can get off track when I start thinking of myself as different from other NA members. The bottom line is that anyone may join us and feel just as much a part of the program as anyone else.

I'll always remember the time I was in a meeting with only one other member. There was a terrible blizzard out, but I happened to live very close to the meeting so I walked there anyway. The only other person there was fifty years older than me. I hadn't even entered the workforce yet, and he was already retired. I had heard him share before about feeling different because everyone else was so much younger than him. That night, we shared about our lives and our experiences. The details were different but the feelings and the spirit were the same. The point couldn't have been made clearer to me. We are a fellowship with a diverse range of experiences and one common identity: recovering addicts.

As a PhD student in pharmacology, his knowledge of drugs almost killed him. Now he is a professor with more than twenty years clean and an understanding that recovery is not a science.

Academic Addict

The squawking voice on the police radio blared a description of me to the authorities. I ran into the freezing morning and began a zigzag trip to my apartment. I turned my jacket inside out so the color would be different. I was crawling through people's backyards in a Midwestern college town, an emaciated, drug-addled junior Rambo. I anxiously asked neighbors if they had seen any police around, my eyes bugging in panic, jacket inside out, sleepless for days. With their nervous assurance that they hadn't seen anyone, I went inside, threw away my stash, and crashed into a deep sleep, despite the looming raid.

That I heard the "police broadcast" in a bathroom of a deserted university building at 4:00 am on the day before Thanksgiving didn't cross my mind. The delusion of my imminent arrest felt absolutely real, and it fueled my panicked and pathetic reaction. I had been mainlining a relative of methamphetamine for three days without sleep, and the overdose had caused temporary psychosis.

I found this particular drug in the pharmacology department where I was a PhD student.[21] It was the latest substance obtained from my continuous foraging. My studies had become a hollow cover story; the search for drugs was my main activity. This went on around fellow students, staff, and professors who were growing increasingly concerned with my strange behavior and worsening appearance. As awareness grew that substances were walking out of laboratories, security measures kept improving. The foraging got harder and my standards got lower, while my

---

[21] "Pharmacology" is the science of drug action.

appetite for drugs kept increasing. I wouldn't call chemically induced paranoid schizophrenia a quality high, but I was way past the point where using had the remotest connection to recreation. Drugs had become the center of my life.

"The Night of the Police Raid" is just one story from the bottom I experienced before I could seek help. The consequences of my using—getting evicted by a girlfriend who had finally given up; my gray complexion; my arms and legs covered with needle marks; the complete decay of my routine; the channeling of all my energy, resources, and creativity to find drugs; endangering the careers and reputations of my colleagues—made it clear even to me that I had a problem with drugs. Near the end, I admitted that death by an overdose would provide an out. That was where addiction had taken me. All I had was fear and the need to take drugs at any cost. My key delusion was that my problem only involved me; either I could solve it, or no one could. Isolation paves the road to active addiction, and it nearly killed me.

My actions did finally bring about a solution, but not the one I imagined. In a bathroom stall I injected one drug to counteract the effects of another. I collapsed, waking to find two freaked-out custodians thinking I was dead. I was put in the hospital, and kicked out of the PhD program with the warning that if I entered the building, the police would be called. My science career ended, and my recovery began.

Getting kicked out of graduate school was the best thing that ever happened to me. No, I didn't suddenly stop using; I wasn't done yet. But something had changed. That loss, together with all the others, made me admit that perhaps I couldn't manage my problem. I had a sense that maybe things could be different, but I still didn't know anything about living clean. That was for other people to show me.

The disease of addiction cuts across all social and economic boundaries. When people have this illness, drugs will find them. The routes can vary enormously, but the destination is always the same. I didn't grow up in an abusive family. I lived in an affluent town and was educated in an excellent public school system. I had a comfortable home and a family that was loving but perplexed by my self-destructive behavior. I had talent, health, opportunities, friends, and material support by any measure. But I am different from normal people; I am hard-wired for addiction. I can see now that some of my earliest thoughts and behaviors gave hints of what was to come.

I found ways to get high, the usual things that people do in school. But for me these experiences felt important. I vividly remember the first time I got drunk, the first time I used each of a long list of drugs. My using seemed controlled, but I got high every day of high school, and whatever drugs were around were part of the mix. In college I regularly did outlandish, selfish, and dangerous things to get high. I loved being a student and learning, but the parallel life of constant using was always there.

The addict inside me is incredibly resourceful at finding and using drugs. When it was time for graduate school, I really did find pharmacology fascinating. But that choice also made drugs accessible to someone with no "street smarts." In the years that followed, a lethal process operated alongside my legitimate interests. Eventually, as goals got in the way of using, they fell by the wayside. The progression of my disease could be gauged by a series of bargains I made and broke with myself to manage my using. "I'll never use during the week" fell to "I'll never use during the day" fell to "I'll never inject drugs" fell to "I'll never let this hurt my career" fell to drugs becoming my career. My academic expertise about drugs was a dangerous hindrance to my recovery. I was convinced my knowledge of drugs would make them more manageable. I now realize that this is like a ballistics expert thinking he is bullet-proof. My arrogance and delusion would be funny if they hadn't come so close to doing me in.

My recovery started with the undeserved kindness of one of the many professors I had screwed over while using. In an act of pure generosity, he found a drug counselor who would not be fooled by my tendency to manipulate people with my education. In my first sessions with him, I looked terrible, sounded crazy, and thought I had it totally together. But somewhere in my deluded brain was the desire to change. That counselor was the first person I had ever met who called himself an addict and had figured out how to live without drugs. That was intriguing; I wanted to know more. He first earned my trust, and then after a few weeks he sprang the trap: "If you want to keep coming here, then you have to do something else." More tests? Reading assignments? Visits to medical doctors? No. "If you want to keep coming to me, you also have to start going to meetings." Although I was skeptical and afraid, I decided I'd better go. A manipulative addict successfully manipulated by a recovering addict!

I went in with my "difference radar" turned way up, finding all sorts of ways I was distinct from those people, not part of that crowd. I was arrogant and judgmental, looking at the superficial differences instead of the underlying similarities. However, there was one difference that surprised me. I had figured the steps would be some sort of instruction set about not using—"Step One: We don't take opiates. Step Two: We don't inject anything...." But when I heard the Twelve Steps read out loud, they didn't even mention drugs! Here was a room full of people who were keeping clean using a set of ideas that had never crossed my mind. Since my ideas about keeping clean had failed miserably, I found hope in the fact that these people were doing something different, and getting different results.

Some people experience recovery like a lightning bolt: a sudden flash of understanding and clarity, an immediate lifting of the desire to use. The effect of the program on me was more like rain or wind, gradually eroding my false beliefs. It is a process that continues each day I stay clean. I gradually learned that I have an incurable, lethal disease, that having it is not my fault, but that seeking recovery is my responsibility. I slowly came to understand that fellowship is toxic to addiction, and that isolation is a prerequisite for relapse. I still need to be reminded that my best information about recovery is heard from others, and not my own loud head. I still struggle with the truth that in recovery, good action often comes before full understanding; it makes the scientist in me bristle. Some days I learn something new, and others I feel like I am making no progress at all. But so long as I stay clean, the slow pace of my recovery is not a problem. There's no end to the process, so there's no need to hurry.

The life I have is the unlikely gift of recovery. I am a professor at a large university. My colleagues are incredibly bright, creative, and energetic; I am humbled to work with them, and honored by their trust and respect. I have long-lasting friendships in and out of NA, a healthy relationship with my family, and the luxury of earning a living doing what I love and respect. I am truly blessed, and it all springs from living the NA way. That doesn't mean my life is perfect. I have problems, fears, frustrations, and a constant struggle with low self-esteem. But I can imagine where I would be had I not gotten clean. I recall a high school acquaintance named Mike. We had very similar paths. We both were interested in science, both ended up in pharmacology departments, both used heavily, both thought our knowledge would protect us. But Mike died from an overdose over twenty years ago. My life is a gift, no matter what the day's details involve, and I owe that to recovery.

"You can have anything you want, so long as you're willing to pay for it." This is an NA "chestnut" we often hear in the rooms. For me, this is not only about what I might want, but also about what I have already received. My sponsor told me that every day I have clean is a debt owed to NA, so I am willing to pay for the recovery I have today. The price of my continued growth in recovery is offering the same gift to others. When I didn't have the experience to know about this path, others, both addicts and nonaddicts, helped me find the way. They were doing my Higher Power's work, and now it is my turn to do the same by participating in the recovery of others. When I think about things this way, it is clear to me why fellowship is the foundation of recovery.

Even with over twenty years clean, I still have to fight the urge to distance myself from people at meetings by focusing on differences. But now I know this is just my disease showing its discomfort with NA. I always try to look for the similarities between me and my fellow addicts. But that doesn't mean we are all the same. In NA, unity is not uniformity, and there is no better example of this than how different addicts can be. NA is a big enough house for every sort of person. We can speak any language, have any politics or ideas about our Higher Power, and come from any upbringing. In this diverse and growing group of people there is someone for everyone, as a sponsor, a confidant, or a trusting newcomer. It is our diversity that makes recovery possible for anyone. No addict ever needs to feel that they don't belong, whether they know the ivory tower or the guard tower.

*When NA first started in Japan, even members didn't believe
a normal life could be possible for addicts, and especially women,
in recovery. As the fellowship matured, this member and
others like her came to realize "there is no model
of the recovering addict."*

What Makes Me Happy Now

It took me about ten years to realize I could be an NA member
and live a normal life. Before I got clean, it seemed that there
were hardly any women in Japan who were addicted to drugs. I
seemed to be alone. No one in my family knew anything about
addiction, and no one around me talked about it. The women
in NA are very special to me because when I got clean I was
the only one. I was told that as an addict, I should avoid having
children. The fellowship thought that if I had a baby I wouldn't
come to meetings anymore. No one had experience to share
about having children in recovery. Now I know that my recovery
is not short-term—this is a life-long program, and there might
be times when I can't go to meetings. But back then, we thought
that if you couldn't go to a meeting every day then you would go
back to using. We had no history or experience.

In those first years of NA, we went to AA meetings as well,
and many members, including my AA sponsor, used to tell me,
"How dare you get married and have kids before you get well?"
Those early members didn't have any role models themselves.
My son, who is fourteen years old now, was the first to be born
from a couple active in the NA program in Japan. Everyone
watched him grow. People said that my husband and I were going to divorce at any moment. We've been together for nineteen
years now. Our life is normal.

When I first joined NA twenty-two years ago, there were about
ten members. The seven of us from Tokyo would take the bullet
train to visit three members in Osaka. Every time we got together

we would talk about how to spread the NA message. In the first five years there was hardly any growth in the fellowship. We had to look for newcomers. When we heard there was an addict in a mental institution far away, we would go there and talk through the bars. We were doing service work with hospitals and institutions and public information on a regular basis, but we had no connections with physicians. My husband would just walk into a mental institution and ask if there were any addicts there. He would go to very small towns in the hills and talk to the addicts in the institutions, even those who had no intention of stopping. Once in a while, a hospital would ask us to come back. We would take the bullet train to go see just one addict. It was very important for us to keep doing that. I would go watch TV with women addicts in mental institutions. Anything. As NA members, what we really needed was more members.

Because there were so few of us, I felt a lot of pressure to try to be a perfect NA member. At that time, NA was where very young men—kids who were fifteen or sixteen—and older Yakuzas went.[22] When I was new in NA I didn't want to be seen with men who had tattoos all over their bodies and lizard-leather shoes, and I was afraid of some of them. It took many years for some of our members to move on from who they used to be, and to understand that being a boss on the street is different from being a sponsor. A perfect NA member attends meetings regularly, but sometimes it can be really scary for a woman to go to meetings.

As the fellowship in Japan grew, we translated more NA literature. Once we were able to read the message in our language, the program became much clearer. I was shocked to read that drugs were not the major problem for us, but that the problem is our obsessive thinking and compulsive behavior. When I read that I thought, *This is it! This is the life I have been living.*

The women in the fellowship were profoundly affected by the NA message. They would talk about hitting their bottom prior to using drugs. When anyone stops using, it means dealing with

---

[22] *Yakuza* is the Japanese mafia.

emotional pain on a daily basis, and women addicts in Japan often have abusive relationships in which physical abuse, on top of
emotional and psychological pain, are part of life. Many women
shared how drugs were a good thing for them, until their using
became unmanageable. I didn't understand this until the new
translation. These women also had a hard time with the word *recover*. In Japanese, *recover* means "to go back to the way you used
to be." Survivors of abuse don't want to go back to the way they
used to be. In recovery, they want to move on and grow. People
who had nothing to start with were afraid that they really had
nothing to recover. As we started to read the new translations, it
clarified that women in Japan were sharing the same experience
as members around the world.

When we share, our stories light the way for other people. If
we don't share, we are alone in the darkness. And when we do
share, our experiences become part of everyone else's experience. Many Japanese women addicts shared in meetings about
their experiences with sexual abuse and domestic violence. It
was always said that nobody is sexually abused in Japan. Holding onto that story kept us alone in the dark. But sharing with
each other in NA has changed the culture in Japan. All of these
women addicts began sharing their stories, and now people talk
about domestic violence and sexual abuse as real problems. Nobody believed us for so long. I couldn't even believe it myself.

I had a hard time when my child was born because I was home
caring for him. My husband was always busy, and so I never
really was a perfect member because I couldn't go to meetings
consistently. What I did instead, for my first ten years or so clean,
was answer calls from NA members at home. Everybody in NA
knew our home phone number, so it was just like the helpline.
On a typical day, I would be taking care of my child and answering calls about where the meetings were. There are many different ways to serve the program. Even though I couldn't get to
meetings regularly, I was still carrying the message.

During this hard time, I found a new sponsor in California. There weren't many experienced NA members in Japan, so it was necessary for us to go abroad to find members who could share knowledge about the program. She was so supportive, telling me, "I am proud of you. You are doing your best. You don't need to feel guilty."

I met a group of mothers at the nursery school, and we helped each other by sharing baby-sitting. This meant I could get to some NA meetings, but then I was obligated to spend more time with their babies. I also put NA events over events at my child's school. He was always involved with NA, and he didn't have enough connections with other kids. Now I know that working the Twelve Steps is the most important thing—as long as I work the Twelve Steps, I can prioritize my life the way that seems right to me.

Recently, I lost a large amount of money in business. It was one of the worst times I have been through, and I didn't know how to get over it. I had something I believed in and it fell apart. I began to lose confidence in myself. Because of this hardship and the loss of my self-confidence, I started to work Steps Six and Seven. Once I started to see my own defects, that heavy pressure I felt began to lift. Six months later, I was considering this idea of sharing my story and describing what makes me happy. What makes me feel really happy is that right in the midst of this really difficult time, I realize that I'm a member of NA. I have the tools I was taught in this program, and I know I can use them to overcome difficulties. I don't know if I call this happiness, but I think that being an NA member who has tools makes it possible to be happy.

These hard times that I think I won't be able to overcome are really a gift from my Higher Power, and when it's over I always feel relieved. I feel the strongest connection with my Higher Power when I've made a mistake. Making mistakes breaks down my false beliefs. My Higher Power gives me an opportunity to see clearly what I really believe in: When I think that I know what success looks like in business or in my personal relationships, my Higher Power always gives me a chance to look back and see how small my thinking has been. The mistakes that I make are the biggest gifts. I know now that the goal is not to be perfect. When I first got clean, I thought it was better not to make mistakes. But now I have deep respect for those people who, no matter how many times they relapse, still come back to the program and try as best they can.

In those early years, we had a misconception about what it meant to be happy in the program. We thought that "happy in the program" meant that we became model NA members. Recently, I was talking with a member who has been in and out of the program for many years, in and out of institutions, in and out of marriages. When I first heard this, I thought his Higher Power wouldn't love him because of his failures. I, on the other hand, kept coming back to meetings for a long time and loved only one man. I had thought that a Higher Power should love a diligent member like me, not him. Thankfully, that way of thinking has completely changed within me through working the program. I said to him, "Who is actually happier? It could be you or me— we don't know. At least I cannot judge."

No matter how many times you relapse, NA still takes you back—that's the NA program. NA doesn't kick you out; instead, NA is always here for you. I really can't tell you who has the better life—the perfect NA member that I've tried to be for the last twenty years or those people who go in and out of the program. I just happened to stay clean because I was involved with the fellowship. I didn't stay clean because I tried so hard to stay away from drugs; I stayed clean because of the fear that I could not afford not to be the model NA member. I'm not that different from those members who relapse. When I think that way, I feel lighter. I feel more respect for those members who are struggling to stay clean. I believe that the Higher Power doesn't discriminate. What makes me the happiest in recovery is to see change in a fellow addict. It's always a great pleasure and surprise to see members change. No matter how many times I witness that change, it still makes me happy.

When he was new in the program, he learned that, despite his
professional background and education, he belonged in NA.
He had stayed clean since his story was published in our
First Edition and revised it himself for this edition.
Sadly, he did not live to see its publication.

I Was Unique

I had nowhere to turn. I felt like no one could help me, as my situation was so much different from others'. I thought that I was doomed to continue in an insane drive toward self-destruction that had already sapped me of any determination to fight. I thought that I was unique—that is, until I found the Fellowship of Narcotics Anonymous. Since that day, my life has had new meaning and new direction.

I came from a white, middle-class background where success was almost assumed. I excelled academically and went on to medical school in California and Scotland. I looked with smug disdain on my schoolmates who were experimenting with drugs; I felt I was too good and too smart for that. I thought that a drug addict was a weak-willed, spineless creature who must have no purpose in life or sense of worth. I would not, or could not, fall into that trap, as I was an achiever, winning at the game of life. I had such great potential.

Sometime after having started my internship at a prestigious West Coast hospital, I had my first experience with narcotics. I thought it was a curiosity; perhaps I was looking for "something better." I was amazed at the way patients in severe pain would relax when a small amount of morphine was injected into their veins. That was for me! Over the next few months my world crumbled around me. Experimentation quickly led to abuse and then addiction, with all the bewildering helplessness and self-condemnation that only the addict knows.

Shortly after I started my residency training in neurosurgery, the delusion that I could control my narcotic use evaporated. I sought help from a psychiatrist. I was hospitalized in a mental institution for a few days. Once I felt better, I convinced my psychiatrist that I was well enough to return to my training program. He was either naive, gullible, or ignorant of addiction, and let me go merrily on my way. I lasted a few months before relapsing. With no changes in my thinking or behavior, relapse followed relapse, and I established a pattern that I would maintain for almost ten years. I continued to try psychiatrists and mental institutions, but after each I would relapse again.

After having performed many surgical procedures while loaded, I was asked to leave my residency. Another hospitalization followed, and I returned to my pattern of relapse. Besides institutionalization, I tried job changes, geographical relocation, self-help books, methadone programs, only using on weekends, switching to pills, marriage, health spas, diets, exercise, and religion. None of them worked, other than temporarily. Based upon my track record, I was told I was incorrigible and that there was no hope for me.

After about five years of heavy using, I developed a physical allergy to my drug of choice. Each time I used, tissue would die around the injection site. Initially I could prevent the process by using cortisone, but it returned. In the meantime, I developed all the attendant side effects of the steroids. By the time I reached my last hospitalization, my immune system was knocked out and I was a physical wreck. Worse yet, I was totally demoralized and suffering from a spiritual bankruptcy of which I was unaware. The denial and self-deception were so great that I couldn't see what a pitiful creature I had become.

I entered a treatment facility. There, for the first time, I was confronted by physicians who were addicts themselves. They asked me first if I wanted help, and then if I was willing to go to any lengths to recover. They explained that I might have to lose all my worldly possessions, my practice, my profession, my wife and family, even my arm. At first I balked. I figured there was nothing wrong with me that a little rest and relaxation could not set right. But instead, I made a pact with them: I would listen and take orders without questioning. I had always been independent, and this was certainly a change for me. This was my first introduction to the tough love that has helped me so much in NA.

During that month in the hospital, a great change came over me. I was forced to go to outside NA meetings. At first, I was rebellious. These people were not like me; they were common junkies, dope fiends, pill-heads, tweakers, and coke freaks. How could I relate to them? They did not come from where I had. They had not experienced what I had experienced. They had not achieved what I had achieved. Yet when I listened, I heard my story, again and again. These people experienced the same feelings, the sense of loss, doom, and degradation, as I did. They too had been helpless, hopeless, and beaten down by the same hideous monster as I had. Yet they could laugh about their past and speak about the future in positive terms. There seemed to be such a balance of seriousness and levity, with an overpowering sense of serenity. I ached for what they had.

I heard about honesty, tolerance, acceptance, joy, freedom, courage, willingness, love, and humility. But the greatest thing I heard about was God. I had no problem with the concept of God, as I had called myself a believer. I just could not understand why He had let me down. I had been praying to God the way a child asks Santa Claus for gifts, yet I still held onto my self-will. Without it, I reasoned, I would have no control over my life, and could not survive. It was pointed out to me that perhaps that was the whole problem. I was told that perhaps I should seek God's will first, and then conform my will to His. Today, I pray only for His will for me and the power to carry it out on a daily basis, and all is well. I have found that His gifts are without number when I consistently turn my will and my life over to His care.

Through the process of studying, writing, working, and ultimately, living the Twelve Steps of Narcotics Anonymous I have been brought down a path which has led me to a new relationship with the God of my understanding. That alone demonstrates the power for change that the program can bring about. And that change, when multiplied through many addicts, will make the world a better place for all, addict and nonaddict alike.

Since all that I have gained from my involvement in Narcotics Anonymous has been freely and unconditionally given to me, it is incumbent upon me to freely give to others as well. I found one way I could do this is through service.

A special form of service for me has been the privilege of sponsorship. In order to remind me of my previous xenophobic attitudes, God in his infinite wisdom and humor has arranged for me to sponsor many men of diverse backgrounds. Many times the only common ground is our common disease of addiction. Differences in drugs used, ethnic origin, socioeconomic background, sexual orientation, or spiritual belief system no longer create barriers to loving, fruitful relationships. Each has taught me more than I can relate here, and it seems that the "two-way street" we speak of in relation to sponsorship is heavily weighted toward *my* personal growth and awareness. My interaction with addicts—who had been the objects of my fears—has enriched me beyond anything I expected when I arrived in the rooms of NA.

I have found a new home in the Fellowship of Narcotics Anonymous. I have found my calling in life, and that is to carry the message to the addict who still suffers. I am so grateful to God and NA that I can do this today.

The perception of differences on which I had focused was just another way my disease could separate me from you and find me "unqualified" for recovery in NA. I have found that you people are just like me. I am no longer better than or less than. I feel a real love and camaraderie in the Narcotics Anonymous Fellowship. My great spiritual awakening has been that I am an ordinary addict—I am *not* unique.

Life on Life's Terms

Recovering from addiction is about more than just not using drugs. As we stay clean, we are faced with challenges and we are graced with gifts. These addicts share about practicing the principles of the program while staying clean and living life on life's terms.

Reflections

Hepatitis C was killing me, so I had to go on medication. I had to learn to live with syringes in my house. I had to learn to *inject* the medicine at the kitchen table with the windows open, not *shoot* it like dope in the bathroom with the door closed. Taking the medication was the most painful thing I've ever done, and I had to do it for a year. That was a living hell. But it made for a damn thorough Third Step. It had to, because the treatment didn't work for me, and I need that faith. The hepatitis is still with me. I'm still an addict. The steps and my sponsor have taught me things I never imagined. I'm at peace with the world. I've got a new way of living. I might go back on the medication. I might not. I'm leaving that to my doctor and God. It'll work out. I've got NA. I've got a life.

A whole new life started when I went to college, seeking a sense of self-worth. Life was interesting, challenging, and enjoyable—pushing against the intellectual and social boundaries I was used to. Although I was broke most of the time, study was an incredible experience. My sponsor grew concerned when my meeting attendance dropped off due to the academic workload. I kept up contact with my NA support network, though, and during breaks I crammed in as many meetings as I could. I completed college with honors and went on to get a university degree. My children and my sponsor were at my graduation, and the memory of how proud they were swells my heart. I am so grateful to NA for the success I've experienced in recovery.

I'd decided one morning to donate plasma so that I could afford a bag of dope. I waited a long time in the plasma center, and it seemed strange they did not call my name. Finally, a white-robed doctor called me into his office. He bluntly said, "You've turned up HIV-positive. You are permanently deferred from the plasma program." I walked the streets, feeling numb inside. I went on a binge of unparalleled proportions. I wound up in New Mexico, nearly dead, and checked into rehab. I remember an addict talking about how much he loved NA and its principles. I broke down crying, admitting I was an addict, and was able to get active in Narcotics Anonymous.

Some time later I got a girlfriend who had HIV, and she ended up dying from AIDS. I had to spoon-feed her and take care of her. It was a horrible experience. I recall going to meetings, saying, "I can stay clean," but really wondering if that was possible. The night she died I called my sponsor and another NA friend. They came over to support me. After she was taken and everyone left, I was scared. What was I to do? And so I started writing on my Third Step, and my Higher Power showed me that if I didn't use and continued to work a program, there really wasn't anything to fear.

I could not believe I was doing this type of behavior with five years clean! I had nothing to blame it on, no excuses to give. I wasn't loaded or young and inexperienced. I was responsible, and with that awareness I felt dirty and hopeless. I came to understand fully the phrase "you're only as sick as your secrets."

The way to stop the affair, it seemed, was to tell my husband. That day began the lowest point in my life; I was intensely ashamed. Not only did I betray my husband and the guy's wife, but my fellowship was betrayed as well by the ensuing disunity the ordeal caused in our small community. I worked the steps through this chapter of my life and believe that I'd never have survived my behavior without the NA program. Eventually my husband and I reunited. He has taught me unconditional love, forgiveness, and integrity. Today we both try to help others in recovery who may be going through this situation.

One day, while peeling potatoes, I noticed weakness in my hands. I dismissed it as my arthritis acting up. Then I had numbness and tingling in my legs and feet. Soon after, I was unable to stand up and walk. I was taken to the emergency room and was eventually transferred to a physical rehabilitation hospital, where I was diagnosed with a nerve disorder. I was unable to attend meetings during this time, and my sponsor helped me so much. I continued to work on my steps and read my Basic Text. I missed meetings so much and was lonely for the outside world. After two years I was able to stand up again and take a few steps. Now I am able to get around with a walker. I am so blessed to have had the support of my sponsor and Higher Power during this tough time. I don't think I could have made it without them.

I was at my mom's, decorating for the holidays. My wife called, and she was loaded. She said awful, unrepeatable things to me. When I got home after decorating, she was on the couch, seemingly passed out. And then I saw my shotgun was lying in front of her body. I called 911 and stood there in shock, crying and cursing God. I prayed for his will for her, that something would happen so she wouldn't have to suffer anymore. I was arrested and taken as a suspect until suicide was verified as the cause of death. I had my one phone call and called my sponsor. He showed up, and the next day the fellowship came and wanted to help any way they could.

As time passed, the grief did not. I knew I had to surrender it. I could not bring her back, but I could seek sanity for myself. Finally someone shared that the answer was faith and not to give up five minutes before the miracle. I followed the advice to write a letter to her sharing my recovery and the unsaid things I needed to say, and felt released from the burden of grief. I let God handle it. Sometimes I take my will back, but the pain isn't as bad as before.

The program has taught me that I can recover from addiction, despite my other ailments. I suffer chronic pain and must accept that hospitals, doctors, and medication are part of my "right now" if I want to stay in NA and out of denial. In the past, I listened to people who told me I wasn't clean and could not join NA because I had to take medication. I allowed others to run me out of the only place I've found relief—the rooms of NA. I've been back for almost two years now, and I'm so grateful that I have the ability to work the program, just like everyone else. I have a sponsor and work the steps. I do service and attend meetings regularly. Meditation and prayer help reduce my pain. I've been able to stay in NA only because I was willing to accept myself. I'm not leaving this time!

When this addict lost a brother and a son to the disease
of addiction, his heart was crushed and his faith was challenged.
Going to meetings and working the steps have helped him
to survive so much loss.

Life and Death in NA

I first came to NA in August 1986. I looked for differences, found them, and used for another year and a half. When I returned, I surrendered with the willingness to do whatever it took to stay clean. I took suggestions and made new mistakes, and the emotional peaks and valleys eventually diminished along with my desire to use.

I came into this program a father of two awesome sons. When I had two years clean I was blessed with a third son. Throughout recovery I have done my best to be a good father. I made mistakes, but I also learned to love, protect, and provide for my boys instead of trying to control, dominate, and fill them with fear as I had done most of my life. I did not want my boys to live as I had, with hate, anger, fear, and disregard for life. No matter what message I carry through words, my boys watch how I act and react to situations. I had to learn to walk the NA walk and do my best to practice the principles in all my affairs, because my boys would mimic my positive traits and my defects of character.

This program works in mysterious ways. My father told me he loved me twice in my life: once after the Chicago Bears won the Super Bowl and once at some New Year's Eve party. But thanks to NA, the last years of his life were different. He was diagnosed with cancer in 1996, and as my boys jumped on his hospital bed they told him, "I love you, Grandpa!" as they did regularly. I was taught to say "I love you" in NA; I taught my boys, and to my surprise, my boys taught my father. That day in the hospital, in front of my own eyes, my macho father responded to my boys, "I love you too." I stayed close through his struggle; he died about six months later. Thanks to NA, Dad left this world knowing that my boys loved him and with my boys knowing that their grandfather loved them. He died at fifty-eight with nineteen years clean.

My brother battled with the disease of addiction for years. He knew I went to NA meetings. I would invite him to come along. He tried other avenues to deal with the disease, but they were only temporary solutions. Addiction always came out on top; he was being slowly sucked dry. I was taught in NA to be there for any addict seeking recovery. He knew I loved him unconditionally, but when he was actively using I had to love him from a distance. He also knew I was there to take him to a meeting whenever he was ready.

On the 21st of June 2001 I received a call from a hospital. I was told that my brother had been in a terrible accident. I wasn't sure how they got my phone number. They wouldn't tell me if he was okay, and I knew that wasn't good. I got to the hospital and was asked to identify my brother because he hadn't survived. He lay bruised and dead: gone forever at the age of thirty-four. He had gone to cop, gotten high, and on the way back home he had slammed into a viaduct at high speed, dying instantly.

The day before, he had come to have lunch with me at work (it had been a safe time and place to meet). We hung out for a while, and as he left he said, "I love you, big brother," and I responded, "I love you too." Because of what I learned in the program, the last words I shared with my brother were "I love you." Later I found out the hospital staff got my name and number because he had my business card in his pocket from the day before — thanks, NA, for reminding me not to completely shut out struggling addicts. I wish he had wanted what we have to offer and had been willing to make the effort to get it.

Once again my heart was crushed, my spirit weakened, and my faith challenged. My sons were devastated. I did what I was taught to do: work steps, pray, call my sponsor, go to meetings, and be there for my loved ones. I needed to be surrounded by loved ones both inside and outside the rooms of NA. My friends in the fellowship were there that day as they had been since the day I got clean. In my heart I know they will always be there.

Up to now this hasn't been too hard to write because I have had a few years to grieve those losses. But what I am about to write I would never want anyone to experience. During the last nine months I have lost my hope, spirit, and zest for life. I feel a void where my heart used to be. I have cried more in the last few months then I have in my entire life.

About two years ago my oldest son came to live with me, and I noticed that he had been using. He knew for the last fifteen years I was an active member of NA. He was no stranger to the disease of addiction and the terror and destruction that come along with it. We bumped heads. I sought help from other recovering addicts to deal with my own son living in active addiction. His using progressed, and my heart broke the first time I saw him nodding. Within a year he shared that he saw no hope for his life or ever getting clean.

He decided to get help and came to NA in March 2004. We went to a few meetings together, but he wanted to attend meetings on his own. He started working a program and began sharing with me on a deeper level than ever before. We cleared up some wreckage of the past, for which I am truly grateful. It felt good to see him trust the program and begin to clean up some secrets that haunted him. He started to get that NA glow.

Our literature tells us that "those who keep coming to our meetings regularly stay clean," but my son chose not to continue going to meetings after I left for Afghanistan. I know I cannot take this program from my soul and hand it to another, even though I hoped I could have handed it to my son. He relapsed in late November 2004. I returned from overseas to see my skeleton of a son curled up in the fetal position in a hospital after an overdose. As he awoke, he told me that he was hopeless, and just wanted to sit in a room and use forever. He said he wasn't as strong as I was and he couldn't stay clean. I assured him that if I could stay clean, so could he. My stomach was in knots.

Because I had been away from the area so long, I decided to do ninety meetings in ninety days to get to know some of the local recovering addicts and get involved again in NA service. I know that if I hadn't done this "ninety in ninety" and strongly refreshed my foundation, what was about to happen would have spiritually crippled me.

My son went into another treatment center in early December, but didn't want visits and rarely called. When he did call me from treatment I asked if he was going to NA meetings. He said, "The guys from NA stopped coming around Christmastime." At the end of January he decided to move to a halfway house in California. I was against the idea when he told me. I told him that he had relapsed so badly the last time, I was afraid I might not see him alive again. I was teary when I went to hug him and say good-bye before he left for the train station with his mom. He saw my watery eyes and asked if I was okay. I was speechless by this time, and nodded yes. He knew I didn't want him to go. I was powerless over his decision.

He left treatment on 3 February and headed for the halfway house on 5 February, the same day I started as panel leader for the new hospitals and institutions meeting we started on the unit my son had just left.

He called me a week later from the halfway house. He sounded really worried and said he was scared because he and his room-mates had relapsed the night before. Then he said the words I was hoping for: "I want to come home." I felt cautiously relieved, because I know using addicts will say anything for money. I sent him a nonrefundable train ticket. He left the next day and was coming home to live with me and my other son. The next day, I got a call from his mother. I thought she was just confirming that I was going to pick him up at the train station. I was wrong.

She was crying hysterically and blurted out, "Our son is dead!" I didn't want to believe it—he was almost home. My heart sank as she told me that he was found dead in a bathroom on the train in Kansas City. My wonderful, fun, outgoing, family-oriented, respectful, loving son is dead at twenty-one. He did one more, and it killed him. I will never hold my son again, I will never laugh with my son again. I will never fish or go to the movies with my son again. My niece says he lives in our hearts. But I am selfish: I want him here next to me. He was supposed to outlive me.

Living with this life-changing nightmare has been challenging. Seeing my own son in a casket ripped my heart out. I have already gone through all of the what ifs, could haves, should haves, and if onlys. I did the best I could. I loved him unconditionally, and was always there for him.

Working steps has reduced the guilt and regret I felt. I have learned to let the people I love, respect, and admire know the impact they make in my life. I also must be there for my family and friends who are dealing with tragedies, even if I am uncomfortable and don't know what to say. I just need to be by their side; no magic words necessary.

The bottom line is that if it weren't for Narcotics Anonymous I would not have had the tools to deal with losing my father, brother, or most of all, my son. The journey continues. More lessons await me in the meetings, and in the meetings before and after the meetings. In the last nine months there have been four deaths from overdose in our area. Death from the disease of addiction is real. This is a serious disease that kills. But today I have a choice.

Yes, there is loss and pain in recovery, but the journey in NA has also been far more rewarding than I could ever have imagined. To name only a few of the dreams coming true, since being clean I am the only child out of seven to earn a bachelor's degree. I have traveled around the world and have been fortunate enough to go to NA meetings in Japan, Turkey, India, and Malaysia. Last year I was in Germany, Uzbekistan, and Afghanistan. The journey continues as I slowly learn to live with the pain of losing my wonderful, outgoing, handsome son. I hope he watches over me and his brothers.

I do not blame God or anyone else for my son's death. He chose to put the needle in his arm; death was the result. He was coming home to me, but somewhere along the trip home the disease of addiction did what it does best.

Now I know that life is precious, and I try to send the flowers before the funeral. I do my best to reach out to the newcomers, always. I continue to do the same things that kept me clean the first ninety days.

Even in a remote corner of paradise, the disease can find us—and so can recovery. She kept coming back, and found freedom through fearless inventory work.

Breath of Life

I have no problem accepting the fact that I was born an addict. It's in my genes. Where I grew up I was the only white kid, or Haole, in my class. In Hawaiian, "ha ole" means without breath or life spirit. With my red hair and freckles, I was so white I felt repulsive. People would look at me and say, "What is wrong with her? She looks sick. She's so white!" I felt a lot of shame. In fourth grade I asked my brother to draw a big chain-and-anchor tattoo on my arm. My dad was in the Navy, and that year we had a Chilean sea captain staying at our house. I wanted to be him—or Pippi Longstocking, who was really rich, was strong enough to lift a horse, had a pet monkey, and stayed mostly alone. She looked like me.

I had been molested by various people—friends' parents, baby-sitters, and people in the neighborhood—since kindergarten. It made me hard inside. I froze my heart and also found my worth. I became an object, and my sexuality became my only power. It's where I got my validation, where I believed I had my strength and my skills.

I was already walking the streets in Waikiki at fifteen years old. I found recovery when I was a teenager, but I came in and out of the rooms for many years. I would sit in the back of the meeting and say nothing. I would ask a woman to sponsor me because I needed a name when someone asked me, "Who's your sponsor?"

Because of my addiction and the ways and means I used to get more, I caused a lot of harm to myself and others. No amount of degradation would kill the pain I carried inside me. I relapsed many times. I lost pregnancies. I was riddled with disease,

315

shame, fear, and anger. At one point I was living in a crack house in East LA and I had one dress. It was actually supposed to be a tube top. I was filthy. I lived like an animal. From my window, I would watch the ladies at the bus stop going to their jobs and hanging laundry in their small, fenced-in yards. I was dying. My spirit was dying. I asked God, "Why can't I have that? Why can't I have just a simple life? I don't need much. I just want to feel ... to be decent." With what resources I could gather I moved to a rural and remote corner of Hawaii. I didn't know anyone there.

I asked God to help me to help myself. I was desperate. I called the hotline and went to an NA meeting. There were three people at the table. They all shared and then they all looked at me! It was time to open my mouth and speak. I began to stick around the rooms. We were a small group. We would hang together: go to a meeting, a movie, to the diner. We'd drink coffee all night and talk. We'd call each other and check in before bed, and wake up to another day clean. I put some days together. I went to gatherings in our region, and I realized that people on other islands were clean. Then I went to a convention and I found there were people in other states, and even in other countries, who are clean! My life in recovery began to expand, and the darkness could not stay. I was letting in the light of recovery.

I made a decision, and a spiritual life became real. I began to feel a little freedom. Suddenly, I had choices. I went back to school and graduated with a degree. I made some amends and got my legal problems worked out. I dedicated myself to service in the program.

At a certain point I became very serious. I was able to focus a little bit better and I used—no, I wielded—the traditions and our policy in service like a sword. Someone told me, "If everyone lived by the rule of an eye for an eye, we would all be blind." I had to stop putting out the eyes of those around me in service. I learned that my life depends on NA unity, and I needed to get tougher skin and a softer heart.

I began to realize that I was still practicing behaviors that were killing me. I had to give it up. I had given my sponsor inventories that addressed crimes against society and institutions, but I hadn't given up the "crimes against me." The results of holding onto that shame of the past had me acting out in dishonesty, violent anger, sexual addiction, serial relationships, gambling, retail therapy, debt, and anorexia-bulimia. It was full-blown addiction without dope. These behaviors are defects of character that stand in the way of my living a full life. I had a taste of what freedom could be, but I didn't know how to get it. I was exhausted.

I had some beliefs stuck inside that were killing me. All of my anger and resentments from the past, my childhood, my mistakes, my grief, my loss—that pain so deep, no amount of beastly behavior could dull it—had to go. If I didn't let go of all of it, I wasn't going to live. In tears, I wrote it all out on paper. I found a sponsor who was like a surgeon when it came to inventories. She said, "Are you ready to meet yourself?" I thought, I don't know. What will happen when I let this out of me? I was afraid. She told me, "HP is right here, right now. We are loved and it's safe." So I gave it up, and after I did I felt relief. I wondered why I didn't do this sooner! I felt alive, and you know what? I felt clean. I realized that clean is the new high! This was step work? I liked it! I learned that I wasn't going to get hurt by this. I also knew I had a lot more work to do. Construction was under way.

I love my sponsor. She helps me to live by spiritual principles. She looks deep into my eyes and reflects me back to me. She has loved me whether I brought grace or petty meanness to the table, and she has taught me to love myself despite it all. I realized that I was not one person; I couldn't be after being so fractured. I am really divided into three people. There is "lower me;" that is the addict. She can be dishonest, can pinch a baby when no one is looking. She's the one who smoked your bail money. This is still a part of me. Then there is "middle me;" she is a citizen. She pays her taxes; pays her bills; is a good daughter, sister, wife, and worker. She is decent. She is a trusted servant. She can show up and be accountable. She is generous and funny and loving. "Higher me" is my exact nature: who my HP intends for me to be. This is the part of me that is compassionate, nonjudgmental, open-minded, and full of grace. This part of me is pure light and pure love. When I first sponsored someone, I asked, "How do I do this? What kind of role is this? What kind of voice do I need? I learned that if I am just human, a recovering addict as I am, and I allow HP to lead us both, it will all be okay. My HP sends me people so that I can learn about myself.

Secure in the love of this fellowship and working the steps, I have begun to heal. I have learned forgiveness for those who harmed me when I was little. This is possible! Those memories sadden me, but I no longer have to carry them as a burden. I have come to understand our four-sided symbol as a framework for living: Self, God, Society, and Service. That is the foundation for how I live this program and how I work the steps.

I have learned how to transform my anger into creative action. I have learned how to disagree and even argue, and still get along. I have learned healthy patterns in relationships and with family. I have learned that goodwill means that I believe that everything another person does or believes in is as important as my own actions or beliefs. That's a simple statement, but it has led to a very intricate path of discovery. Some very surprising things have happened, and I know that this is the magic of recovery. I will be working a step, and the moment I am ready, a veil will be pulled from my eyes and I will see the truth. This is a path to freedom.

I feel high on life. I laugh from the bottom of my belly with my mouth wide open. I feel joy and unselfconsciousness. I feel on a very deep level. I have conscious contact. Prayer and meditation have brought me a connection to others and to my HP that addiction had made impossible. Addiction separates me from life. NA has allowed me to find my way to my heart, to listen to it, to think from it. My heart isn't frozen anymore. It's warm. It feels like the difference between sitting in the shade and sitting in the sun. I am so grateful. I have been given the breath of life. Thank you, Narcotics Anonymous.

This Indian addict believes "there are no bad days, only good days and learning days," and he has learned a lot in recovery. Perhaps most importantly, he has learned how to love and to trust the process.

Just Say Yes

I grew up in a traditional Indian Sikh family, where even smoking cigarettes is taboo. The Sikhs are a martial people, and "Sardar," the Indian word for Sikh, means leader. Because Sikhs can be identified by their turbans, I was a very visible user. A Sikh who smokes is a disgrace to the community, and I was using. Even the dealers called me "Smacky Sardar."

I lived at least two lives, my professional life and my addict life. I graduated from a very good school, though I had managed to get suspended for a year because, on an impulse, I took off to the mountains with an urge to "do mushrooms." In the beginning, I worked in go-getting corporate environments, and then, because it became harder and harder to reconcile the demands of work with the needs of an addict, I went to teach in the mountains. My rationalization was that I didn't want to be in the rat race. I gave impassioned lectures to anyone who would listen about doing something meaningful. But I think what attracted me most was the laid-back lifestyle, and the great marijuana that grew outside my cottage. A cottage on a cliff in a residential school was an easy place to isolate. At first it was fun, and then it became hellish. I couldn't handle the loneliness, so I went back to the city to look for a job.

With each switch, assimilating into the new environment got harder. From the beginning, guilt, shame, and fear were part of my using. I did many geographics in active addiction to get away—from the people who loved me because I was unable to bear looking into their eyes, from the jobs I could no longer keep, from the friends I had let down. I thought if I changed my

320

circumstances, I would finally get my life together. I believed that my problem was that I was just born in the wrong place at the wrong time—I was supposed to be a rock star in sixties California; instead I was an Indian computer software guy in the nineties. And you know the story: Ultimately I couldn't keep juggling. For me, hearing that my life had become unmanageable was a relief: You had given my condition a name.

I came to my first meeting like most addicts do—hopeless, desperate, and suicidal. I got there just as the meeting was ending. As I walked in, two people on either side grabbed my hand and said the Serenity Prayer. I learned an important lesson that day—put one hand in the hand of a newcomer and one hand in the hand of an experienced member, and you don't have a hand to pick up. Outside the meeting, a man spoke to me and shared his story. He started saying things I had felt, things I hadn't told anyone. Finally he described things I hadn't even told myself, but when I heard them, they resonated in the depths of my being. He had given voice to my feelings. Someone understood. And he said, "You never have to feel like this again. You never have to be alone again. Just keep coming back." He became my first sponsor. I haven't used since that day.

The next day I told my best friend, with whom I'd used for ten years, that I'd been to a meeting and asked whether he'd like to come. I don't know why I asked him, or, more remarkably, why he said yes. I had my first successful twelfth step call even before I knew there were Twelve Steps! Getting clean and staying clean with him has been one of the pleasures of my recovery.

Like many people, I came to NA an agnostic. When my sponsor asked me to pray, I said I didn't believe in God and so I considered praying to be hypocritical. He laughed so much that tears came from his eyes. But he asked me to pray anyway— "Just say the words." And I did. I was hurting so much I was willing to do anything. And one day I woke up and I believed in a power greater than me: A loving, caring Higher Power became the God of my understanding. I discovered the principle that action comes before feeling. Prayer had to come before belief. To all the slogans we have in NA, I want to add one: The Cornier It Sounds, the Better It Works!

Twenty days after I came to NA, I lost my job. My sponsor said that was probably what I needed. I had little to do but hang out with NA members, go to meetings, write my steps, and get involved with service. My recovery motto became "Just Say Yes." Whatever you asked me to do, I said okay. I was willing to go to any lengths.

When I was a year clean, I moved to Qatar in the Persian Gulf. Suddenly I was in a new job in a foreign country and with only two meetings a week—of AA. The first few months I spent half my salary calling my sponsor in India. He didn't just tell me stuff; he held my hand and walked me through the day—on some days, minute by painful minute. I'd wake up with a knot of fear in my stomach and just want to die. I'd call my sponsor 3,000 miles away to hear him say, "Have a shower and call me back." I'd call him back and he'd say, "Have breakfast and call me back." I discovered that breakfast is a spiritual principle: With honesty, open-mindedness, willingness, and breakfast, we're well on our way.

I'd get to work and be okay for a while. Then the paper would get stuck in the printer and I'd look at the paper and think, "What am I printing? What am I even doing here? This is meaningless. I should just kill myself." In those days, I used to go from serene to suicidal in three seconds. I couldn't control the feelings, but each time I felt that rage and frustration, I would run to the toilet. I spent a lot of time in the toilets as I did in my using days, only this time it was for the privacy to pray.

My sponsor suggested that I get someone in Qatar to sponsor me. The idea of developing another sponsorship relationship, establishing intimacy with another person, seemed overwhelming. Despite my resistance, I was willing and took action. There was no NA in Qatar so I asked someone from AA to sponsor me. I worked the steps from *The NA Step Working Guides*. Every morning I sat for an hour and wrote answers to the interminable questions. My new sponsor made a copy of the guide and studied it so he could help me. He was a tolerant and humble man. When I looked at what I wrote, it all seemed wrong and meaningless and I couldn't see what the benefits of all this writing would be, but I know now that's not the point. What was important was the hour I committed to my recovery every day. By doing it every day, I have progressed through the steps, not perfectly but to the best of my ability.

I believe what really helped me was that I was willing: Because there were only two meetings a week in Qatar, I started going to NA meetings in Internet chat rooms. I even had a service position; I was the secretary of one of the online meetings. Even if no one else showed up, I'd do the meeting protocol, type my share, and think, "And this is what they call being restored to sanity!"

A year later I moved to Oman. It was hard: Moving every year meant building new relationships, trusting new people every time. I found another recovering addict, and we started an NA meeting. People started to come to the meetings. My friend whom I'd twelfth-stepped moved to Oman, and we had an NA Fellowship. My home became the NA hangout. We met, talked about recovery, had meetings, and discussed hospitals and institutions and public information initiatives. I had a sponsee, and we worked the steps together.

Then I got involved in an unhealthy relationship. I was in Oman, a foreign, Islamic country, and the price of getting caught in that relationship was unimaginable, but I could not stop. Once again, I knew the meaning of powerlessness. I felt fear, guilt, and shame, and one of the most precious gifts of recovery slowly disappeared: I no longer felt good about myself. My contact with the God of my understanding was poor. I went to meetings, but I could no longer share honestly. I believed what saved me was sponsorship. I continued to share honestly with my sponsor. I made many attempts to break this obsession, but each time, I failed. Finally, my sponsor said, "This is too dangerous—for your recovery and for your life. Quit your job and go back to India and start over." I wanted to argue, fight, rant—I had worked hard and did not want to give up my professional success. But I've learned to listen for guidance. That day I went home and prayed, "God, if this is your will for me, then I accept. But if there is a way, please take this obsession away. I can't do it."

The next morning, my boss called me to his office and told me that our company had gotten a big contract in Bahrain, and I would have to move immediately. God's solutions have always amazed me. A friend of mine said, "There are no bad days, only good days and learning days." In every situation I can ask the God of my understanding, "What is your will for me? What am I supposed to learn here?" I can practice this in all my affairs. Even at work I can ask, "What can I bring to this situation?" rather than "What can I take away from it?" When I practice this approach, I usually end up a winner.

My sponsor made me write about this fascination I had with attached women—my fear of commitment. "The only way to live is to walk through fear. It's time for you to get married," he said. I had always held up my willingness as a flag, and so I said, "Okay. But it takes two to be married."

"Do it the traditional Indian way. Ask your mother to find you a girl," he said.

"What about love?"

"Love is action," he said. "You'll learn love. You will propose to a part of the anatomy, but your mother, she will find you a woman with whom you can make a life, spend a lifetime."

He also asked me to tell her about my addiction and about NA. I thought that would be the solution. I'd tell her my war stories, and she'd say, "Who the hell wants to marry this maniac?" and that would be that. I could follow my sponsor's directions, and I wouldn't have to get married. That was my plan. God's will was obviously different. She heard my story, and she was supportive and empathized with me immediately. We were married shortly after.

The day before my first wedding anniversary, my wife's bags were packed. She was ready to leave the next morning—for good. I remember thinking, man, you took the willingness thing too far that time. You shouldn't have gotten married.

That evening, I went to a traditions workshop conducted by someone who was visiting. I wasn't really excited by this workshop. I thought of the traditions as dry. But I was miserable and confused, and I thought I would kill some time there. I heard something I will never forget: The person sharing on the First Tradition said, "As long as staying clean is more important than getting loaded, you stay clean. As long as preserving your group is more important than being right, you'll be okay." I went home, hugged my wife, and said, "I'm willing to put in the effort to make this work." From that day our relationship changed and I fell in love. I never thought of the traditions as dry again.

When I work the Eleventh Step and ask for my sponsor's help, whatever decision I make is the right one. I learned that at a traditions meeting, too. At our NA group, a member worried that in this country, where we were likely being watched, guys who were still using could endanger the meetings. The group discussed the First Tradition—our common welfare must come first, without the meetings no one will recover; the Third Tradition—the only requirement for membership is a desire to stop using; the Fifth Tradition—our primary purpose is to carry the message to the addict who still suffers. I got the opportunity to speak to someone from world services at a workshop, and asked him what decision he would have made without telling him what we'd done. And he said, "It doesn't really matter what you eventually decided. I already know you made the right decision, because your group used the tools—you had a discussion, talked about the traditions, and then arrived at a decision." It was a huge lesson for me—trust the process.

Where I live now, the NA Fellowship is rapidly growing. I don't think I have felt as much at home anywhere as I feel here. I shared my intimate secrets with NA, and did not get rejected. So I started to open up even more. Through these relationships, I am learning intimacy in my other relationships—with my wife, my colleagues at work, and my parents. I have learned to trust, make myself vulnerable, and ask for help, especially in things I have had no experience with—from what to do for my wife's birthday to how to make amends to my father.

One day at a time, I have come to understand that love is action. I have a life and a partner, and every day I am faced with choices. I find making decisions hard. They say that with continuing recovery we will have a clearer idea of who we are and what we want. But it's still not automatic for me. Getting married, moving house, working abroad—in all my big life events, I have been supported and helped by the fellowship. Not only has NA changed me, it has made me comfortable with change.

When she had years clean, depression almost killed this
recovering addict. But a renewed commitment to recovery
brought relief and a deeper relationship with her Higher Power.

Inside Job

My using was much the same as anybody else's; my drug of choice was more! As long as I was out of reality and didn't have to face life, it was okay with me. But after a while I lost the will to live. I was constantly in court for crimes that my addiction made me commit. I progressed from shoplifting, to picking pockets, to stealing my own children's presents, to crimes I cannot mention. I didn't care as long as I achieved oblivion.

My children lived my addiction with me; they saw the drugs, the crime, the death, the police raids, the illness, the isolation, the misery of an existence that I had the cheek to call "life." As long as they were at school every day so I could go make money, I didn't care, even when they were ill.

That's nineteen years in a nutshell: day after day the same sad reality of living with a disease that wanted to kill me, and torture for those who had the misfortune to be part of my life.

I reached a living hell. My partner had gone, my kids were being taken away, and I was on my way back to prison. I had been offered help over the years but had always refused to take it. Pride, stubbornness, and the love of drugs were killing me and my kids. A doctor said that if I didn't stop using he gave me six months to live. "Yeah, yeah," I thought. "They always say that." But it stuck. Something (now I call that something "God") told me, "Change or die." I asked for help, and my journey into recovery began.

And what a journey! In treatment I was told I had to attend a Narcotics Anonymous meeting. I was so terrified, I can't begin to describe the fear. I hid in the wardrobe; I was not going to any meeting, and what did the bastards do? Grassed me up[23] (life savers, more like), and I was put on the bus. I sat in that meeting but didn't hear a thing besides what was in my own head. I was so crippled with self-obsession that I was afraid to go to the toilet. It was hell. I kept going back, at first because I had to, and thank God I did have to. Somewhere in that time I started to hear, and started to have some hope, and started to laugh, and started to understand a little bit, and started to want to live!

Then treatment ended; it was down to me. I attended two meetings a day for the first year, raised my hand for all commitments, completed none of them, changed sponsors four times because it was time to do Step Four! Like I was going to tell them who I was; I didn't bloody know who I was. So this was my first year: meetings, sponsors, making friends; learning very slowly how to shop, dress, eat, communicate, pay bills; learning how to be a mother—basic living skills. I would drive illegally and think that the police wouldn't pull me over because "they should know how well I am doing!" That's insanity, but that was my thinking in the first year, and you know what? I loved it! I felt like I belonged somewhere at last.

I was pretty much nuts, but started to get a life together. I attended meetings regularly. I got a new sponsor and made a decision to turn most of my will over. I knew that I needed to move forward with the steps or I would stay mad and possibly use again. This was the beginning of real honesty, open-mindedness, and willingness for me, and practicing these principles opened the door for growth and healing.

I went to college for four years and got a job I was good at. My children returned to live with me. I traveled. I had and lost my first clean relationship. Life was fun. I loved being clean, being part of a fantastic fellowship that really did feel like a family.

Then, all of a sudden, I started to sink. A depression set in on me. It got bleak, dark, hopeless. I carried on, thinking, "This too shall pass." I attended meetings daily, shared, talked to friends,

---

[23] Informed the authorities; snitched (UK slang)

went to work, and tried to live as normally as I could. But it didn't pass. Two months went to three, four, five, and I was working and going home to bed, not attending meetings, not answering the phone, not eating. It felt like I was in a black hole and couldn't climb out. "It isn't supposed to be like this," my head screamed. I remember sitting on the bottom of my stairs and rocking, holding my ribs because of the physical pain, it hurt so much. I was sobbing and shouting, "Help me." I thought about using, anything to relieve the pain, but I knew that using was not the solution. Using would only make it worse. Then I thought the solution was death; I wanted to die. I was seven years clean and hit an emotional rock bottom in recovery. I had tried everything to fix me except truly getting a loving higher power in my life. Work, shopping, boyfriend, sex had been my gods, and I didn't even know it. I phoned my sponsor and asked for help. I started to go to meetings again.

Since this time I have worked on the most important relationship in my life: the one with my higher power, God. I have come to realize that no people, places, or things can ever make me whole, but the program of Narcotics Anonymous will. The phrase "it's an inside job" was so difficult for this addict to understand, but it is so true. I am involved in more service than ever. I was the chairperson of our area convention last year and am involved again this year, and I am vice chair of the area service committee. I love it and the relationships I make doing service. I regularly attend meetings, help the newcomer, and try to be grateful. Today I seek peace of mind and contentment through working the program of Narcotics Anonymous.

Among the challenges this addict has faced in his thirty years clean are cancer and open-heart surgery. From it all, he has learned about surrender and love.

God Walked In

When I first came to Narcotics Anonymous I didn't think I could go without drugs for thirty hours, let alone thirty years. I was terrified NA wasn't going to work for me. I had tried religion and psychiatry and the military. Being a veteran, I thought that the government would and could save me, but they couldn't. I walked into my first meeting of Narcotics Anonymous alone— behind me was jail, hospitals, violence, foster homes, a sick mother dependent on food stamps and government welfare, and a dad who abandoned us. A couple of members took me to a house where there were other addicts living clean. I didn't eat or sleep for days, but I found the message of recovery.

One of the gifts I've received in NA has been falling in love and getting married to my wife. We have been together now for twenty-six years, and we have been faithful to each other all these years. Before I met my wife, I was a pretty rough and reckless guy; there's no question that working the steps has helped me have a relationship with her. After we had been together for five years, my wife told me that she needed intimacy. I wished she had asked me for a million dollars—giving her that would have been easier for me. And at first I thought she meant sex, but it wasn't about sex; it was about sharing who I am with her. The steps have given me the courage to be honest and intimate with another human being.

Narcotics Anonymous has also given me the ability not only to hold a job, but to work my way up from the bottom of a company to the position of vice president. I never got out of ninth grade, so to be vice president of an industry leader was an accomplishment. I showed up to work every day, I was disciplined, and I was trustworthy. When I went to work it didn't matter if I was going to be accepted or promoted or hired or fired; what mattered was staying clean and trying to go with the truth I found in the steps.

When I was two years into my job, the company hired a clinical psychologist to pick everyone's brain. I told my wife that they were going to find out who I was and fire me. When I went to meet with this man I had told myself I was going to lie, but then he started to ask me all these questions and I ended up sharing the equivalent of my inventory with him. After it was over I knew he was going to have to give me up. But he said that although the company executives did need to hear about what I had told him, they also needed to hear what he was going to tell them—that he had never felt the same kind of honesty and integrity that I had shared with him from anyone in his whole career. He wanted to thank me, and said he would hire me in a heartbeat.

I have also been blessed with opportunities to serve and give back to the fellowship. One of the most profound things that happened for me was when I had procrastinated and had no speaker for an H&I commitment, forcing me to do the panel at a hospital detox unit by myself. Even though I had time clean, I was still intimidated to go there by myself. It was a coed panel with dually diagnosed addicts—most of them with physical challenges and many who were wartime vets. I was setting up the literature and taking everyone's inventory because I was afraid and it made me feel better. A guy would walk in and I would say to myself, "I've done more than him;" a woman would walk in and I would say, "She's going to think I'm weak." Finally, God walked in. And God walked in in the form of a person who looked like he came from the same clan I came from—he had similar tattoos, he combed his hair in the same way, and the only difference between him and me was that he was escorted in by two orderlies. He was what they call a frozen addict. He had put a needle in his arm with synthetic heroin, and it had frozen him for his entire life. Inside this man, his mind was going a mile a minute, but on the outside he was drooling all over himself. He would never be able to speak to another person, let alone pick up the phone or write a step. How could I take this man's inventory? At that moment I knew, in a way I hadn't before, that we are all in this together, and there but for the grace of God go I. I knew that if I could do anything for that man it would be to think of him when I feel like complaining about not wanting to do an inventory or pick up the phone. When I spoke at the detox that night, tears were coming out of his eyes—this man changed my life.

When I celebrated twenty-two years clean I hit a series of difficult situations. First, after being with my employer for twenty years, I was terminated in a corporate downsizing. I was given a few hours' notice, and I was gone. I felt abandoned, embarrassed, and ashamed. A week went by and my mother-in-law, whom I loved deeply, died. My wife was then physically attacked by a family member, and it took all my strength not to attack back. I struggled to find a permanent career for about a year and a half, and my finances were seriously affected. And just when I was meeting with some executives for a big job, my eyes went crossed and I couldn't see straight. I had a stroke. In the hospital, I was told I had had three strokes due to a heart defect. I had a hole in my heart and would have to have open-heart surgery so they could close the hole and save my life. I got real angry at God and felt like I didn't get clean to experience this misery. One more time my sponsor reminded me that we must handle life on life's terms and that we are blessed to have the support of a loving God and a program of recovery. After I had my open-heart surgery I was in intensive care, and there were all these tubes coming out of me. I was coming off anesthesia and the pain was insane—I couldn't speak, and I was so thirsty. I had my family and loved ones around, but there was this one person in particular—I knew it was a male figure—who seemed like he could read my mind. If I was thirsty he would swab my mouth; when I was in pain he rubbed my feet. Eventually I found out that this man was an addict whom I hadn't seen in many years. He had heard that I was in intensive care and worked his way through the hospital and got in with my family and just kind of took over. My family was watching this man be so loving to me—I still get emotional about it. To me, that sums up this program.

I wish I could say it all got better after that. It did in a deep spiritual way, but I continued to have physical challenges. Two years after my open-heart surgery I was diagnosed with cancer. I was still not working steadily, and found out I had an aggressive cancer. I prayed and cried and talked, and then one more time I surrendered to a loving higher power. It was so humbling and freeing at the same time. I had radical surgery and was informed that all of the cancer was gone. With all my physical challenges, one of my biggest fears was getting hooked on prescribed medication. I read *In Times of Illness* and had my medication monitored by my sponsor and sponsees; the miracle is that I did not get an obsession to use.

Recently I found out that the cancer has come back and that the last three readings have been higher and higher. The last time I saw the oncologist I was told that they want me to go through eight weeks of daily radiation. They tell me that chances are very good that I'll be cured from this cancer. I'm still surrendering. All of this has changed me profoundly. And yet, the truth is that the fear and anxiety that go along with being diagnosed with cancer and having open-heart surgery pale in comparison to how I felt when I walked through the doors of NA. The fear, loneliness, and isolation that I had back then were way worse than what I'm going through now. I've been very well supported by my friends in NA, particularly the oldtimers. I did have some sponsees pull away—one who, when I told him about the cancer, jumped up and said, "How can you do this? My father did this same thing." I knew where he was coming from. He started crying and tried to leave, and I said, "This is not about you; you know that."

There have definitely been challenges in dealing with all the illness. When they start taking out your prostate and your lymph nodes and other parts, having sex is an issue. What bothered me, even though my wife and I don't have children, was that I could never father children. It just blew me away. All these things were hitting me at once. I had to work on surrendering to the reality that I'm not going to have any children and that my name is not going to carry on. What I've received from this process is a deep feeling of wanting to be of service—not only to the fellowship of NA, which I love so much, but to humankind. As a result of being clean all these years I have had the opportunity to grow older physically and experience what all human beings have to face: health issues, financial ups and downs, family and friends going through life's challenges and changes, and ultimately facing our physical mortality. I have been blessed to move through all of life's colors over the years, but without the steps, my NA family, and the principles that I have learned, these life changes would have been much more difficult to cope with and also celebrate. I believe that the longer I'm on this planet, the more wisdom I develop, but I also believe that that wisdom deepens and I end up going full circle to a profound state of innocence, and what a freedom that innocence brings.

I've been through a lot and I want to get mad at God, but I know all of this is not about God or being mad at God. These challenges have taught me about Love. The Love has been the hardest thing for me to accept in my recovery. And what's even harder is accepting and giving myself that Love. What a profound gift—to Love and be Loved. I thank NA, my sponsor, and especially the Twelve Steps for continuing to teach me.

Writing her story from a hospice, this HIV-positive lesbian
tells how she survived great adversity to find grace
in some unlikely places.

One Potato

I am writing this from an AIDS hospice in Toronto, Ontario, Canada, where I am currently residing. I surrendered to the disease of addiction and found recovery in 1983. When I first walked into our rooms, I found every reason possible to not want to be there. I was the only lesbian, the only native person, and there were so few women! It wasn't until after about a month of attending daily that I realized I wasn't that important—that others in the rooms didn't care who I was, where I was coming from, or what I had used. They only cared about me, as an addict seeking recovery.

I always arrived late and left before the Serenity Prayer at the end. There was no way I was going to let anyone hug me, let alone get to know me. And there was no way I was going to pray to a God who, in my opinion, had never done anything for me. I had prayed daily as a child—praying that God would stop the abuse, praying that God would help my mother stop drinking, praying that God would bring my daddy back to me. Those prayers were never answered, so I wasn't about to pray to God now.

When I was about ten days clean I packed up and moved across the country. I ended up in Seattle, where I had lived before. My first stop was at an ex-partner's house, knowing she would have drugs. It had been a few years since I had seen her, and she looked different. I told her I was hurting bad and needed a fix. She looked at me and said she knew exactly where to get what I needed. We headed off in her car to a large yellow house. Imagine my surprise when I realized that she had brought me to a recovery house, where meetings were held daily! It was a speaker meeting that night, and my ex was sharing her experience, strength, and hope. She ended by suggesting to all newcomers that they find a home group, get a sponsor, and attend ninety meetings in ninety days.

I looked around the room and saw a woman I could relate to. I figured she would make a good sponsor, so I asked her to sponsor me. She told me she would, and we should get together to talk about it. That very night, she and two others got high and ended up in a car wreck. Those with her died instantly. She hung on. When I found out the next day at a meeting, I went to visit her in hospital. What I saw shocked me. She had lost her arms and legs in the crash. I looked down at her and thought, "This is my sponsor." She died the following day.

When I was ninety days clean, I again packed up and moved to Portland, Oregon. There, the first person to greet me was a military police officer in recovery. After the meeting she invited me to join her and others for coffee. I was amazed at the fun we had that night. We laughed a lot, we talked about everything—not just about recovery—and I learned that there were many other single parents in the rooms. I was gifted with a Basic Text when my home group members realized I didn't have one. I attended meetings daily, bringing my children with me when necessary. I contributed to the Seventh, and I think I may have volunteered to do a reading—once.

No one knew when my first anniversary came up because I never shared. My children were having a sleepover at a friend's house, so I attended a meeting that night, but turned down offers to go out for coffee. I had other plans. I went home and hung myself in my basement. The God I didn't want saw fit to have a flood take place in my home that night, and when the plumber arrived he found me hanging in the basement. I was immediately cut down. I woke up in hospital several days later to find that woman from the meetings sitting by my bed.

She was holding my hand and telling me to hang on, praying to the God she loved to give me one more chance. Once I was coherent enough to speak, she asked me if I had called my sponsor before trying to kill myself. I shook my head no and told her I did not have a sponsor. Knowing I would never ask, she said, "Well, you do now! I will temporary sponsor you until you can find one."

She ended up "temporary sponsoring" me for the next eight years. That relationship ended only when her God called her home. About six months after she began sponsoring me, I went to make an amends. As I was driving along the highway, I found myself talking out loud. This "Higher Power" stuff was heavy on my mind, because I heard it every day at meetings. Having been raised Catholic, I knew about miracles, and I asked that if there was a God, I would be given some sign. I said this aloud. Suddenly, the truck ahead of me lost its load. Bushels of potatoes fell all over the highway. I parked my car and got out to help the farmer. He was very grateful and offered me a bushel. I said, "No, thank you—but can I have ONE potato?" He didn't know why I wanted one, but said, "Sure!"

When I got home I immediately called my sponsor. "I think I found my Higher Power," I told her. She invited me to come over to talk about it. I packed up my potato and walked into her home. I held out my hand. She looked at the potato, looked at me, and in her wisdom asked if it had a name. I told her its name was Spud. She smiled at me and said, "How wonderful! SPUD—Special Protection Under Direction!"

The topic at the meeting that night was, of course, "Higher Powered." I shared my experience. Nobody laughed at me. After the meeting, I allowed members of our fellowship to hug me for the first time. I began working the steps, and found myself getting a cake and a keytag for the anniversary I had not celebrated. Members also gave me many gifts—potato chips, a potato hat, gift certificates for French fries, and bags of potatoes.

It was during this time that Patrick came into my life. He attended many meetings but had been gone for some time. Everyone assumed he was out using. When he returned to the rooms, he was very thin and obviously unhealthy. He shared that he had spent months in hospital with AIDS-related complex, and that he was dying. I didn't know Patrick well, but he had shared that he had no family, and I had just enough recovery in me to know that no one need die alone when he is a member of NA. I reached out, offering to be on his care team. Patrick taught me a lot about living during the next four months. I held his hand while he took his last breath, and the fellowship made sure he had a decent funeral. Patrick showed me how to live and how to die clean.

When I was two years clean, I was working my Ninth Step. I knew in order to continue recovering I had to get real honest with my sponsor, and then I had to surrender to police on old felony charges. In 1980 I had kidnapped my own children, attempting to protect them from further abuse by their father. I was wanted on a total of five felony charges as a result. My sponsor didn't judge me. She only asked if I was sure I had to do this, and if I could handle the consequences. I didn't feel I had any other choice. I knew if I was going to recover I had to be willing to go to any lengths, and making amends was something I had to do.

In order to surrender to police, I had to return to Canada. Standing in front of the judge brought back many memories for me. But this time I was clean and my prayers to God were not "Please keep me out of jail, I promise not to do this again!" Now I let go and asked God to decide what would be best. After a long trial, the jury found me guilty. I was facing a total of fifty years in prison. I knew it would be tough, but I also knew that members from hospitals and institutions committees would attend the prison, bringing messages of recovery inside, and that we could hold meetings of our own in prison. The judge, however, saw that I was in recovery and overturned four of the five guilty verdicts.

She sentenced me on only one charge, "harboring." At sentencing, she said she had no doubt that I felt the need to harbor my children, and that I was in recovery, and had offered honest information that I could well have denied. I ended up living in Ottawa, Ontario, working in a shelter. There I reconnected with my native roots and spirituality.

I was seven years clean when I was raped and stabbed during the Oka crisis.[24] My doctor stitched me up and gave me an HIV antibody test. The test came back negative. So did the next test six months later. I found it extremely difficult to remain in Ottawa after the attack, and moved to Rochester, New York, where I had many friends in recovery. I knew they would help me deal with this violence against me, and help me continue to recover.

A month after I arrived in Rochester, a friend shared that she was scared to go for her HIV test. I agreed to go with her. Her test came back negative. Mine came back reactive. I asked the doctor what this meant and he told me that I had HIV, and would develop AIDS and die. I told no one. For six weeks I sat alone in my apartment, not answering the phone or door, not attending meetings. Even though I knew I had contracted HIV through the rape, I was filled with shame. It felt like a bomb had been dropped in my lap. I was terrified of what lay ahead, having seen so many friends die from AIDS.

I made the decision that rather than bring shame to my family or hurt those in recovery who loved me, it would be better if I died. I didn't want to use, so I went to a bridge. I was about to jump when I felt my father's energy around me. I swear I could even smell Brylcreem! I remembered the words he used to tell me as a child: "If you ever doubt the love of your Creator, go hug a tree!" Slowly I stepped off the bridge and made my way to an old tree on the shore. I sat, hugging it, and cried. I attended a meeting the next day and shared.

About a year later I decided to return to Canada, hoping that my illness would help to bring my dysfunctional family back

---

[24] In 1990, there was a three-month-long armed conflict between the Mohawk Nation of Kanesatake and the government of Quebec in the town of Oka.

together. I thought I needed to be near my children and my grandchildren. I soon learned that ongoing contact with my family would only keep me sick. Nothing was going to mess with my recovery. I decided that if God saw fit for me to have HIV, I was going to do Her or His will, and take care of me first. I also got training and became an AIDS educator. I traveled across the country doing AIDS prevention and education workshops, bringing the message of hope to those still stuck in the disease of addiction that it was not too late for them, that they COULD recover! It has been fifteen years since I was infected with HIV. This disease has taken its toll, but I did what was suggested. Most importantly, I did not use!

It was not until a doctor told me that I was going to die that I truly began to live. Each day, I thank Creator for another day of life, another day of recovery, and ask what I can do to help someone that day. Hopefully, sharing my story will help one addict find recovery.

*Neither the military nor prison nor hospitalization helped
this Russian addict clean up until some members brought
a meeting—and a Basic Text—to the hospital. Reading the book
gave him the willingness to try the NA way. Now he's been
clean and working the steps for five years.*

Mosaic

Looking back on my life to tell you this story, I can see that individual situations that seemed to have no connection interweave to become part of one picture, like a mosaic made whole from small fragments.

I grew up in a southern republic of the Soviet Union. I don't remember any significant commotions in my childhood. My first disappointments came from girls: I was short. One simply told me: "First you have to get taller; then we might be friends." I thought I had to prove my adequacy. Constant street fights and conflicts with my teachers and parents made life pretty extreme. Feelings were too much for me. My scandalous reputation led me to bad company, where drugs and crime were used as medication to avoid reality.

By the time I was eighteen, my addiction was obvious. I tried repeatedly to solve the problem with medical help, without success. Military service was compulsory, but those who had health problems, including active addiction, could have an exemption. I willingly went into the army because I thought that it would solve my problems with the law and drugs. I met other addicts, and they told me where I could find drugs. My service became the endless search for drugs and money. I gathered opium in the poppy fields and stole money in town. In the fall there was no opium in the fields; in desperation I robbed a pharmacy and was caught by the police.

At twenty-six I was released from jail for the second time. Major changes had happened while I was imprisoned. The

Soviet Union had fallen apart, and my parents had moved away to Russia. It was clear that I had to change too, as soon as possible. My relatives tried to help me. I was baptized and moved as well, but neither religion nor geographical changes solved my problems. The new town was only fifty years old, and living there, I was depressed and melancholy. I felt like I was forever separated from my motherland and my friends. I met a girl, and I devoted myself completely to her. When she left I could not overcome the pain. Again my life became a vicious circle of crime and using.

I ended up with another jail sentence. After that there was another try to start my life over again. But I woke up in intensive care, hooked up to a ventilator, and understood that I had been in a coma after another overdose. As soon as I was discharged from the hospital I was back on the streets, looking for drugs and money. My interrogating officer let me go until sentencing under the pledge not to leave town. My first thought was to go into hiding, but the life I was leading wasn't worth such effort. I was calm when I went to court, and I received a surprisingly brief sentence.

I continued to use in prison until I realized that I hadn't willingly surrendered to the authorities just to get high. That night I collected all the drugs I had left, and threw everything away. I made a firm decision to quit using. I had my first sincere prayer experience. I was not religious, but in my own words, I asked God to help me. I was ashamed to ask to be rescued from the results of my own actions. I believed that many people who suffered from my actions needed God's help much more than me. I asked God to help all people to solve their problems. Soon I was paroled.

I was shocked when I started using the first day I was released. It started with one drink. I reached my bottom within four months. I got so scared that I stopped again.

I met an old friend, and she invited me to go to Narcotics Anonymous with her. The girl was pretty, so I said yes. I was not impressed by the meeting. When the secretary announced the First Step as the topic, I was surprised. I thought they were all still on the First Step. I didn't realize that this topic was for me. I was sure that my clean time was the result of my willpower. I stopped going to meetings, and soon I was back to using.

My next treatment was not easy. The doctors thought I was incurable. I was totally discouraged. One day I was talking with another patient about Narcotics Anonymous, when some of the people I saw at my first NA meeting came in. They were full of energy and sincerely tried to help. At that time the NA Fellowship in my city was just seven months old. There was only one copy of the Basic Text, and they left it for us in the hospital. I read it almost from cover to cover. The visit from NA members and reading the book had an effect on me. I started to work my First Step.

I wrote down the most vivid evidence of serious problems, but when the time came to acknowledge my powerlessness and unmanageability I flatly refused to write about it, thinking that it was absolute nonsense. I asked everybody to explain why the step was worded this way; maybe it was a mistake. Explanations didn't help until I realized that all my life I had dreamt of being healthy, rich, living in a beautiful house in the city. I dreamt of love, and always wanted to be sophisticated. But in fact I had ruined health, a criminal record, and social instability, and at that moment I was in a hospital of a certain kind, which speaks for itself. It was the first time I could see the difference between my dreams and reality. What I learned stunned me. I gave up: All my attempts to control my condition had been worthless.

My First Step helped me face my fears. I started attending NA meetings regularly. I didn't have any more problems recognizing my powerlessness and insanity. It was the right time to ask for help. I tried to apply everything I heard in meetings. Besides going to meetings every day, I wrote my steps, talked with my sponsor, shared honestly, and analyzed my day and my feelings in the evening. It worked: My life started to change. Most surprising was the way I felt. I gained confidence and inner strength, backbone. Those principles that I heard in meetings were beyond doubt for me.

The Third Step confused me. I needed to turn my will and life over to the care of God? I thought I could never achieve such readiness and faith. I talked about it with other NA members. Not saying a word about religion, they shared about God, love, and the perspective that emerges in the Third Step. I couldn't understand what they were telling me. I wrote about it, attended meetings, and thought a lot about the concept of turning my life over to the care of God.

Meanwhile, I got into a conflict involving a girl I had feelings for and another person. I was ready to take drastic action to solve the conflict. Instead, I decided to trust my God—and waited for the results with great interest. My relations with my friends didn't revive, and the girl stopped talking to me, but I experienced amazing tranquility. I found out that I am able to be above my impulses and live without doing harm to myself or people around me. The experience taught me to be honest in seeking my goals and leave the results in God's hands.

My home group was pretty young, and sometimes we had meetings with only two people present. When we had questions, we called other cities. I attended conventions of neighboring NA communities. The group grew a little, and then there were a series of relapses and again the group became really small. I had been close to those who relapsed. I couldn't understand why it happened. If there are no guarantees, what's the point of recovery? I was not satisfied with the answers I heard. I was depressed for weeks.

One day, sitting by myself in a meeting room, I noticed that the walls were covered with scraps of paper, and that nobody had cleaned the floor for a while. The books we used were in poor condition, and some of the literature wasn't related to our fellowship. I thought that I had found a reason for relapses. People didn't get what they came here for, because we were not ready to give it to them. I started coming earlier to clean the floor. For decoration I chose key phrases from our literature. My need to understand why the development of the group slowed down pushed me into studying the traditions.

I started to understand that my service was not only for my friends. There are those who don't have the opportunity for a change, and we can give them this chance. Reading about the creation of the Basic Text, I learned principles of service. The words "with Gratitude, Love and Dedication" were a call for action.

Understanding the necessity of personal recovery, I continued working the steps. Afraid of the Fourth Step, I took precautions. I ordered a small wooden box, cut a furniture lock into it, kept my notebook with the inventory in that box, and carried the key all the time. The Fourth Step allowed me to see the true reasons for my actions, which were not always pleasant. Sometimes, when I analyzed yet another resentment that was so similar to the previous ones that it hurt, I started to lose the point of what I was doing. But trust in my Higher Power and the program helped me to move forward. From experience I knew that pauses in working the steps can be dangerous. I knew I had to write regularly, even if in small portions, but to write.

When I was working the Fourth Step, I started looking for someone to work the Fifth Step with. I asked God for help, and my prayers were heard. A person I recognized from another city's group anniversary came to our group anniversary. He shared his experience of the Sixth Step. After I described my situation to him, he shared his experience of working Steps Four and Five and we made a plan to meet. My new sponsor listened to me the whole night. When I was done reading the last page, he said that he understood my feelings and shared about similar situations that he had had. Nevertheless, he noted that in his opinion

I was not thorough enough in one area. He recommended that I study and write some more.

To start writing again I needed to overcome my fear of my listener's opinion. I came to understand that confession to myself and God is not any less important than sharing with another person, and that person suffered because of my fear of being misunderstood. Our next meeting was very productive. He asked me: "What are your feelings from the work you have done?" I said, "I am not just a drug addict. I have an addictive personality. My sexual life has the same symptoms of addiction as when I used drugs."

While working the Sixth Step I practiced such principles as self-acceptance and honest recognition of the character defects that were the core of any conflict—internal or external. Understanding the need to move forward, I started the Seventh Step. I was sure that I was "entirely ready," but I didn't notice changes in my behavior and thinking. I realized that my desire to get rid of the character defects expressed in words on paper did not always have agreement in my heart. I went back to the Sixth Step and then worked the Seventh Step again. I needed more than a year to understand the choices made in Steps Six and Seven. These discoveries were the beginning of a new relationship with God.

Now, in the fifth year of my clean life, I understand that it is necessary to take responsibility for my actions. The Eighth Step, no matter how much I want to delay it, is a landmark in my recovery, proving that I am on the right track.

Sometimes I have moments in my recovery when it seems that all my efforts are in vain. Reality makes me despair, the words of my friends don't comfort, meetings seem annoying, and prayer is not sincere. In such situations I just try to live through the feelings. And life goes on: People trust me, professional activities bring satisfaction, new perspectives appear, and love comes with time.

My recovery is not just a series of senseless coincidences. Whether I am engaged in service on a committee, or practicing the Twelfth Step, or simply living the program, I find values inside myself which would be impossible to replace with something external. My life is a mosaic, and Narcotics Anonymous is the structure and foundation of that mosaic. Each time I look at my life I see more pieces being added to that mosaic, and a bigger picture becomes visible—as well as the greatness of the one who has made beauty from broken pieces: the God of my understanding.

As a parent, sometimes recovery means accepting
your children's disease as well. This woman helped
her sons find their way home.

Family Disease, Family Recovery

With ten years clean I was facing a crisis in my family. Living the program of Narcotics Anonymous had given me the tools to create a good life for myself and my children. I wanted them to participate in their lives and thrive. But despite all my efforts and attention, the counseling and consequences, my two teenage boys were out of control with their use of drugs. I was at a loss as to how to help them.

Raising two boys is challenging in any case, but when I had one son under two and was pregnant with our second boy, I came home one day to find my husband dead of an overdose. My life was painful and exhausting, but I put my head down, held my boys close, and pressed on. The effects of my husband's death can still sneak up on me in surprising ways—grief washing over me as I get a scent of his cologne while leafing through a magazine, or when I realize the only memories our boys have of him are stories and pictures.

A few years after his death, I could no longer hold down the grief on my own. My long history of casual using rose to a new, unmanageable level. A year later I gave up on my career and quickly deteriorated—mind, body, and spirit. I did not lose my home or my children, but I lost my enthusiasm, my compassion, and my energy.

I was not able to emotionally connect with my boys, so I brought in a mentor and caregiver to take care of their physical needs. He proved to be my family's angel. He fed and dressed my young boys when I was debilitated, combed their hair, and took them to day care and school. He became the one person they could count on. Then he became part of the solution to my real problem: He was involved when my family held an intervention for me. I went to treatment, and while my family cared for my children out of state, he wrote to the boys every day. He remains a part of our family, living in our home and mentoring the boys, a vital part of our lives.

I first heard of NA in treatment, and I doubted that it could be the answer for me. I became involved with Narcotics Anonymous reluctantly. I did not join groups, I did not know how to ask for help, I did not have a higher power or want to find one, and I did not get along well with other women. Growing up in the home I did taught me to be independent and to hide my feelings. But I continued to go to meetings, and I was eventually able to hear the message. I finally got a sponsor, and she suggested I get to know some women, get a service position, and start working steps. This was the beginning of real recovery for me. The women in the program have shown me how to love and be loved, how to ask for help, how to be of service in all areas of my life, how to find my higher power in everything, and how to experience joy in my everyday life.

I began living my life in recovery. Our home was filled with people from the fellowship. My friends in NA were in my life on a daily basis. My service commitments kept me involved, and I secured my place as a member of the NA community. I attended lots of meetings and felt like a good example of a person living recovery.

Unfortunately, I was living with the mistaken belief that by being a "good enough" recovering addict, I could shield my children from ever experiencing active addiction. Having lost my husband and both parents to the disease of addiction, I committed myself to ending the cycle of addiction with my own recovery. I intended to protect my children from active addiction. This, however, was beyond my control.

It seemed our lives were always in chaos. Whenever the phone rang, I cringed and wondered what crisis awaited. I spent my days trying to keep track of where they were and who they were with, hoping to ward off trouble. I spoke to teachers, counselors, mentors, parents, my sponsor, and friends in recovery. Always one to paint a rosy picture, I acted like things were okay. I tried to minimize, justify, and deny that things were as bad as they were. I practiced "magical thinking," telling myself that everything would work itself out. The reality was that my children were both sinking.

It was in my power to be there to help them when they were ready to be helped. At fifteen, my youngest son made a resolution to quit using. I promised to help him if he was unable to do it alone. When he couldn't stay clean by himself, we took him to an adolescent treatment center. I didn't know if there was any way to help my seventeen-year-old, and in some ways I had given up on him. Family therapy was one of the treatment center's primary components, and we all attended the sessions together. I began to regain some hope. We continued the counseling, each of us individually and our family as a whole, and began to unravel the unhealthy behaviors that led to our turmoil.

All the while, I prayed and worked steps. I went to meetings, tended to my service commitments, and stayed close to my community. I looked to the people in NA who had been through similar experiences. I got the message, again and again, that my children have a higher power too, and that our lives are unfolding perfectly. It didn't feel like it as I watched my elder son struggle with his commitment to stay clean for the sake of his little brother. When my younger son completed the treatment program, we all went to pick him up. We left his older brother there in his place. We continued on the path we had begun with ongoing family therapy.

We are among the many who have found the way to Narcotics Anonymous by various paths, and I am present to the miracles that brought us here. The important thing is that we are here, and we are all in recovery now. We have had to learn how to be supportive of each other while maintaining separate programs. Our family is on a different path, and we have new ways of relating to one another. It is not always easy, but it is always better than what we knew in active addiction.

For many years I have been grateful to Narcotics Anonymous for what it has done in my life. Now, as I see the love of the fellowship surround my sons, I am grateful beyond measure.

*This Canadian addict had years clean before he was willing
to face his addictive behavior in recovery. He now knows
he doesn't have to talk clean and live dirty anymore.*

Enough

With all that I had left in me, I cried out, "Enough!" I couldn't
count the number of times I had said that. I sincerely didn't
want to use any longer. Yet I reached toward the table, toward
the very cause of my pain. I hadn't willed this action, yet there I
was, reaching for another fix. "No!" my words echoed, but I was
alone. I heard a faint voice: "Do you want to live, or die?" I sat
there looking down at my seemingly endless supply of destruction. I wondered if I had finally lost my mind: Had I actually
heard death's ultimatum? Had God spoken? I felt an abrupt shift.
My spirit, with what must have been its last ounce of strength,
dragged me battered and beaten toward life. Memories of empty
promises flooded into me, of all the people I had let down, and
all of those I had hurt. I had truly hoped it would be different this
time. I stared at the clock and prayed for God to help me. Finally,
at 6:30 am, I reached for the phone.

That was over seven years ago. I was introduced to Narcotics
Anonymous through hospitals and institutions meetings while I
was a resident of the local detox facility. I had a short relapse after five and a half months clean. After that I got clean and began
working the steps, got involved in service, stayed in contact with
my sponsor, and began to apply my recovery. After returning to
school in order to pursue a career, I moved to a nearby city and
found a job that I love and still work at today. From the beginning of my recovery I began to have feelings of belonging, hope,
and peace. I remain extremely grateful for the life NA has helped
me to develop. Gone are the endless days of desperation, loneliness, despair, and shame.

When I had a few years clean, after a relationship failed, my sponsor prompted me to begin addressing relationship issues through step work. I started to see a pattern in the kinds of difficulties I had in relationships with women. I began to understand the reasons I pursued unfulfilling relationships: This allowed me to focus blame outward, rather than look at myself. Yet instead of facing these issues, I started another relationship with another woman in recovery before finishing the previous one. I was willing to look at my pattern of pursuing women in order to feel valued, but I brushed off the persistent tap on my shoulder telling me I should examine the role sex played in my life.

During this latest relationship I was still secretly acting out sexually, rationalizing and justifying these behaviors to myself, using my clean time as a defense against the rising tide of guilt. A steady, secret shame was growing inside. Sex allowed me, for a brief time, to feel wanted and desired. After I had acted out, once the pleasure subsided, shame would again set in. I still wasn't talking about this.

When my girlfriend said that my addiction was running rampant, I would resist, blame, derail, rationalize, and then begin rambling about freedom of self-expression, topping all of my defenses with justification. I would act out again, with the same result: temporary pleasure followed by nagging guilt I tried to ignore. Slowly, each sexual fix created a tolerance that required a larger "hit" to create the same experience of escape. At the time, I did not see the similarity between this and my drug use. My defenses and secrecy kept me blind to my behavior. Inevitably, I began to think about how drugs could add to my sexual experience. At first this thought tempted and appealed to me, and then I disregarded it as an annoyance. The day I brushed aside the devastating power of addiction, I became a conscious contributor to my disease.

One night, while I was again out cruising the local drag, I started to look out for a dealer. This time the thought was anything but subtle. A craving to use drugs hit me with a deadly force, a force I had forgotten. It was as if I went on a brief mental vacation. I could still sort of see myself as I was, but it was like I was an observer of my own actions. I saw a parked ambulance, and the attendants were loading someone into the back. The thought occurred to me that this was probably related to addiction, an overdose perhaps. As I continued to drive, I noticed four police officers walking the beat. Then, as if a missing part of me had returned, I found myself feeling shocked and afraid, questioning what I was doing in this area of town. I headed straight home.

As soon as I got home I went to bed. Old tapes began looping in my head: "What's the matter with you?" "You're sick!" "What were you thinking?" "Don't tell anyone." "Just give up." I felt alone, worthless, hopeless, and desperate. I ached for relief. I prayed for help, and through my prayers I began to understand what I needed to do.

The next day I connected with another NA member, a sponsee. In spite of my fears, I told my friend about the events of the night before, and about my secrets. He shed genuine tears of concern, and I felt accepted, understood, and unconditionally loved. In spite of my shame I made a commitment with him to attend a meeting that evening. I stayed close to him all day, attended the meeting, and then made a commitment to connect with him the next day as well. I went to a meeting in the morning and shared directly about my recent experience, and exposed the dark secrets of my shame to the light of recovery before a group of men. I cried. After this meeting I stopped at my sponsor's home and began the process by getting honest with him. Several men in recovery called me on a regular basis expressing their love, concern, and encouragement. One day I arrived at a meeting and realized that I had not made a commitment to anyone to attend that meeting. For the first time since nearly using, I was at a meeting for myself.

Soon I got honest with my girlfriend. I acknowledged my behavior and validated her concerns. In talking about my secrets, I took the first steps toward changing my behavior. Today I am admitting my addictive behavior and working this out through the steps. One thing I've learned from this is that the feedback I get from those closest to me and how I react to it are a direct indication of where I am in my recovery. We are each other's eyes and ears, and building relationships with other addicts in Narcotics Anonymous gives me the support I need to face myself and grow in my recovery.

During much of my recovery I have stayed involved in service, attended meetings regularly, joined and completed step groups, and formed relationships with other addicts in the program. And I have prayed. As a result, I had a huge support system in place to help me when I needed it the most. It's one thing to apply this program when I want to stay clean, and another thing altogether to apply this program when I want to use again. This is how the program works for me.

I believe that the night I was out cruising, my loving Higher Power kept me safe. The work I had done in my earlier recovery laid the foundation for me to build a deeper and more meaningful program of recovery today. I now understand that I can talk clean and live dirty. I've had enough. Today I not only want to be clean from drugs, I want to live clean.

He enlisted in the navy to avoid a second jail term, but kept using until he finally hit a bottom. He got clean when NA was new in Colombia, and twenty years later, he and the fellowship have grown up together.

It Is Worth It

When I was a child, my older brother had mental health problems which everyone said were caused by his drug use. I felt ashamed that other kids knew he was my brother. I was scared of drugs, but instead of rejecting them, I felt attracted to them. Besides the physical sensations, I felt like I belonged to a *parche*; I felt older.[25] I believed I could control my drug use; my brother's psychiatric problems wouldn't happen to me.

As a teenager I was increasingly involved with drugs. I was lazy and irresponsible; my only interest was to use drugs and to hang around the street corners of my *barrio*.[26] I felt more intelligent than everyone else. I dreamed that I would get so rich that I could use drugs without affecting anyone else, without anyone else bothering me, without having to work. I wanted to enjoy life, and the only way I could imagine that was by using and by acquiring material possessions. My dream was to become a member of the mafia so I could own everything I ever wanted. In reality, I was too cowardly to risk becoming a trafficker; I was afraid that I would end up in jail or be killed.

When I was eighteen, I went camping with friends along the Bizcocho River, and the police arrested us with a pretty large supply of drugs. I went to jail for the first time, and my life changed dramatically. For the first time I experienced starvation and being deprived of my freedom. But drugs were always a relief, an escape. After I got out of jail, the judge issued another warrant for my arrest and I ran away. I thought it was cruel that the police chased me just because I enjoyed using. I didn't think

---

[25] A *parche* is a close group of friends.
[26] A *barrio* is a neighborhood.

I was harming anyone—I didn't even realize that I was harming myself. Drugs separated me from my family, my studies, my neighborhood, and my friends. I felt that this was just my fate; I didn't question my drug use at all.

Looking for a way out of this legal mess, I volunteered to serve in the Colombian navy. My family hoped that military discipline would change my ways. My ego took a blow when they cut my hair and made me wear a uniform. I was a number, a rifle, a toy that marched, but inside I was still a dreamer who felt different and more intelligent than other people. With drugs I escaped, and I could find people who were like me; life seemed less hard.

A month before I finished military service, one of my friends told me that he wanted to stop using. We talked about it and planned to quit—after we got out of the navy. Two days later, he committed suicide. It affected me so deeply that for the first time I consciously decided to stop using. I began to think that I wanted a normal life, without drugs. I stopped using with great difficulty, and when I returned home a month later I felt like a different person. I slept in a clean room, alone, after such a long time! To be able to take a bath and eat Mom's *frisoles* felt like heaven.[27] My family got me a job, and I thought that the nightmare was over.

But addiction had other plans for me. A new substance arrived in my life, and it was love at first sight. Things changed. I had a constant need to use. I felt desperate when I ran out. This drug cost a lot more money than I was earning, and I began to steal at home and from work. I lost my job and my family again. When I used drugs I always lost something. This time I didn't share drugs like I did before. I just hung around other people until they gave me some, and then I would leave and use alone.

Soon the drug didn't give me any pleasure; instead I got permanent pain: anguish when I didn't have any more, fear, paranoia, guilt, lies. I walked the streets alone until dawn, ashamed

---

[27] *Frisoles* are a popular regional dish.

that people would see me asking for money in the streets, willing to do anything so I could get high. I wanted to stop using but I didn't know how. All my attempts and promises failed.

My father passed away and I returned home, but everything was much worse. I felt guilty and empty. I was using more and more, and I wanted to die. Finally my mother knelt down in desperation, and as she cried she handed me a knife. She asked me to kill her once and for all, not little by little like I had been doing. My brothers threw me down the stairs and out of the house, and I went out into the street, intending to commit suicide by throwing myself in front of a car. This was the darkest day of my life. I hit bottom, and looking for help, I arrived at NA.

When I got to NA, the fellowship was just beginning in my country. There were three people with very little clean time and no literature who gathered in a room in a church twice a week. I didn't understand much in this meeting, but I felt that they were people like me who had suffered because of their drug use and who wanted to help me unconditionally. For the first time I felt hope: If they could do it, why couldn't I?

What helped the most in the beginning was learning that I suffered from a disease and that I could recover if I wanted to. The only thing I needed to get started was not to use that first dose, no matter what happened, just for today. I was not alone—these people would help me. The next day one of the group members called to find out how I was, and he invited me to a new meeting. I wanted to stay clean with all my heart. I only left the house to attend meetings. My only priority was to stop using. I began to feel that recovery was possible, and I began to live the miracle of not having to use.

My experience had shown me my powerlessness. But little by little I began to discover that my life was unmanageable. I was filled with guilt. I was afraid of having to face life, of assuming responsibilities. I believed that the world should reward me for staying clean. The group taught me that stopping using was not the total goal. I began to believe that the Power that was freeing me from the obsession to use could also help me to change.

I began to ask God to transform my life, and a powerful desire to be of service was born in me. I had not yet worked on my defects of character; I still allowed my impulses to run my life, but I felt an enormous need to give, and began to serve with the conviction that it was God's will for my life. I desperately wanted other addicts to have the opportunity to know the program. There was a lot to do. Almost no one knew that we existed; we didn't have literature or a structure. There were only two meetings in the whole country. When we worked in unity, the groups began to grow and multiply. Sometime later we contacted world services and we discovered that we were not alone, and that there was help available. When we received the first translations of the NA steps we were able to acquire our own identity as a fellowship. The message gained more power with the literature, and more addicts were able to identify with us and stop using.

Thanks to my Higher Power I kept coming back, and I've witnessed miracles. I've seen those four initial members become hundreds, and from that one little group, the only one we had in Colombia, grew more than 80 groups providing 300 weekly meetings. Our first contacts with NA members in other cities in Colombia and from other countries brought us indescribable joy. We'd share translations and literature, and hope the message would take root. When Colombia hosted the world convention, we truly felt that we belonged to a universal fellowship.

My recovery has always been tied to service. In the beginning, my responsibilities made me feel that I wasn't useless; my life had meaning. On occasion, being responsible for opening the meeting kept me from using.

There has also been difficulty in service, but from that difficulty I learned to listen to my heart. In the beginning the group followed the Second Tradition; then the group started to become an extension of the leader's personality. It was very painful and confusing; I had to choose between loyalty to my sponsor and the principles of the program. Should I keep quiet to maintain unity, or express my conscience as I had been taught? We lost many members, but with the help of the literature and members outside the region, the few of us who remained were able to move forward in harmony with our principles, and once more we grew.

Sponsorship has taught me to commit to the steps and to trust the process. Working the steps helped me to discover a person who I don't want to be any longer, and to develop a vision of the person who I aspire to be. Today I really believe that God wants me to stay clean and be happy; to give and receive love; to live here and now, accepting life on life's terms; and to change my old way of reacting when things don't turn out as I had hoped. I have developed a relationship with my Higher Power which has opened my mind, so I can better relate to myself and others. I am learning to forgive others and to forgive myself. I experience the miracle every day I stay clean and when I do what I have to do with joy. I don't have to look for happiness anymore. If I follow this path, my life is destined to be more serene and happy.

This program has become a way of life for me. I have the freedom to choose according to principles. I know that I am not alone. I have a lot of gratitude, and I express it by being of service. It was worth going through all the horrors of active addiction so I could participate in the development of NA here in Colombia. From my heart I want to continue as a member of NA for the rest of my life, because I cannot find a better place on the planet.

When I first heard that recovery was a lifelong task, it seemed like too much. It seemed impossible to think that I would always have to work this program. Twenty years later this is what I like the most: to know that it never ends, that I will always have a place in NA, that I will never stop learning.

Addiction is not the only disease this member has had to deal with. Diagnosed with schizophrenia, she has journeyed in recovery from suicidal patient to mental health counselor.

Becoming Whole

Hi. I'm an addict and my name is.... I say I'm an addict first because if I don't remember what I am, it won't matter who I am. Today was a good day at work. For a person who was once on Social Security disability living in government housing, this is truly a miracle of recovery. Now I work with people who, like me, have been diagnosed with major mental health disorders.

When other counselors at work talk about their clients, I think, "If they only knew I used to have all of those symptoms and I've used all of those drugs." On a low-self-esteem day, sometimes I still feel so transparent, as though others can see right through me and they are just tolerating my existence as some sort of pet project. The good news is that those days pass. Sub-zero self-esteem used to be a way of life for me.

When I first came into recovery I tried it with no medication and just meetings—with no God, no sponsor, and no steps. At ninety days clean, I went home the day after a vicious fight with my using husband to find him dead. I continued to go to meetings, but working the program my way and with no medications drove me, eleven months later, to a full psychotic breakdown and another suicide attempt clean. It was painful to learn that I am powerless over life and death. My attempt did not kill me—nor did it stop the incessant psychotic thoughts that I experienced. I thought people could read my mind and were putting thoughts into it. I even had a notion I had been captured by aliens during a hostile takeover and you guys in the meeting were part of the conspiracy.

I was so sick, not just with addiction, but with another disease called schizophrenia. I had been diagnosed many times with many different types of schizophrenia, including paranoid schizophrenia. After several more months of torture in my mind, in which I lived horrors still unbelievable to me to this day, I finally turned myself in to a psychiatric ward, where I got stabilized on some medication. How wonderful that I was no longer agonizing, trying to not hear the voices. I got some relief through psychotropic medication.

Shortly after that last hospitalization my father died. I believe he knew that finally I would be taken care of. I had started doing all of the basics in NA and have never stopped doing them. Plus, though I had formerly been a devout atheist, I became a spiritual explorer of sorts, trying all faiths on for size. The suggestions I heard from the fellowship at meetings helped me to develop a positive working relationship with a Higher Power. I stayed on my medication for about a year and a half while I learned some new tools. I had lots of outside help and was finally authorized by my doctor to try to live without the medication and to have regular checkups, which I have been doing ever since.

One of the major themes in my life is my search for family. I was an only child and never bonded with my mother. I was always given mixed messages and felt damned if I did and damned if I didn't. I was taught that kids were seen but not heard. I lost my innocence when I was very young. By the time I was thirteen I was using every day as well as bingeing and purging. Since I had not been validated when I was growing up, I felt visible to the eye, but not to the heart. My life before Narcotics Anonymous was loveless and lawless.

A lot of my sick behaviors were unhealthy ways to try to recapture the innocence that I lost and to create family. I wanted a new family that would be there whenever I needed them, who would love me unconditionally. When I made abandonment and loss my "lower power," I relived my youth in dysfunctional relationships, returning to the source of my pain for comfort again and again.

I have come to understand that in NA I am in a large extended family where I don't get mixed messages. Thank goodness it's a simple program. In NA I find the clarity and direction I have always sought. Thank God for the simple spiritual messages and collective wisdom found in NA. At home the rules had always changed. Reassuringly, these simple spiritual principles never change.

Narcotics Anonymous has helped me arrest my disease on a daily basis. I have not used, binged, purged, or self-mutilated for the fifteen years I have been in NA. I have not, since that early suicide attempt, heard any voices. I have had lots of outside help to deal with my mental health issues, but I address the residual symptoms of my disease through recovery. The times when I have felt suicidal, I haven't acted on those urges. At those times I tell myself maybe in the future, but not today, and then the feelings and desire pass. Suicide is a permanent solution for a temporary problem. The Fifth Tradition leaves me never purposeless and never alone; as a group member I can always carry the message of recovery to the addict who still suffers.

I have learned in NA to feel my feelings and become an integrated, whole human being. Today I know that the consequences of not feeling are much worse than the consequences of feeling. My feelings are there for a reason. They are not just there to torment me to extremes. When I am attentive and mindful, I can see what they are telling me. Then I don't have to make emotional decisions, reacting to or running from the pain and fear. I own it, and then let go and let God.

I was dumped recently, and instead of dwelling on the rejection, I took inventory. I shared and shared. Tired and abandoned, I deepened my surrender, and felt God's grace and love fill me up more than ever before. I know that for me to live I must give and forgive—give back what was so freely given to me; forgive and not hold onto my patterns of victimization in relationships. I have relationships today that are grounded in respect and equality.

I have learned in NA that the more I let go, the freer I am, and when I do this in relationships I am finally able to give and receive unconditional love.

With the help of others and the steps, staying teachable and reachable, I am not afraid. I have a strength that is not my own. The steps have helped me become an empowered woman. I have learned that my story is continually unfolding, with each day being a few pages in the book. Knowing that more will be revealed excites me: Each day is a mystery in my Higher Power's hands. My human experience is not always my disease, and I don't have to blame my disease for every human experience. There is no shame in living today. I have the right to be happy, sad, fallible, joyful, ignorant, stupid at times, in debt or out, dumped by a guy or happy together, and so many other things.

Earlier in my recovery somebody told me to keep a miracles diary. I see so many coincidences and miracles each day that I cannot deny the value of my life anymore. So I would like to reach out and say, don't quit before the miracle happens. Life on life's terms is rich with miracles.

A string of "coincidences" led this addict to find a sponsor and to see that our acts of service can have far-reaching effects.

The Good We Do

Sometimes I get the distinct feeling that I'm exactly where I'm supposed to be, that people are put in my life for a reason, and that coincidences are, well, not coincidences at all. Our actions have consequences we can't always see. We'll never know how our small efforts will reverberate through the world. Sometimes the smallest selfless act takes on a life of its own and makes a difference in the lives of countless other people.

After winding up in a treatment center in my hometown, I went into a halfway house about a thousand miles away. By the time I left the halfway house, I was a part of the local NA community and had a job, so I stayed. When I was close to four years clean, I returned to the city I'd grown up in. I had recently lost my sponsor, and knew that I needed a new one to help me through all the stresses and changes of relocation. As luck would have it, an NA convention was being held a few miles away one week after I relocated. I went to the convention hoping to meet new people and perhaps find a sponsor.

I didn't know anyone there, felt very alone, and wasn't having a good time. But I stayed, remembering that my purpose at this convention was to find a new sponsor, even if I felt alienated. I'd been clean long enough to know that recovery sometimes requires doing things I don't like to do, such as getting to know new people even if I feel too scared to talk to them. Sometimes I just need to do a little bit of footwork, face a little fear, and hope for the best.

My first few years clean had also shown me that those members who are committed to service in NA are often people who have strong recovery, so I went to workshops on the Twelve Traditions. At the workshop on Traditions Ten through Twelve, the second speaker introduced himself as Jim. He had a lot of good things to say; he also seemed vaguely familiar. As I listened, it dawned on me that this might be the same person who had brought a meeting into the treatment center I'd been in. My memories of those first few days clean were fuzzy, so I wasn't sure if he was the guy from four years earlier.

After the meeting, I approached him. This was intimidating: He had a lot of clean time, and was already talking to a bunch of other people. I asked if he had brought a meeting into the treatment center I'd been in about four years earlier. He said yes, and after four years, I had an opportunity to thank the nameless guy who'd first carried the message to me. I told him that he was the one who'd introduced me to NA, that the hospitals and institutions meeting he'd spoken at had made a profound impression on me and helped me to grasp the First Step, and that I'd been living clean, a thousand miles away, for the past four years.

Though I hardly knew him, I trusted that we'd been brought together for a reason, and asked him to sponsor me. "I'd be honored," he replied. He invited me to join him and some friends for dinner. The more we talked, the more confident I became in my choice of a sponsor. He sponsored me for the next eight years, and served as a model for me in many areas of my life; we remain close today. What were the odds of me running into this man during my first week home, out of several thousand recovering addicts in the region? How did I wind up in a workshop where he was the speaker? Why was the convention so conveniently held just a few days after I relocated? In a flash, I saw the string of coincidences that led up to this moment.

It occurred to me then that we never know the good we do. One act of service can make a profound difference, and one addict's good work can ripple outward in ways we can't foresee. There's something magical about that for me, something that helps me to continue to believe in a power greater than myself. He didn't know I'd stayed clean, had become a responsible member of society, and had been carrying the message into hospitals and institutions myself; I was just one of many addicts he spoke to in the course of a year-long weekly service commitment four years before. The full cycle of recovery—one recovering addict helping a newcomer get clean, and that newcomer growing and himself starting to carry the message—had taken place, all without his knowledge. Since that moment, I have never doubted that my service efforts are worthwhile.

She was one of the first women in Iran NA when she got clean.
Five years later, the fellowship had grown, but she had drifted
away from the program. When her husband died, she relapsed.
Now, clean again, she has true peace and self-respect.

Sacred Places Inside

I am one of the first women who found recovery in the NA program in Iran.

I was born to an upper-middle-class family in which everyone was pretty well educated and successful, but I felt different. I was afraid of expressing myself since I did not want to be exposed as different or weird. I wanted to be a good daughter and worked hard to please others, but it seemed like I never could. I would be successful for a little while, only to lose hope and feel guilty and powerless to change. I hated myself for most of my life because of these feelings.

As I got older, my feelings of discomfort and isolation kept getting stronger. My inability to belong was the source of some of my most painful feelings. I couldn't find anyone to feel comfortable and close with. I did anything to get attention or approval from others. Sometimes I was loud and active; at other times I was very quiet. I kept looking for a place to belong. No one in my family smoked, drank, or used drugs. I started smoking cigarettes when I was sixteen and kept wanting to try new things.

While I was attending college, I decided to get married to fill the hole that I felt inside me. In my second year of marriage, my daughter was born. My feelings of loneliness followed me into adulthood. I kept looking for new things to fill my emptiness. Every time I found something new I thought it would fix me. However, anything that I tried kept my interest only for a short while and eventually led to more problems and headaches. On the surface I seemed to have a good, comfortable life, but on the inside I was ready to explode.

368

I found drugs when I was twenty-eight. At the beginning my husband and I used occasionally for pleasure. As our using progressed, I felt alarmed and tried to control my using. However, my disease had become active and gradually spread to different parts of my life. My compulsion to use grew dramatically. I was in love with drugs. I used more than people who had been using for a long time. I believed that I had finally found what I had always been looking for and didn't know how I could ever live without drugs. I was in conflict with my using and myself.

The first few years of using were enjoyable. But after that, all that was left was pain, isolation, and guilt. I did everything in secret. I had to deal with the painful reality of my life; the pretending was killing me. After seven or eight years of using, the only bond left between me and my husband was the drugs. Finally I came to the conclusion that the only way to free myself from drugs was to separate from my husband. I was tired and hated everyone and everything. Today I can see that my whole life was about self-centeredness. Both my marriage and my separation were based in self-centeredness. All of my biggest decisions amounted to running away, escaping reality, and staying in denial.

After my separation, I escaped back to drugs. This time I used until I nearly lost my mind. I felt like a wind-up toy, a sleepwalker. I reached complete desperation.

For the last few months of my using, I cried every night. Since I had tried quitting a few times in the past, only to go back in very little time, I believed it would take a miracle for me to get clean. One night I begged God until nearly morning to show me a way to save myself. The next day I was watching satellite television and saw this person talking about addiction and getting clean. He was saying unbelievable things about himself and about recovery. At the end of the program he gave a phone number in Iran. I called the number many times at all hours, but no one answered. After a few days, I started losing hope and began to think I was just gullible, and that the show was probably a commercial and a bunch of lies. However, I continued calling the number every few days, until finally one day somebody answered — and told me that he didn't have time to talk! But he gave me another phone number to call. Full of fear and doubt, I called. The person who answered is one of my best friends in recovery today.

I had called looking for some sort of a medication or a simple way to quit without having to suffer a lot of pain or taking time off from work. I was afraid, so I didn't talk a lot about my using. Still, the miracle happened. He told me I needed to get clean and go to meetings. When I asked him about a way to detox, he asked me if I knew any doctors. My answer was no. Then he shared with me that some of us detox without any medication. Even though I was using a high dose of drugs, I started from that day. For fourteen days I stayed home and went through the pain of detoxing. My only connection with the outside world was with three people in recovery who called me regularly from Tehran.

After fifty-one days I went to Tehran and attended a meeting. There were no women and only about ten men in that meeting. We didn't have a place to meet, so we met in the middle of a park, standing even in rain or snow. I didn't know what I was doing there, I was afraid, and yet something kept taking me back. Since I had no other options, I kept going to meetings and stayed hopeful. I worked the steps and stayed clean for five years. At that time I didn't know of any women in recovery in my city, and was scared of going to meetings there. Every so often I would go to Tehran for a few days to attend meetings. I would go to meetings morning, afternoon, and night; and then I would go back home. After five years clean I started believing that I could stay clean forever. I stayed away from meetings and got separated from the program. I got involved with everyday life and forgot why I had ever used drugs. I forgot that I had a disease and more importantly that the disease is progressive and difficult for me to detect. I had forgotten that I needed to protect my recovery at all times, work the steps in my everyday life, attend meetings regularly, and be a part of the program.

I would only go to my home meetings in Tehran when I had time or when it was easy for me. By this time in Tehran the meetings had grown and there were many women. I was no longer alone, but I had become distant and separated. At some point during this period, I lost my husband whom I dearly loved. His death was unbearable for me and I relapsed. I still think that if I had really been committed and involved in the program, maybe this would not have happened. My relapse didn't last very long; I only used a few times. But I stopped believing in myself and returned to complete isolation. I wanted to die.

During the five years I had been clean, I had built a close relationship with God. I felt as if God was always with me because everything was going well, and things were going my way. After my relapse, I cursed God for a long time. I felt that because I had stayed clean, He should have protected me from relapse. Ultimately, I had to come back to God and ask for help. One more time God showed me His miracle. I moved to Tehran where my home meetings were, but still I would not go to them. I was immersed in hopelessness.

My original friend in recovery appeared in my life again. With his help, I went back to meetings, got a sponsor, and started working the steps. This time I knew that I needed to get more in-depth with the steps and my recovery. With a new level of open-mindedness, I gradually got more and more involved in the program. This time I understood that I couldn't live without NA. I started sponsoring others and getting involved in service work. The miracle happened for me one more time. My relapse had become a turning point for me, and within a short period I grew much more than I had done in the first five years of recovery. This time, since I have surrendered to the program, I am learning how to live. Before my relapse I had everything:

family, money, love, and a comfortable life. After my husband's death and my relapse, when I came back to NA I had lost many things, including my husband's love and my financial security. Gradually, I have earned much more important things. I have a sense of satisfaction about my life. I have peace of mind, faith, and a positive outlook on life. I have realized that I have deep, sacred places inside, and that events cannot strip them from me. My fear has subsided tremendously. I have all of these not just because I have stayed clean, but also because I have been willing to work the steps in my daily life and actions, live the principles of the program, and truly become a member of Narcotics Anonymous.

Because my parents were well known in their community, I was always afraid of doing something that would hurt their reputation. In my first five years of being clean, I never had the courage to attend a large gathering or admit that I was an addict in front of others. Today, I go to meetings and conventions, and whenever necessary, I let others know that I am an addict. I discuss my addiction and my recovery with my parents without fear. Today I can be myself and do not have to hide my feelings. I am not sorry for my past, and I'm not afraid of tomorrow. I don't live with my fears. NA has offered me a life that I never expected.

I believe I needed to experience my relapse in order to take recovery seriously. I realize that relapse is not an easy matter and not everyone makes it back. I experienced horrible days and lost many things that were important to me. Today I know that I cannot stay away from meetings, that I need to move on the path of recovery on a daily basis and make steady progress. I realize that in order to keep what I have, I need to share it with others. I have come to know unconditional love and have more balance in life. I experience serenity and know that NA really works.

Recovery has allowed this inner-city addict to get
an education and a rewarding career. Through giving back,
he found that his relationship with his community
and his God are the keys to real success.

I'm So Grateful
that God Still Hears an Addict's Prayer

My story is similar to many who have come before me and to many who will come after me. It is unfortunately typical of far too many urban, African American men. It includes a childhood characterized by crime, intravenous drug use, and a disease-imposed spiritual blackout: As a child I knew God, but during my active addiction my disease prohibited me from having a relationship with him.

Growing up, I was attracted to the people in my community who lived the street life. I looked up to them and aspired to imitate them. This was certainly not the attitude of everyone else in my community. Several of my friends saw these people as nothing more than "community bloodsuckers," worthy of neither praise nor respect. I had a sister and a brother with graduate degrees who served as excellent role models, so it is difficult to explain why I was drawn to the streets. Maybe it was the loneliness and emptiness I felt as a child. Or maybe it was my longing for acceptance, or my need to feel like I "was somebody." Whatever the case, my obsession with the "streets" would ultimately lead to years of pain and misery.

As a child I felt isolated from my family and community and never really fit in with any particular component of society. I was always sad and depressed, and pot, to a small degree, freed me from my isolation, pain, and loneliness. Also, I was a puny kid who needed others in my life for protection from bullies and to feel accepted; using provided me protection and acceptance. I never enjoyed smoking weed. It made me paranoid, caused me to act "silly," and gave me the munchies. In spite of these unpleasant feelings, I continued, because being accepted by my peers was an important value in my life at that time.

In high school, I experimented with heroin and it instantly replaced marijuana as my drug of choice. It seemed to relieve all my pain, anguish, and feelings of hopelessness—in the beginning. It freed me from the need for "protection," because it gave me a false sense of toughness and courage. I committed crimes in order to support my habit. I would never have had the courage to do those things before. My addiction led to isolation from my family, association solely with other addicts, trouble with the law, and a complete disinterest in school. I dropped out of high school and traveled the country, trying to "find myself."

I moved back and forth to Atlanta on three different occasions, the final time in 1984. I prayed that this time I would settle down, get myself together, and overcome my drug use. However, this disease had an agenda of its own. I returned to using drugs daily. I shared an apartment with my nephew and a friend. They were also addicts, and the three of us used together. One day, after nearly overdosing and reaching the point where I became "sick and tired of being sick and tired," I dropped to my knees and prayed that famous prayer, "Please, God, help me." I'm so grateful that God still hears an addict's prayer. Shortly thereafter I went to my first Narcotics Anonymous meeting. Since that day, God, the Twelve Steps, my sponsor, and the fellowship have all worked together to help liberate me from a life of active addiction.

Early in recovery, I learned the value of being involved in the fellowship and became active in NA service work, quickly becoming committed to helping others. I held a wide variety of service commitments. From these experiences I gained confidence in my abilities to serve.

My first "real job" was as a counselor. However, because I had less than a high school diploma, I was professionally limited. I was constantly being told that I did not have the credentials. My resentment prevented me from pursuing a degree. I believed that my life experiences and personal recovery were more valuable.

Acting on a suggestion from my sponsor, I finally decided to pursue my education. With this decision came several barriers and challenges. I had not been in school in almost twenty years, and I literally did not know where to begin. I dropped out of high school because school interfered with my mission as a full-time addict. Early in recovery, through prodding from many of the "older" members of the fellowship, I earned a GED.[28] But I was thirty-five years old and felt I was too old to be starting a college career. I figured I would be somewhere in my forties by the time I graduated. And I had no earthly idea of how I would attend school and financially support myself. However, I knew God had not delivered me from active addiction to leave me stuck in a dead-end job.

I should have never made it to this point in my life. I should have been dead and buried, but because of God's grace and mercy I was blessed with membership in Narcotics Anonymous. I was able to stay in his good favor because of the direction I received from my sponsor, the Twelve Steps of NA, and my friends in recovery. Each had convinced me that God had positive plans for me, but I would have to remain obedient and trust him. This trust could only be exemplified through daily practice of the principles of NA.

College was extremely difficult. I had poor study habits (actually, I had no study habits at all), and I didn't read very well. I could read the Basic Text and literature from the NA program, but no other literature held my interest. I was forced to become active in study groups, and this proved to be an additional challenge. My cohorts in study groups had no "program," and it was difficult for me to interact with them. Studying in the library was hard for me. The silence would literally drive me crazy. Instead of studying, I would often find myself daydreaming. In spite of all of these obstacles, through daily prayer and meditation I was

---

[28] A high school equivalency degree

able to graduate with honors and get accepted into the master's program at a leading school of social work.

Graduate school presented a new set of challenges for me. I wondered if I was smart enough and suspected my professors and the other students believed that I was there not because of my abilities but because of affirmative action. I had issues with the relatively small number of African American students on campus. I did not believe that the white students could identify with my experiences. I had similar experiences during the early years of my recovery when there were only ten to twelve African Americans active in NA in my community. When race was raised as an issue, we were quickly reminded that addiction was an equal opportunity disease and that it affected us all regardless of race. If we were to recover, we needed to discover a strategy that would allow us to do so in a manner where the influences of race and/or racism would not impede our progress.

In spite of these challenges, I graduated with a master's degree in social work. In one lifetime God has allowed me two chances to live, and I am in a position to help others avoid some of the painful experiences I suffered through. To me, this is the greatest gift I have received. As a member of NA and as a social worker, I am charged with the responsibility of helping others.

I mentioned that during my early days in Atlanta I lived with my nephew and a friend. In 1991, my nephew died from complications of AIDS. Shortly thereafter, my friend was sentenced to twenty-five years to life in prison. Today I am celebrating more than twenty-one years of NA recovery. I am pursuing a PhD in social work. In addition, I serve as executive director of a recovery-based nonprofit organization that I founded. None of these accomplishments would have been possible without my higher power and the Fellowship of NA.

In the first seventeen years of my recovery I managed to gain every material thing a "brother from the 'hood" could dream of having, including a four-month internship in South Africa, where I was blessed with the opportunity to help grow the NA Fellowship. However, during this period of material gain, I felt like I lost my soul. I had a "higher power" in my life but I had no real relationship with him—not the kind of relationship we discuss in our Eleventh Step.

One day when I was clean and miserable I was introduced to other members of NA who spoke openly about their love for God and a connection between their belief in God and their recovery from addiction. They talked about spiritual progress rather than spiritual perfection, and that was important to me because I never believed I could meet or maintain the standards that people of faith appeared to live by. Today I don't compare my NA recovery, faith walk, or love for God with anyone else's. My relationship with the higher power is real and it's personal. My agreement with him is that I will do the best I can a day at a time and he will continue to help me along the way. Understanding my responsibility has been the spiritual awakening that I've discovered through working the Twelve Steps of Narcotics Anonymous.

This member from Ireland grew up quiet and withdrawn,
but recovery helped him overcome his fear of speaking
in public to find his voice and himself.

Speaking Up

I was a quiet kid. Being quiet worked for me. When things got difficult, I found that an impenetrable silence was usually my best defense. I have a photograph of myself aged about ten, which shows a very solemn little boy gazing up at the camera. It reminds me what it was like growing up in the kind of home where it was often wiser to keep to myself. Even at that age I constantly sought an escape, and spent much of my childhood lost in reading.

The times I pulled my head out of a book long enough to speak up, my fears were only reinforced. At the age of eleven I was chosen to do a reading at the service where I'd be confirmed into the Catholic Church. My family were all there, as well as the local archbishop. Although I wasn't overburdened with faith, I knew this was important and really didn't want to mess it up. When one of the priests came over and asked in a whisper if I was ready, I immediately launched into the passage. Spoken in a loud, clear voice, my amplified words echoed around the huge church. When the reading was finished, I sensed something was wrong and looked up to find the archbishop staring at me over his glasses. I felt a sudden stab of shame as I realized I'd been supposed to wait for him to speak first. It was one of those moments that seem to go on forever. As they began the ceremony in earnest I felt very small and very wrong, and I hated it. This helped instill in me a dread of speaking in public. Later on in life, I found out that many people were more afraid of public speaking than they were of death. That made a lot of sense to me.

This phobia was only made worse when my hormones kicked in and I suddenly found myself the owner of what was, for a thirteen-year-old, a remarkably deep baritone voice. I was very self-conscious about the subsonic rumble that came out every time I opened my mouth and the effect it had on people when they first heard it. I also started using around this time. All the reading had paid off—I'd done lots of research into the different kinds of drugs, and I was already looking forward to working my way through the menu. I told myself as long as I didn't cross the line by taking one particular drug, I'd be fine.

As my teenage years progressed and I got more heavily into drugs, I found that when I used, it helped me to talk to people. Of course, when I say people, I really mean girls. When I wasn't using, I would fall back into a rigid silence. After a while, all I could talk about with any degree of confidence was drugs.

In my adult years the only reason I wasn't fired from my job was that I was self-employed—though it wasn't very helpful to my professional reputation being regularly searched on the street by the local drug squad. I could only put so much of my unmanageable behavior down to my "artistic temperament." When my family and colleagues tried to find out what was going on with me, they were met with a stony-faced silence. The only people who really knew what kind of a life I was leading were the people I used with. I was experiencing terrible feelings of inadequacy and self-loathing that even the drugs didn't seem to be able to mask anymore. I had long since crossed the line I'd set myself. All I had to look forward to was crossing lines I hadn't even thought of.

Then one of my friends started going to NA meetings. Although I desperately wanted to get clean, the idea of spilling my guts out in front of a roomful of strangers filled me with such acute anxiety that I resolved to find another way. I tried substituting drugs, only using when I had a certain combination of drugs, and started seeing a counselor. Nothing worked—I could stop using, but I couldn't stop thinking about drugs. It seemed that the only way to stop thinking about them was to use them.

Of course, as soon as I used, the next thought would always be "I have to stop doing this."

Eventually, I couldn't see any other way, so I called my friend and she took me to my first meeting. When I got there, I recognized the people in the room. Some of them I'd met before, from school or from using, but in a way I recognized all of them. They were like me, and I was like them. In one way they weren't like me in that they didn't seem to take themselves as terribly seriously as I did. In fact, some of them were actually laughing, and at themselves. And more significantly, they were talking about all the feelings, fears, and insecurities that I had been carrying around all my life. I had always thought that I was the only one who'd ever had them. It was a very profound experience, and I felt at home for the first time in a very long while. This feeling was rapidly replaced by mounting horror as I realized that the meeting was a round-robin. The sharing was making its way around the room toward me. I remember wishing as hard as I possibly could that the meeting would finish before they got to me. Of course it didn't, so out of politeness I said my name, that I was an addict, and that I really didn't like talking about myself. That's all I could say at my first NA meeting. Even though I felt that I was only calling myself an addict to fit in, when I said the words something shifted in me. I didn't know it at the time, but I had just started working the First Step.

Now, I would love to say that as soon as I started to experience the love and acceptance that came to me from the people in the rooms, it immediately took away my fear of speaking publicly. But it didn't. I had to overcome something in me in order to be able to share. If anything, once I realized that what I needed to talk about was myself, sharing in meetings became even more difficult—because I hated not knowing what I was talking about.

Around that time it also became apparent that for me, "sharing was comparing." I was surrounded by people who seemed so much more clever, more articulate, and funnier than me. Every time I opened my mouth I struggled to speak through an avalanche of "not good enough" thoughts. Obviously, a lot of these thoughts were reflected in what I was sharing. There was more than a little of "beating myself up" coming from my corner of the room. It seemed that when I shared, what popped up to the surface first were all my character defects, to the point that I sometimes thought that they were all that I had inside me. In hindsight I can see that this was a pretty useful process, though it wasn't too comfortable at the time. As well as my voice, my accent marked me out as someone from a different part of town from many of the people in the meetings. At first I was tempted to adjust my accent to fit in better, but even then I could see that this was just another way of not feeling good enough.

For the longest time I was unmerciful with myself when I shared, obsessing about what different people in the room could be thinking about what I'd said. It took quite a while for me to realize that many of them were probably just as self-obsessed as I was. At nearly two years clean I went to a European convention, and was sharing in my usual low murmur at a marathon meeting when a brash voice called on me to speak louder. As I went up a notch in volume (to a quiet murmur), I had the awful thought that for the last two years maybe no one at home had heard a word I'd said, but that they'd all been too polite to tell me and I was going to have to start all over again.

The thing was that even though on some deep level I felt that I'd never be any good at sharing, and that I'd never have the ease that I heard in other members around me, it was vitally important that I continue to try. All the times that I opened my mouth and nothing that seemed to make any sense came out—or even worse, the many times I just dried up completely—and even though inside I died a little every time this happened, I knew I had to keep going, because I needed to share to be a part of NA. Deep down I knew I needed to be a part of NA if I was going to survive. Up until then my way of looking at life had been pretty simple: If at first you don't succeed, give up. It was most unusual for me to be faced with this constant failure, as I saw it, and nevertheless to keep going. One thing that really helped was when I started to realize that all the criticism was coming from inside me, and that what I was getting from the people around me in meetings was encouragement and approval.

After the first few years passed, I even began to let go and accept that an easy, expressive way of sharing would always be beyond me, but that just because I couldn't share as well as the people I admired didn't mean I was any less of a recovering addict than they were. I started really working the steps, and one of the immediate ways that I could see the benefits was that the more I worked them, the easier it became for me to share openly and honestly.

So, as had already been happening in many other areas, the miracles started happening in this part of my life. A lot of it had to do with practice, which is the only way I've ever become good at anything in recovery, including working the steps, sponsoring members, and doing service. Rather than always seeing it as a necessary evil, I started to feel more relaxed about sharing in meetings, and actually started to enjoy it occasionally. I was even asked by my professional association to chair some of their meetings, a skill I'd learned through doing service in NA. Then, when my grandfather died a few years ago, my family asked me to give a eulogy at his funeral—having been the black sheep during my using, being asked to be of service like this meant a great deal to me. I prepared a short eulogy, adding the words "speak slowly" in big, block letters on the top of the page. As I walked up to the pulpit I prayed for the ability to do what I needed to do. When I got there I took a deep breath and spoke from the heart about this man I'd admired so much, and how proud our family was of him. When it was over, the congregation applauded and I walked back down to sit beside my mother. Her eyes were shining with pride, and I felt very grateful to NA for all the help I'd been given in rising to the challenge.

The miracles continue to this day, and show no signs of letting up. Last year, long after I'd given up on ever being asked, I was the main speaker at our regional convention. As the moment of truth approached, my nerves were jangling. An oldtimer at my table leaned over and said quietly, "Just be yourself." I took his advice, and to my surprise and delight I actually enjoyed speaking in front of pretty much all of the local fellowship. As I neared the end of my share, there was polite applause when I mentioned that I've done everything right in recovery. This was followed by laughter when I pointed out that I've also done everything wrong. And when I pointed out that the greatest mistake I've ever made in recovery was thinking that I wasn't good enough, I could feel the waves of identification from the members washing over me with their applause.

I am very grateful to Narcotics Anonymous for so many things, not least for the ability to survive long enough to truly get to know and value myself. There have been many awakenings and miracles along the way, and one of the most important for me was that through the meetings and program of NA, I have found my voice. And through finding my voice, I have found myself.

This Portuguese addict was planning to abandon his young daughter and go buy drugs when a group of NA members invited him to a meeting. Now his daughter is grown and sees what NA has taught him about intimacy, respect, and love.

NA Is a Road Map

My friends say that I am protected by God. My story should have ended in a jail, mental institution, or cemetery. I have been to the first two, and I have seen my younger sister and many of my friends die from overdoses. But I have been in recovery for almost seventeen years and, due to a strange coincidence, I was born in 1953, the same year Narcotics Anonymous was born to the world. Maybe my friends are right.

I was born in Lisbon, the only male in a family of six women— my grandmother, my mother, and four sisters. I felt protected by my family and my neighborhood; life seemed to be about either demanding things to happen or using my strength to get things done. When I left the protection of my neighborhood to enter secondary school I was scared. Anger became my best defense and, at the age of fourteen, I found drugs. They became my best allies.

In 1974 I ran away to Holland to avoid arrest. A few months later, the Portuguese dictatorship was overthrown. The revolution made it possible for me to return home. During that time of anarchy and confusion I found pride and security dealing drugs with a gang. If you close your eyes and imagine everything an addict can do to feed his obsession, you can be sure I did all that.

Narcotics Anonymous found me in a mental institution at the age of thirty-six, during one of the many detoxes I had undergone in twenty-two years of active addiction. A group of addicts decided not to go to the beach in the heat of the Lisbon summer, and instead carried the NA message into an institution. When I left that institution I went with a friend to my first NA meeting.

384

After my third meeting I decided that Narcotics Anonymous groups were a good place to deal drugs safely, because everybody said they had the desire to use, they seemed to have money, and they spoke about confidentiality. At my fifth meeting they explained that the rooms were not a place to sell drugs; they were a place to learn to live without them. I decided NA was not for me, and left.

I had spent more than half of my life using; I was sick and tired and could not live with or without drugs. I wanted to stop using but did not know how. At that time I didn't know I had a disease; all I knew was that I could not stay a minute without using. When I couldn't sleep I would hurt myself so that physical pain would distract me from the distress I felt inside. I continued using for another year.

In June 1990 I decided to camp with my seven-year-old daughter in an isolated part of southern Portugal. I thought that because I loved her, I would be able to not use. But each night I left my child alone in the tent and drove as much as 600 km in order to use "just one more time."[29] Soon I had no more money. My daughter cried for food. I went to a restaurant and asked for food for her and wine for me. I had a plan: While my daughter ate I would steal a car and drive to Lisbon. With the sale of the car I could use again. I convinced myself that because she could say her mother's phone number, she would be safe.

When I walked through the door I heard people laughing. Insane as I was, I believed they were laughing at me. I headed for their table to beat them and make them stop. When I approached the group, I recognized them and they recognized me: They were NA members who went to that meeting where I had arrived a year earlier. Like a miracle, my anger was gone and they invited my daughter and me to sit with them. They paid for our dinner, listened to my complaints, and told me that I needed a meeting. I tried to convince them that I needed money to buy drugs. Finally I agreed to a meeting, hoping I would make them change their

---

[29] 373 miles

minds. They got a Basic Text from the car, and we had a meeting in the woods by the road. During that meeting—which today I consider my first—I cried my soul out. I cried for all the years of anguish and desperation.

They put gas in my car, and I went home with the promise that I would go back to meetings. I went, even though I couldn't stop using. With the help of a friend in NA, I was institutionalized, and have not used since. My first year in recovery was fabulous! Learning to taste the basic pleasures of life and the simple fact of being clean—to be able to sleep, to eat, to bathe, and not have diarrhea—was more than enough. The meetings were an enchantment: the laughing, the sharing, the shame of my first dance in recovery, the friendships, the availability of other members, service meetings, the "fights" for a service position, the enthusiasm to carry the message to the still-using addict—everything was a wonder.

During my second year in recovery my sponsor was diagnosed with cancer, and I moved in to take care of him. I admired his recovery, and he was the one who helped me believe I was capable of staying clean. He didn't want to take painkillers even though his pain was enormous. I was confused; it seemed unreasonable to endure such suffering. I was frightened, insecure, and tired. I worked during the day and took care of him at night. Because I did not leave him alone, I no longer went to meetings. I needed my sponsor, but he was ill and needed me. One sleepless night, I considered killing him. The strength of that thought scared me: I no longer used drugs, but anger still lived in me and manifested itself every time I was invaded by fear. I started to see myself again as a bad person, without principles, capable of doing terrible things.

Finally he was hospitalized. I was alone and scared and began to have one relationship after another. I didn't want to use again, but I needed something to take away the anguish. I started a vicious cycle: The more I avoided drugs by using people, the more shame and resentment I felt. Service became a tool to impose my will on others. I fought with a member in front of the group, and people started to criticize me. I was avoiding meetings.

When I was offered a job outside of Lisbon, I did not think twice. I ran away. I didn't go to meetings—the closest one was 250 km away[30]—and did not speak to my sponsor. I got involved in another relationship, but I didn't even know how to live with myself. When she left me for someone else, I felt lost and meaningless.

A few days later my sponsor called to ask how I was doing. We spoke for hours, and I told him that NA didn't work for me. He asked, "How can you say that if you did not give the program a chance? How about giving yourself a chance, too? Why don't you start working the steps?" Those simple questions flashed like a lightning bolt!

I started to work steps with my sponsor, who helped me to realize the depth of my disease. When I was six years old, I had been paralyzed with rheumatic fever. My healing took a long time, and I couldn't run or play. I felt different from the other boys; I felt crippled, and couldn't understand the difference between limitations and deficiency. Remembering that I quit the treatment for that disease as soon as I could, and the obsessive way I started to compete with others to be the best, no matter what, helped me to understand the power of my denial.

When I started working Step Two, I needed to trust something outside of me; I needed to be with other addicts. I accepted an opportunity to work with addicts professionally. At the same time a friend and I started an NA meeting. At the beginning there were just the two of us, but little by little the newcomers arrived. We did hospitals and institutions service work at a jail. A day at a time, a meeting at a time, we grew. We formed an area and organized our first convention. I felt alive again and had an objective in life.

---

[30] 155 miles

But I started to have problems with my boss, who wanted to stop me from going to NA meetings. I refused. Twice I had turned my back on Narcotics Anonymous and my life had become a nightmare. I would not make that same mistake again. I was fired and returned to Lisbon. I felt insecure and afraid of what people might think of me. But this time things were different: I had Narcotics Anonymous in my life and the desire to change. I found that the Twelve Steps of NA are a road map that show me the best direction to get to my destination: to view others with respect and consideration, to learn to value myself and accept life on its own terms, and to stop living based on fantasy — to abandon the idea that I am the center of the universe.

In Lisbon I kept doing service work and going to meetings regularly. I was welcomed in the rooms with open arms, and if there were critical voices, they did not touch my heart. I found a group where I felt comfortable, and it is still my home group. My life became a constant exercise in awakening and learning. I learned to forgive myself and to take responsibility for my change and growth. The spirituality NA talks about is for me the quality of the relationship I build with myself, with Life (God as I understand Him), and with others. Working the spiritual principles of this program with the help of Steps Five, Six, and Seven is the vehicle that helps me travel this path.

When I had nine years clean two things happened: My sponsor relapsed, and my daughter, who was then sixteen, came to live with me. The loss of my sponsor and the happiness of having my daughter with me were contradictory emotions that I lived simultaneously. I came to realize that life is a constant sum of good and bad moments, and the only thing I can control is my attitude. The traces of my character will never leave me, but I can learn healthy management of them.

Living with my daughter has helped me learn to share my space and to accept others as they are. Involvement in service has helped me too — to accept that other people's ideas are as important as my own. NA is not a place for "me" and "others," but rather for "us." My faith in Narcotics Anonymous was refreshed by the hard work and dedication of our work together for the evolution of NA. For me it was a spiritual awakening to realize that in spite of our differences, our common purpose is the same, and is what actually binds us together. For many years my perception of fellowship was only a bit wider than my country's boundaries. The opportunity to live the reality of a Universal NA is a great spiritual experience that is difficult to put in words. I owe my life to NA because it did not let me die from drugs, but also because I was reborn as a human being.

On my daughter's twentieth birthday, my father died. Once again life was offering me good and bad, happiness and grief, death and life, side by side. I had the chance to be with my father in his last hours of life, to be friends with him again after being separated from him by my addiction. Our eyes met and we were able to say good-bye without having to use words. That same day we celebrated life, my daughter's birthday, at a family dinner.

Today I feel like a different man, capable of respecting my family. I am a proud father and a happy man. I am privileged: I like my profession, and I enjoy the material goods I've been able to acquire. More important, my family and friends love me and respect me. My fellow NA members help me to be conscious that I have a disease that never rests, and that only through the Narcotics Anonymous program can I learn to keep it from taking over my life again.

For three years I was unable to establish a relationship with another sponsor. I was one of the members with the most clean time in my country who still went to meetings and did regular service work. I tried sponsorship at a distance, but that didn't work. For me intimacy is still very difficult, and distance and lack of personal contact make that task even more difficult. During those years the rooms, service, and my sponsees were my support system. A year ago I started a new sponsorship relationship—it isn't easy, but I won't give up because I want to keep on working the steps and growing as a person.

Recently, at another birthday dinner for my daughter, I managed to ask her a question I had had in mind for some years: What kind of father had I been? She answered: "You taught me values, principles, and to live with dignity." My heart almost burst with love and gratitude. I can only give what I have, and if I gave her all this it is because I first received it from you, the Fellowship of Narcotics Anonymous.

His recovery journey brought him from a job as a pharmacist to
one working alongside recovering addicts and has given him the
tools to deal with life's challenges—illness, grief, and intimacy.

The Gratitude
Side of Circumstance

I was most afraid for my recovery when I had twelve years
clean, and this intense fear lasted for the next four years of my
personal journey.

A series of deaths in my network of loved people happened in
close succession: my brother, my mother, my father, and a close
friend who I helped into recovery. It felt like twenty-four-hour-
a-day grieving on a forever basis. In the middle of trying to cope
with these losses, I contracted a life-threatening infection and spent
ninety days in the hospital, able to move my limbs only with great
effort. I didn't leave the bed for sixty continuous days. A breathing
machine inhaled and exhaled for me in a loud, pounding rhythm
for five weeks, and I had a frightening leg wound open to the bone
that had to be cleaned and dressed every few hours. It all seemed
too much at once. I lay there, feeling no courage, no faith, and no
hope for anything good to happen ever again. I kept thinking that
if I wasn't hospitalized, I probably couldn't have stayed clean. Being captive gave me no choice, in a sense.

I spent the next couple of years gradually learning to walk and
work and function again. It was all-consuming, requiring everything I had and everything that others gave me: support, love,
time, and tears. Encouragement came from other NA members,
from my sponsor and his wife, and from my own devoted wife
and three sons.

These were the straightforward challenges, the unavoidable challenges. I call them "no-choice challenges." I had to do
whatever I could to gain some degree of function and comfort.
There were other challenges, though. Chief among them was the

question of how I could find what I needed in the Twelve Steps of NA, the NA meetings, and the support offered by friends. It wasn't obvious to me at all.

My sponsor, along with his wife, was my inspiration in overcoming these. They shared with me about living with limitations, living with medical problems, and just about daily living. We talked of this additional second chance, how it was a new opportunity to live when I might well be dead, and how it was so much like getting clean in the first place. We talked about the obligation we all had—that is, to carry the message to others in order to stay in recovery ourselves. All I could think of was how hard that was to do when I was consumed with wishing that something was different. I looked for some opportunity to find gratitude for my life and to surrender being obsessed with my own troubles. How could I carry any message of recovery unless I could get to the gratitude side of my circumstances? This was the impetus for my path from then until now. Every day I try to allow myself to be absorbed with self for a definite period of time, a little longer on a bad day, and then I turn to a more positive perspective.

Reviewing Steps One to Three every single day means that I go through the process of acknowledging how powerless I am, confirming my belief that a Higher Power is there to help me, and surrendering my self-will. This takes me to the place of gratitude and hope and helpfulness so that I can work on the remaining nine steps. That's what I do each day and how I stay in recovery today. It's the foundation of my program.

I remember when I started using just like it was yesterday. I had been sidelined with a chronic intestinal illness on and off for years, and I struggled each time with staying on painkillers and going off the medication. For twelve continuous years, I had been hospitalized for many weeks each year and tried to stay off painkilling medication, with little success. After a very painful series of events, my only daughter became seriously ill.

She died immobilized in a hospital room after extensive surgery and prolonged suffering. I had carried her into surgery, and that last image of the real her has never left me. I distinctly remember making a conscious decision at that very moment that I would do whatever it took in order to never feel that way again. I came pretty close to achieving that goal for a short time, but soon found that I had an unexpected problem: I couldn't stop using drugs, even when I wanted to. Before long, I lost all hope and was convinced that I would die using, and soon.

After being treated for an infection from a dirty needle and being ostracized from my job and family, I came to NA in Boulder, Colorado, at the age of thirty-five, in January 1981. I'd wound up in a local treatment center where every day was filled with opiate withdrawal symptoms, unprovoked crying, and a constant craving for narcotics. They gave me a tape of a recovering addict talking about staying clean and told me I had to go to both NA meetings in our town. I did that and was not surprised that I didn't find any other health professionals there. However, I did find other addicts there, and some had track marks on their arms just like me, so I felt okay about being there. One thing was certain: I didn't know how to be at home without using. The addicts at the meeting shared with great passion about the despair of not being able to stop using drugs, how they had alienated everyone close to them, how they'd lost all hope and didn't know how to stay clean until they came to NA. It soon became obvious to me that I felt much better at NA meetings than I felt anywhere else, and so I went to NA meetings as often as possible.

The other addicts in my NA meeting told me that I might have to think about giving up my profession in order to stay clean. It made sense to me because, once I stopped using for a few weeks, I was terrified of going back to being a pharmacist and being around all the medication. I couldn't imagine working around narcotics and syringes without eventually self-medicating. After choosing not to use drugs that day, my first significant surrender to recovery was to give up my total investment in my profession and my identity as a pharmacist because I wanted to stay clean more than anything else in life.

So I followed the path of the thousands of addicts who came before me. I went to meetings, read literature, asked my sponsor to help me find ways to make the steps meaningful to me, and got involved in our new local NA fellowship. After I was clean about two years, we started a regional committee and a phone-line. The other addicts told me what to do and I did my best to do what they said. NA meetings grew in our state from two meet-ings to over 100 as a result of the NA phoneline. It was my first experience with NA service and trying to do something good for another addict. At that point I didn't even know that I absolutely had to do it to stay clean; I just wanted to do it because I wanted other addicts to find what I was finding. Later, I noticed the parts of our literature that told how we must "give it away to keep it," and I related to that for the first time.

I enrolled in school in hopes of finding a new way to earn a liv-ing. While there, and with five years clean, I applied for a job that involved working with other NA members. I went to work and stayed there for eighteen years, working in situations that gave me the privilege of interacting with many elements of Narcot-ics Anonymous all over the world. This work situation quickly became both a gift and a curse. It was rewarding and special to work in that capacity, but to my surprise, it was emotionally and spiritually draining and often challenged my personal recovery in ways that I never imagined. I was with many strong person-alities all the time. I had to learn to question my motivation con-stantly in my work; was I really working to help others, or was I just trying to accomplish what I thought should happen?

My sponsor was a great help to me by teaching me some simple guidelines to use every single day—for example, figure out exactly what my responsibilities are and do my very best to accomplish them, but do not get involved in peripheral issues or service politics. He also taught me that my job could not be my recovery under any circumstances. I had to maintain my recovery outside of work and after hours, or else I couldn't be successful at my job and maintain my personal integrity.

Some of the most significant things I've learned in my recovery have been in the area of family. Today I am still with the woman I was with while using. In fact, I've had three relationships with this same woman: before using, while using, and in recovery. Each period has been distinct in so many ways. My own levels of commitment and honesty have differed in each phase in some obvious ways, but also in some very profound and perhaps less obvious ways that my step work helped me to address. I learned, after too many years of recovery, that just because something pops into my head, I don't need to say it to my spouse in the way I'm thinking it. Sometimes it's best if I don't say it at all, and I actually can turn and leave the room rather than say something hurtful. Further, I have a responsibility to honor this very special woman and to communicate to her with honesty but also with great sensitivity. It isn't only about me any longer. I can and should give to her in the same ways that I give to addicts; in fact, I have an obligation to give 100 percent of my best self to her and to my three sons. It's a goal that I work toward every day, and my relationship with all of them is better for this effort.

There's one vivid memory from before I ever came to recovery that stays in my mind always. It happened even before I started using, while I was practicing pharmacy at a local drugstore in my community. I was very committed to public health and always took the opportunity to "bust" addicts when they brought in phony prescriptions for drugs. I was convinced that I was doing a good thing for them and for the community. One night an addict came in with a prescription for a narcotic, and it was obviously forged. When I called the police and an officer came, the addict broke down crying and sobbing. "Please kill me now, just shoot me now," he kept pleading. His passion was genuine and touched us all. Soon we—the addict, the policeman, and I—were all crying for him because it was obvious that he would rather die than not be able to get what he needed. I didn't fully understand it then and for a long time afterward. Today I understand it from deep inside my soul, because I've felt the same thing and with the same passion. This is one of many reasons that I am dedicated to helping other addicts. Maybe someday I can even help that very addict, the one who came in the drugstore that night, to find recovery in Narcotics Anonymous.

While each new day is the most important one in my recovery, I have found great value in staying clean for an extended period. I came to recovery at age thirty-five; now, at the time of this writing, I am in my early sixties. Many difficult things have happened in my life over those years, but my recovery program has allowed me to meet the challenges without causing hurt and damage in most cases. Loss of loved ones, physical and emotional setbacks, and other hardships are certain to be part of our lives as we grow older, and I am so very grateful that I've been in recovery for most of them in my life so far. I've learned, with a lot of help, to practice spiritual principles in my affairs and to find some inner peace.

Even though the person I used to be is still inside me in many ways, I'm no longer known for being him; my identity is much more about who I am and how I live my life now. My recovery is my first priority, even after all these years. I do what's required to live with my physical limitations and problems, and I get the strength to do that from working one-to-one with other addicts. I have a definite message to give: An educated professional with a life-altering illness can stay clean in Narcotics Anonymous if he helps others do the same and continues to ask for help.

Others have characterized the message of my story in much fewer words than I've used here—the story of how a regular guy can be consumed by addiction and find recovery from it in Narcotics Anonymous. It's simple and it's my door to freedom from active addiction. I like that.

Index

addiction (*continued*)
  institutionalization and, 119
  is all encompassing, 20
  is a disease, xviii, xxv, 3, 5
  isolation and, 98
  to legal drugs, 4, 23, 119,
    142–46, 270
  obsession and, 87, 89, 166
  powerlessness over, 11, 13,
    15, 224, 248, 278,
  progression of, 3, 5, 123, 158,
    172, 179, 193, 209, 255,
    265, 287, 298, 310, 374
  Step One and, 19–22
  Step Seven and, 36
  Step Eight and, 38–39
  Step Eleven and, 46
  Step Twelve and, 51
  stigma of, xv, 89
  Tradition One and, 62–63
  Tradition Three and, 65
  Tradition Six and, 70
  Tradition Ten and, 74
  without drugs, 151, 317, 346
  See also disease of addiction
addicts, xviii, xix, xxi, xxii,
    xxiii, xxiv, 5, 7, 9–10, 11,
    13, 14, 18, 56, 59, 81, 88–89,
    90–91, 95, 98, 102, 159, 161,
    163, 178, 195, 234, 247, 249,
    257, 273, 301, 355, 387
  characteristics of, xxvi, 3–4,
    6, 30, 55, 71, 80, 82, 86, 87,
    97, 102, 128, 190, 271, 291,
    321
  description of life of, 14–15,
    294
  identification as, xxv, 8, 20,
    56, 77, 105, 168, 184, 204,
    237, 285, 359, 393, 395–96

Step One and, 22
Step Two and, 23–24
Step Three and, 25–26
Step Five and, 32–33
Step Seven and, 36–37
Step Nine and, 41
Step Eleven and, 46–47
Step Twelve and, 49–53
Tradition One and, 62–63
Tradition Three and, 65
Tradition Four and, 66
Tradition Five and, 67–68
Tradition Six and, 69–70
Tradition Seven and, 71
Tradition Eight and, 72
Tradition Ten and, 74
See also using

agnostics, 94, 321–22

alcohol, xxv, 4, 18, 138, 206, 267
  as first drug, 122, 128–29,
    136, 245
  See also drugs

Alcoholics Anonymous (AA),
  xxv, 87–88, 161, 256, 292, 322,
  323

amends, making, 38–42, 85,
  112, 119, 233, 267, 316, 338
  direct, 169–70, 201–02, 226,
    280
  indirect, 41, 212–13, 226
  See also Step Eight, Step Nine

anger, 27, 89, 97, 102, 209,
  218, 235, 238, 268, 272, 309,
  316–18, 384–86
  Step Four and, 29
  Step Six and, 34
  Step Nine and, 41
  Step Ten and, 43

fear *(continued)*
  nothing to, 93, 100, 306
  of rejection, 55, 346
  of relapse, 103, 247–48
  Step One and, 22, 91, 343
  Step Two and, 25
  Step Three and, 27
  Step Four and, 27–31
  Step Five and, 32
  Step Six and, 34
  Step Eight and, 37
  Step Nine and, 40
  Step Ten and, 43
  Step Eleven and, 47
  Step Twelve and, 51
  of taking medication, 333
  Tradition Twelve and, 76
  of the unknown, 16, 274

feelings, 58, 68, 88, 91, 104, 132, 138, 144, 159, 204, 214, 225, 239, 261, 265, 322, 341, 346
  common, 15, 55, 280, 300
  facing, 85, 205–06, 363
  full range of, 16, 101, 352
  hiding, 214, 349, 372
  of inadequacy, 128, 135, 151, 379
  painful, 5, 15, 236, 368, 374
  relapse and, 81–82, 86, 195, 217
  sharing, 98, 271–272, 285, 321, 345, 380
  of a spiritual nature, 33, 105–06, 210
  Step Four and, 30
  Step Five and, 32
  Step Ten and, 42–43, 104, 343–44
  Step Eleven and, 47
  trap of good, 43

  using to cover, 13, 14, 117, 130, 208–09, 224
  will pass, 82, 182, 363
  See also anger, compassion, courage, empathy, fear, grief, guilt, happiness, hope, humility, isolation, love, pain, patience, pride, resentments, self-pity, self-respect, serenity, stress, tolerance, trust, worry

fees, 9, 10, 117
  See also Tradition Seven

Fifth Step
  See steps

Fifth Tradition
  See traditions

First Step
  See steps

First Tradition
  See traditions

forgiveness, 97, 163, 190, 307, 363
  amends and, 226
  of others, 318, 360
  self, 196, 360, 388
  spirit of, 12
  spiritual principle of, 211
  Step Eight and, 38–39

Fourth Step
  See steps

Fourth Tradition
  See traditions

Fourth Step inventory
  See inventory

G

HOW principles (*continued*)
  See also honesty, open-
    mindedness, willingness
humility, 85, 97, 160, 195, 202,
  233, 273, 300, 323, 333
  defined, 101
  through seeking help, 98
  service with, 182, 242, 284
  as spiritual principle, 12, 211
  Step Five and, 218
  Step Six and, 34, 35
  Step Seven and, 36–37, 276
  Step Eight and, 37
  Step Nine and, 41
  Step Eleven and, 49
  Step Twelve and, 51, 52
  Tradition Twelve and, 75

I

identification, 77, 113, 183, 237,
  271, 383
  as addicts, xxv, 8, 88, 115,
    184, 250, 359
  honesty and, 85, 98
  meetings and, 11, 131, 184
illness, 103, 271, 327, 332–34,
  392, 396
  disease of addiction, 3, 5, 10,
    16, 87, 272, 287
  hepatitis C, 182, 267, 305
  HIV/AIDS, 265–68, 306,
    339–40, 376
  of loved one, 201–02, 280–81,
    309–10, 386, 392–93
  mental, 254–60, 361–62
insanity, 5, 55, 86, 126, 147, 167,
  185, 192, 298, 328, 385
  Step One and, 22, 342
  Step Two and, 23–24
  Step Ten and, 43

intimacy, 83, 234, 322, 326, 330,
  389
inventory, 119, 169, 227, 317,
  332, 363
  daily, 97
  Step Four and, 27–31, 133,
    252, 345
  Step Five and, 31–34
  Step Seven and, 37
  Step Ten and, 42–44, 227
isolation, 84, 187, 254–55, 265,
  274, 368, 373
  of addiction, 4, 15, 19, 20, 98,
    200, 287, 327, 333, 369, 374
  preventing, 85
  returning to, 80–81, 102, 290,
    371
  Step Four and, 32
  Step Seven and, 37
  Step Eight and, 39

J

just for today, 106, 164, 217, 274
  living, 50, 52, 55, 82, 91, 94,
    96, 99, 106, 133, 225
  reading, 93, 100, 159
  staying clean, xxiii, xxvi, 54,
    148, 149, 177, 189, 248,
    249, 358
Just for Today daily meditations
  book, 252

L

leadership, 256
  Tradition Two and, 63–64
legal drugs, 4, 14, 23, 119, 142,
  151, 171, 245, 255, 257–60,
  271, 305, 308, 333, 361–62,
  370, 392–93

love (*continued*)
  of career, 249, 252, 290, 352
  of the fellowship, 91–92, 97,
    101, 104–05, 118, 127, 150,
    157, 162, 190, 194–96, 202,
    205, 217, 273, 301, 345, 351
  of God, 105, 133, 134, 141,
    218, 233, 244, 258, 296,
    339, 363, 377
  hurting those we, 13, 165,
    188, 193, 215, 241, 245, 320
  labor of, xxi
  lack of, 20, 102, 121, 198, 204,
    362
  loss and, 112, 167, 178, 191,
    233, 247, 314, 332, 371, 396
  need for, 122, 135, 186, 255
  from sponsor, 131, 196
  Step Two and, 24, 248
  Step Five and, 226, 317
  Step Nine and, 41
  Step Eleven and, 47
  Step Twelve and, 52
  tough, 300
  Tradition One and, 62,
    324–26
  Tradition Two and, 64
  unconditional, 103, 117, 231,
    263, 281, 307, 313, 354,
    364, 372

M

medications
  See legal drugs
meditation, 17, 218, 308
  emotional balance and, 95,
    103, 256, 259, 375
  improving conscious contact
    through, 227, 257, 318

Just for Today, daily
    meditations book, 252
  spirituality and, 130, 243, 276
  Step Eleven and, 44–47, 212
meetings, 9, 54, 143, 202, 211,
    265, 279–80, 295, 306, 314,
    350, 361, 389
  attending one's first, 15, 152–
    53, 158, 159, 173, 177, 181,
    184, 189, 203–04, 209, 217,
    224, 231, 242, 321, 327–28,
    330, 335–36, 370, 374
  attending ninety in ninety
    days, 55, 190, 222, 256,
    267, 312, 336
  attending regularly, 82,
    118–19, 185–86, 223, 226,
    266, 293, 296, 308, 311,
    328, 349, 355, 388
  described, xvii, 10–12, 88,
    181, 198, 236, 239, 318,
    345, 380, 386
  identification at, 19, 113, 160,
    232, 236–37, 250, 273, 278,
    283–85, 291, 315, 358, 380
  in institutions (H&I), 147–50,
    168, 172, 235, 259, 352,
    366, 384
  learning from, 94, 212, 219,
    272, 313, 325, 343–44, 362
  missing, 79, 174, 192, 251,
    267, 292, 305, 307, 329,
    338, 339, 387
  purpose of, 9, 56, 84, 98–99,
    127, 200, 249, 251–52, 372
  as relief from pain, 56, 86,
    235, 282, 310, 393
  returning to after a relapse,
    83, 138, 157, 194–95, 371

relapse (*continued*)
relationships and, 195, 267
reservations and, 5
returning after, 77–78, 83, 85,
138, 192–97, 217, 296, 352,
372
Step Nine and, 40
Step Twelve and, 50, 83
related facilities and outside
enterprises, 5, 7, 8, 21, 55, 72,
79, 119, 120, 137, 138–39, 150,
157, 158, 159, 161, 162, 170,
172–73, 189, 193, 194, 196,
209, 217, 218, 222, 223, 225,
233, 236, 242, 245–48, 250,
255, 256, 257, 259, 262, 279,
284, 293, 299–300, 311, 312,
327, 328, 330, 331–32, 335,
342–43, 349, 350, 352, 365,
366, 384, 393
Tradition Six and, 69–70
relationship(s), 15–16, 82, 183,
253, 326, 328, 330, 388
in active addiction, 7, 136,
157, 165, 180, 187–88,
204–05, 246, 247, 271, 294
with family, 13, 41, 56, 104,
118, 166, 170, 290, 309–14,
348–51, 395
with Higher Power, 12, 24,
95, 98, 99, 133, 211, 242–
44, 282, 301, 329, 346, 360,
362, 371, 373, 377
honesty in, 85, 232, 344, 395
learning to be healthy in,
143–44, 206, 212, 281, 296,
318, 363–64
as manifestation of the
disease, 317, 323, 353–55,
386–87

in NA Fellowship, 91,
181–82, 251
relapse and, 192–96, 267
with sponsor, 57, 178, 251,
274, 301, 322, 337, 389
Step Four and, 29
Step Eight and, 38
Step Nine and, 41
Step Ten and, 42
Tradition One and, 325
Tradition Six and, 70
Tradition Seven and, 71
Tradition Eleven and, 75
See also friendship, God,
Higher Power

resentments, 4, 16, 82, 97, 102,
135, 169, 190, 209, 211, 235,
264, 317, 375, 387
relapse and, 79–80, 162,
192–93, 267
Step Four and, 29, 30, 280,
345
Step Six and, 34
Step Nine and, 41
Step Ten and, 43
Step Twelve and, 238

reservations, 5, 21, 36, 54, 55,
79, 131, 184, 185, 247, 281

responsibility, 15, 86, 101, 106,
214, 366, 377
accepting, 13, 97, 104, 127,
196, 220, 251, 306, 346,
376, 395
avoiding, 79, 122, 123–24,
220, 274, 356, 358
of group, 57
for recovery, 91, 103, 207,
290, 388
service and, 211, 237, 359,
394

of sponsorship, 57–59
Step One and, 21
Step Eleven and, 48
Tradition Eight and, 72–73
Tradition Nine and, 73

S

sanity, 41, 43, 129, 221, 266, 307
restoration to, 17, 23, 25, 186, 218, 225, 248, 249, 273, 275, 323

Second Step
See steps

Second Tradition
See traditions

security
NA environment of, 92, 105, 205, 318
personal, 34, 41, 349, 372, 384

self-acceptance, 58, 101, 239, 346

self-centeredness, 4, 20, 46, 63, 86, 95, 97, 99, 130, 192, 211, 268, 277, 369

self-deception
See denial

self-esteem, 15, 33, 79, 99, 208, 290, 361

self-obsession, 55, 97, 107, 153–54, 328

self-pity, 4, 27, 29, 34, 55, 80, 82, 102, 202, 207, 218, 264, 267, 268

self-respect, 16, 52, 103, 105, 262

self-sufficiency, 62

self-will, 19, 64, 80, 93, 105, 128, 300, 392

self-worth, 16, 244, 305, 317
serenity, 95, 169, 243, 256, 260, 300, 372
developing, 47, 120, 212, 322, 360
Serenity Prayer, 266, 321, 335
service, xxii, 59, 60–61,149, 293
being of, 159, 173, 178, 211, 227, 238, 250–51, 252, 257, 266, 280, 282, 294, 308, 322, 334, 350, 352, 371, 394
importance of, 12, 98, 182, 190, 238, 250–51, 312, 359, 374–75
making commitment to, 157, 186, 201, 316, 323, 365
outreach, 162–63
outside of NA, 104, 256, 376, 382
purpose of, xxvi, 57, 58, 98, 154, 198, 219, 225, 242, 244, 253, 275, 277, 284, 344–45, 349, 355, 387–90
ripple effect of, 366–67
spirit of, xv, xxiii, xxvi, 102, 117, 301, 318, 331–32, 347, 359, 360, 386
Step Nine and, 212–13
Step Eleven and, 212
Step Twelve and, 51
Tradition One and, 201
Tradition Two and, 64, 260
Tradition Four and, 66–67
Tradition Five and, 67
Tradition Seven and, 71
Tradition Eight and, 72–73
Tradition Nine and, 73–74
world services, xvii, xxi–xxii, 325

Twelfth Tradition
 See Tradition Twelve
Twelve Steps, the
 See steps
Twelve Traditions, the
 See traditions

U

unity, xv, xix, 10, 61, 359
 lack of, 306, 360
 of NA Fellowship, xxi, 201,
  238, 291, 316
 Tradition One and, 62–63
 Tradition Five and, 68
 Tradition Seven and, 72
 Tradition Eight and, 72
 uniformity vs., 111, 291
unmanageability, 13, 21, 58,
 162, 216, 221, 294, 321, 348,
 379
 admitting, 15–16, 93, 96, 265,
  287, 358
 Step One and, 19–23, 81, 280,
  343
 Tradition Two and, 63
unrealistic expectations, 32, 82,
 106, 137, 144, 194
 Step Two and, 23
 Step Five and, 32
 Step Six and, 35
using, 11, 83, 89–90, 102, 117,
 128, 136–38, 151, 161, 191,
 199, 255, 267, 292, 320, 361,
 362, 371, 392
 centering life around, 3–4,
  13, 119, 166–67, 188–89,
  214, 220, 242, 261, 287,
  315, 356, 373, 379

desire to stop, 9, 10, 65–66,
 85, 96, 152, 177, 184, 186,
 207, 224, 263, 284, 335,
 342, 350, 352, 357–58, 370,
 380, 385, 393
desire to use, 77, 81, 82, 84,
 91, 103, 178, 196, 222, 264,
 273, 311–12, 333, 354
disease of addiction and, xix,
 55, 86, 106, 132, 180, 187,
 208–09, 240, 259, 293–94
dreams, 196
impossibility of controlling,
 5–7, 20, 78–80, 157, 168,
 179–80, 193, 209, 215–17,
 220, 225, 241, 246, 262, 271,
 283, 288, 299, 327, 343, 374
living without, 93, 100, 107,
 119, 158, 162, 202, 212, 236,
 248, 256, 257–58, 265–66,
 301, 329, 339, 340, 346,
 353, 363, 370, 395
people instead of drugs, 99,
 137, 386–87
progression and, 14, 121–25,
 129, 171–73, 245–6, 278,
 341–42, 348, 369
social, 6, 14, 119
Step One and, 19–22, 210
Step Two and, 23–24
Step Three and, 25, 306
Step Four and, 28, 32
Step Five and, 31
Step Eight and, 39
Step Nine and, 41, 213
Step Ten and, 42
Step Eleven and, 46
Step Twelve and, 50, 52